ULTIMATE

Walks & Hikes

AUSTRALIA

LAURA WATERS

Hardie Grant
EXPLORE

Top Bondi to Manly Walk, NSW

INTRODUCTION

I think it was Sunday bushwalks as a kid with my family that first sowed the seed. The ritual always began with a barbecue and ended in Tim Tams, but somewhere in the middle a bushwalk would drop me in a wondrous world of fern-filled forests, waterfalls, goannas, lyrebirds and wildflowers, perhaps in the Dandenong Ranges, or the granite playground of Hanging Rock. My young mind would be blown by new discoveries and then at day's end I'd flop into bed with satisfaction, legs having done something and lungs flushed with oxygen.

Since then, the bush has always been my happy place but it wasn't until my thirties that I tried my first overnight hike. A friend guided me on a jaunt through the rainforest near Cairns, while I carried a borrowed canvas backpack stuffed with far too many possessions. The experience was memorable and not long after, I headed out to traverse the rainforest, rivers and beaches of Hinchinbrook Island (on the Thorsborne Trail, *see* p. 236), discovering the satisfaction that comes with self-sufficiency and the bliss of simply walking.

A decade later, I catapulted into long-distance hiking – 3000km from one end of New Zealand to the other on the Te Araroa Trail. I crossed countless unbridged rivers, traversed trackless terrain and got blown off my feet by gales. It wasn't easy but I've also never been happier than I was with one bag of belongings on my back and the sole task to just walk. Those five months opened my eyes to the healing power of nature and the manifold benefits of rising to the challenge of an adventure.

Since then, I've walked thousands more kilometres, through dusty canyons in Jordan, over glacier-carved mountains in Patagonia, and through villages in Nepal while snow-capped peaks towered over me. Solo, I tackled the Bibbulmun Track – 1000km from Perth to Albany (*see* p. 152) – and dozens of other Australian trails.

The joy of hiking has never gotten old; if anything it's only become more firmly embedded in my psyche. Walking in nature has the ability to ground us, to reconnect us with something far bigger and more powerful than ourselves. You don't have to travel far to feel it; even a few hours spent ambling in a misty forest, sun-drenched beach, or coastal cliff-top is enough to revive the soul and inspire creativity.

In this book, I've outlined 40 of Australia's most inspiring walks and hikes. In a country that spans 7.6 million square kilometres, it was no easy choice to select them and I make no claim they are the best – there is no way to classify this – however my aim is to showcase some of Australia's incredible diversity, from rainforest to outback, mountains to coast. You'll find some classics that are well known, for good reason, and hopefully some lesser-known trails you might not have considered. Some are easy rambles, while others are more challenging trails that anyone with a reasonable level of fitness and the desire to get out there can achieve.

Each chapter outlines why the walk is special, the planning and resources of each walk, plus you'll find local knowledge, an overview of what it's like to hike and the scenery you'll be rewarded with.

Never has getting your feet on the earth been more important than it is now. It is the soothing salve for our modern lives, the bridge to appreciation of this amazing planet.

The world needs more hikers. Get out there.

Laura Waters

Bottom Wandering Tasmania's Tarn Shelf *Opposite* Sunset in the Glasshouse Mountains on the Sunshine Coast

MAP OF AUSTRALIA

Route Map Legend

PERTH/BOORLOO	○	Capital city
BONDI BEACH		Suburb
BUSSELTON	○	Major city/town
Noosa Heads	○	Town
Willaura	○	Other population centres/localities
Telegraph Saddle	○	Start/end of walk

Walking route

- - - - - - - - - - Optional Walk   – – – – Ferry

🍴 Best eats   ● Point/Attraction

⊢⊣ Best sleeps/Accommodation   ▲ Mountain

⛺ Camping area

WESTERN AUSTRALIA

Kalbarri ● Loop Trail

Gabbi Karniny Bidi ●○ **PERTH/BOORLOO**

Bibbulmun ● Track

Cape to Cape ● Track

Bluff ● Knoll

● Bald Head

Australia Map Legend

○ **CAPITAL CITY**   ● Walk

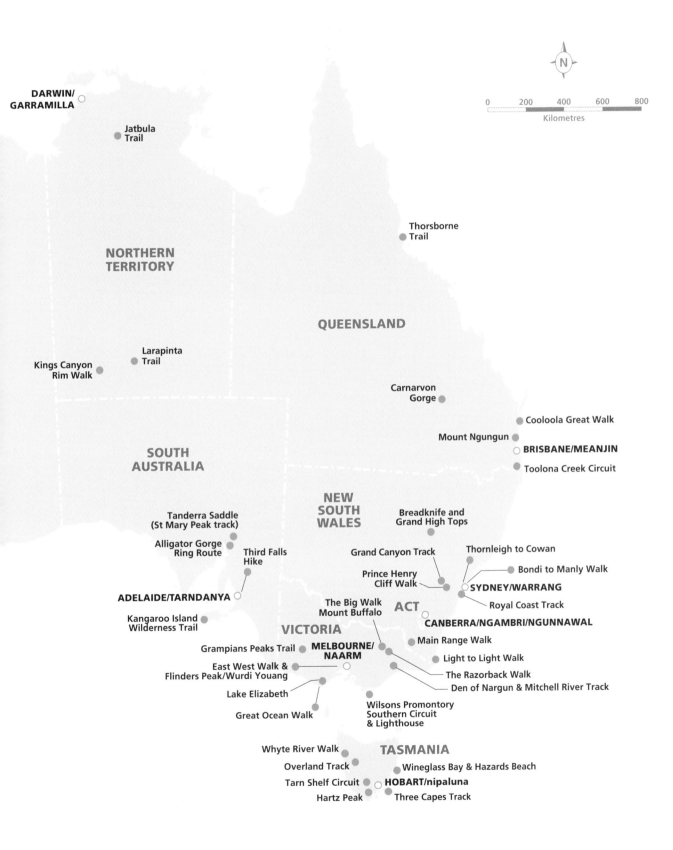

DARWIN/
GARRAMILLA

Jatbula
Trail

NORTHERN
TERRITORY

Thorsborne
Trail

QUEENSLAND

Kings Canyon
Rim Walk

Larapinta
Trail

Carnarvon
Gorge

Cooloola Great Walk

Mount Ngungun

SOUTH
AUSTRALIA

BRISBANE/MEANJIN

Toolona Creek Circuit

NEW
SOUTH
WALES

Breadknife and
Grand High Tops

Tanderra Saddle
(St Mary Peak track)

Alligator Gorge
Ring Route

Third Falls
Hike

Grand Canyon Track

Thornleigh to Cowan

Bondi to Manly Walk

Prince Henry
Cliff Walk

SYDNEY/WARRANG

ADELAIDE/TARNDANYA

The Big Walk
Mount Buffalo

ACT

Royal Coast Track

Kangaroo Island
Wilderness Trail

VICTORIA

CANBERRA/NGAMBRI/NGUNNAWAL

Grampians Peaks Trail

MELBOURNE/
NAARM

Main Range Walk

East West Walk &
Flinders Peak/Wurdi Youang

Light to Light Walk

The Razorback Walk

Lake Elizabeth

Den of Nargun & Mitchell River Track

Great Ocean Walk

Wilsons Promontory
Southern Circuit
& Lighthouse

Whyte River Walk

TASMANIA

Overland Track

Wineglass Bay & Hazards Beach

Tarn Shelf Circuit

HOBART/nipaluna

Hartz Peak

Three Capes Track

BEST OF THE BEST

Top Grampians Peaks Trail, Vic *Opposite* Great Ocean Walk, Vic

GETTING STARTED

Whether you're a seasoned hiker or just starting out, there are a few tips, tricks and habits worth cultivating to help you have a fun adventure in the great outdoors. In these next pages, I cover off things I've learnt after years of experience walking on different terrain and in different conditions.

First things first

More often than not, Australia is described as eight states and territories but in truth this wide brown land comprises scores of nations as identified by those who have lived here for at least 65,000 years. Look at a map like AIATSIS or Gambay that shows First Nations Country, and you'll see the complex divisions between nations, many of them encompassing clan groups with their own distinct culture, customs, law and language. This book recognises and respects this is their land and identifies the Country that each walk is on. Some walks visit important cultural sites and sacred areas. Take opportunities to meet with Traditional Owners and do local tours that enhance your understanding of First Peoples. Please treat First Nations Country and culture with respect. This means not entering sacred areas, not touching rock art and ensuring that you follow trail signs.

Choose your adventure

Each of the 40 walks in this book has an overall rating of difficulty, from easy to hard, however easy, moderate and hard mean different things to different people. Some walkers have good aerobic fitness but might not be so comfortable on uneven or rocky terrain, while for others the reverse is true. Other factors, such as ease of navigation or trail length, can also influence difficulty. As such, you'll find included extra details on terrain, elevation and other relevant info so that you can make your own call.

Plenty of hikes in this book offer options for shorter variations and many of the longer walks can be tackled in sections, which means you can opt for a day hike, a weekend adventure or tick off an entire long distance trail section-by-section over months. Options are outlined in the 'Walk it' section for each hike.

If you don't have time to venture far, every state and territory intro features a trail where you can get feet on dirt within 'cooee' of the city. These are outlined in the City Walks chapter (*see* p. 1).

Find your way

Most of the hikes in this book are fairly well defined and marked, but there are still some tools and habits worth cultivating that will help you stay on track.

Even on short walks, it's handy to have a visual on where you're headed. Basic trail information and maps can usually be downloaded from the relevant national parks office before you go or, alternatively, take a photo of information boards and basic maps at trailheads for easy reference. These will help you keep track of progress, alert you to any highlights or potential places to break for a snack, and help in the event you're unsure at a track junction.

For multi-day walks, you'll need more detailed route information and a topographic map. The ever-changing array of smartphone mapping apps are super handy but it's wise to back it up with a paper map as technology can occasionally leave you in the lurch with random glitches or battery failure. It's worth stopping in at visitor centres or national park offices to get local maps, or obtain online before heading out.

It's good practice to stay aware of your surroundings and always have a rough idea of where you are at any given point. In the event you suspect you've wandered off track, retrace your steps to the last point where you were confident you were on track and review instructions again.

Wildflowers on the Larapinta Trail

HIKE SAFE

It's easy to get blasé and adopt that favourite Aussie philosophy: 'she'll be right', but remember that no one intends to have an accident when they do. They are, by definition, unplanned so take precautions.

Let someone know before you go

Leave your travel plans with someone at home (someone who cares), who can raise the alarm if you don't return as planned. Let them know where you're going, your intended route and expected return time. And then remember to let them know when you've returned safely. This is important for short hikes, as well as multi-day ones.

Safety on the trail

Some of the walks in this book involve the odd creek crossing or exposed cliff-top route. Take extra care in these areas. Hiking poles can provide really valuable extra stability when crossing creeks. Be careful not to tackle any that are in flood or look too fast or deep to manage safely and note that if, on the rare instance a creek is flowing high, you may only need to wait a few hours for water to subside to a safe level. Cliff-top trails provide epic views but make sure you don't get too distracted by them and wander off course. Cliffs often have unstable or crumbly edges so stay well back from any sheer drops and remember that gusty winds in these areas can sometimes give you a sideways nudge. Again, hiking poles can provide extra stability. Some trails involve beach walking. That sweet spot of firm sand can vary from beach to beach but take care not to get too close to rushing waves. And if you're thinking about a swim, visit beachsafe.org.au for safety tips. Many beaches are unpatrolled and may have rips, making them unsafe for swimming.

Check conditions

There's nothing more annoying than making plans to do a hike only to discover, sometimes after a long drive, that the trail is closed. It's a good idea to check the relevant state or territory national parks authority website before you leave home for current conditions, with respect to track closures, road closures, safety issues or maintenance works. See this list:

National Park authorities

NSW: NSW National Parks and Wildlife Service
         nationalparks.nsw.gov.au
ACT: Parks and Conservation Service
         environment.act.gov.au
Vic: Parks Victoria
         parks.vic.gov.au
SA: National Parks and Wildlife Service South Australia
         parks.sa.gov.au
WA: Parks and Wildlife Service
         parks.dpaw.wa.gov.au
NT: Parks and Wildlife Commission of the Northern Territory
         nt.gov.au/parks/find-a-park
Qld: Queensland Parks and Wildlife Service
         parks.des.qld.gov.au
Tas: Tasmania Parks & Wildlife Service
         parks.tas.gov.au
General: Parks Australia
         parksaustralia.gov.au

Check the weather

Check the forecast. Extreme heat or cold, high fire danger, gale-force winds, snow or electrical storms (particularly in alpine areas), or even plain old rain (if your route includes rock scrambling which gets slippery in the wet) can make venturing outdoors risky. If conditions aren't ideal, rethink your plans.

Bushfire risk

Australia has seen some unprecedented bushfires in the past decade or so, and bushfire risk is increasing. Prevention is better than cure, so check the forecast and don't head out when bushfire risk is high (including hot, dry or windy days) or to locations particularly prone to bushfire. If the worst should happen when you're on the trail, stay calm and call the emergency number of 000 if you have reception. Don't try to outrun the fire. Head to lower ground - fires travel uphill - and seek shelter in hollows, rivers, damp gullies or to rocky outcrops or barren ground where fuel is low. Keep skin covered (non-synthetic fibres only) and cover your mouth with a damp cloth. If all else fails and you need to make a run for it, take a deep breath, cover your face and move quickly through the flames (only if less than a metre deep and high) to already burnt ground.

Walk with friends

It's always nice to share the experience with someone and infinitely safer to have the security of backup in the event of an incident. If you do happen to be walking alone though, be conservative. Pay attention, don't take risks, and definitely let someone know where you're going and when you'll be back.

Choose the right hike

Select a route that matches the fitness and ability of yourself and those you're walking with. No one likes getting left behind or feeling pressured to rush. You're only as strong as your weakest member, so pick a trail that you can all enjoy and share together.

Allow enough time

There's nothing worse than having to power-walk a trail because you're worried about running out of daylight (except maybe *actually* running out of daylight). Check ahead of time how long your chosen trail is expected to take, then allow time for rest breaks, snacks and photos. And remember, you're only as fast as your slowest walker.

Carry a phone and PLB

In any emergency, your first option for help should be dialling 000 on your mobile phone. If you don't have reception right where you are, see if there's an option to walk up a short hill or into a clearing. If you're tackling a remote route or one where mobile phone reception is questionable (and there's plenty in this book), it's wise to carry a Personal Locator Beacon (PLB). These can be rented from outdoor shops and some national parks offices. Remember that calling in the choppers is for proper dire emergencies – not for when you're feeling a bit tired or you've run out of chocolate.

First Aid

Carry a first-aid kit and get some skills. There are plenty of reputable websites and training courses that offer tips and training on First Aid and Wilderness First Aid.

How big your first-aid kit is and what it contains might vary depending on where you're going but at the very least some painkillers, adhesive plasters, pressure immobilisation bandages and a whistle are a good starting point. Longer, remote or multi-day hikes, where you're far from help, might warrant supplies expanding to include anti-inflammatories, non-stick gauze dressings, bandages, stick-on wound closing strips, insect bite gels, rehydrating powders, or whatever else you feel is appropriate. Do your research and ensure you know how to use whatever supplies or medications you're carrying.

One common malaise for walkers is the blister – a small thing that can turn into a massive problem.

A misty morning on the Pieman River, Tas

On Blisters

Friction is the enemy. There are a bunch of things you can do to avoid it, as well as actions to take if things do go pear-shaped:

- Make sure footwear is worn in so it's had a chance to soften up and mold to your feet. Feet often swell on the trail so avoid shoes that fit too snugly.

- Trim your toenails so they don't dig into soft damp skin.

- Choose well-fitting socks that don't bunch up or have thick seams. Wearing an inner layer, such as an anti-blister sock that creates a slippery buffer, can help.

- On long hikes, airing your feet regularly to keep the skin dry can make them more resilient to abrasion.

- You can minimise friction by stuffing hikers' wool inside your socks or applying powder or petroleum jelly to the skin. If you're particularly susceptible to blisters, you might want to consider some pre-emptive taping of the feet or toes.

- Treat hot spots as soon as you feel them to stop them turning into big painful problems. Ideally you want to apply a second-skin, such as tape or adhesive gel pads like Compeed (stick-on plasters have the potential to create more friction).

- If you do end up with a fat blister, the most sterile approach is to leave it alone – however that can be painful. The alternative is to relieve the pressure by lancing it. Give your hands and the blister area a good wash first, then sterilise a sharp needle (I use a safety pin) using an antiseptic wipe. Rather than stabbing the bubble head-on, it's better to come at it from an angle, gently 'lifting' the skin with the tip of the needle until it just punctures the blister. The smaller the hole in your skin, the less chance of any nasties entering. Drain all the fluid from it, wipe it clean and then cover with a non-stick dressing.

Leeches

You'll generally only come across these blood-suckers in damp forests or rivers. Covering up the skin and spraying your socks with insect repellent will largely avoid interactions but if one should latch on, don't rip it off in a panic (or burn it with a cigarette end, cover it in salt, etc). These methods will freak them out and cause them to regurgitate bacteria-filled blood back into you – this is when infection can occur. Simply slide a fingernail under the head and flick it away.

Snakes

Although many Aussie snake varieties are venomous, the vast majority of the time they will do their best to avoid you. Keep your eyes open – especially around long grass or when stepping over logs. Don't provoke snakes, and if you see one give it a respectfully wide berth. Note that snakes don't have eardrums but they do feel vibrations. In particularly snaky areas, you may want to consider wearing leg gaiters for a little extra protection.

If you get bitten:

- Lie down and don't move. Venom travels via the lymph system which pumps fluid around the body via muscle movement.
- Stay calm and call emergency services.
- Don't wash the bite area. Any venom on it can help with identification and choosing the most appropriate anti-venom. In any event, a generic anti-venom will still be effective.
- Apply a pressure immobilisation bandage: Wrap a 10cm wide bandage directly over the bite, firmly but not so tight as to cut the blood off. Then apply a second bandage moving upwards of the bite the full length of affected limb (e.g. from toes to groin, or fingers to armpit) to prevent the venom moving to the rest of the body. Applying a splint will prevent any movement of the limb.
- Mark the location of the bite on the bandage.

GEAR

The right gear can make the difference between a fun day out and a survival experience. What you need will vary depending on the walk you choose but there are a few universal factors to consider.

Footwear

Many walkers are increasingly opting to wear trail runners or hiking shoes over hiking boots. Whether you go for waterproof or non-waterproof is another choice to make. It's all personal preference but here are a few points to think about:

- Boots will give you more ankle support than runners and will generally have a firmer foot base which reduces fatigue on the feet over uneven ground; they stop you feeling every little rock.

- Boots can be overkill if the terrain is flat or well graded, leading to your feet feeling more tired and uncomfortable than they need to be.

- Trail runners are definitely more comfortable than hiking boots, however over a multi-day hike they can sometimes lack the structure and arch support required – particularly when carrying a load. Having said that, I've worn runners on long hikes where the terrain was easy and my feet have been happier for it.

- It's often said that trail runners will dry quicker than boots if you have to cross a stream or you get caught in torrential rain. Conversely, boots with a Gore-tex (or similar) lining are far more likely to keep your feet dry in the first place, negating the need to dry out.

Hiking poles

I'd never used poles until I started long-distance hiking but now they're with me on every multi-day trip (i.e. when I'm carrying a load) and on day hikes where the terrain is steep or slippery. They significantly reduce knee strain, help hoist you on the uphills, provide stability (I can't tell you how many times they've saved me from a face plant when I've tripped) and are super handy when rock hopping rivers, testing the depth of mud/puddles, or pushing aside trailside foliage to check for critters.

Day hikes

Short walks are pretty straightforward but you can still end up with quite a load, particularly if you're carrying lots of water, or helping to lighten the burden for kids or a buddy. Look for a pack with around 25-30 litre capacity. Having some structure to it will ensure it doesn't flop all over the place, plus it helps spread the load. Wearing the hip belt and chest straps done up helps keep the pack nice and snug against your body, reducing stress on your shoulders and back.

Gear checklist for day hikes

- Plenty of food for lunch and snacks (*see* p. xvii)
- Plenty of water - minimum 2L per person for a day hike (in warm weather or hilly terrain you will drink more)
- First-aid kit (*see* p. xii)
- Insect repellent
- Sunscreen
- Hand sanitiser
- Rain jacket (or a light windproof or spray jacket if the forecast is good)
- Warm clothes (if the location and forecast requires it. Bear in mind it's often surprisingly cool in windy places or up high; the weather in alpine areas can change rapidly)
- Toilet paper/tissues
- Mobile phone (loaded with navigation app and offline map of your route)
- Paper map (*see* p. x)
- Whistle

Multi-day hikes

You'll obviously need to be self-sufficient on a multi-day hike, which means a bigger pack and more in it. There's often a lot of trailside talk dedicated to the topic of gear but know that there is no one perfect, definitive set of equipment. Everyone has their own preferences and needs (some people feel the cold while others don't, some need a plush sleeping mat while others are happy with a flimsy sheet of foam), so do your research and select what works for you.

Lighten your load

The one thing all hikers agree on is to aim for as light a pack as possible. It's tempting to bounce one piece of equipment in the palm of your hand and think it doesn't weigh much but if there is a lighter alternative, take it. If you can shave 20 per cent off every item in your pack, it might end up saving a few kilos overall and you will definitely notice that. The commonly quoted rule of thumb is to have a total pack weight no greater than a third of your body weight, but ideally aim for much less. Bear in mind that drinking water will add a kilo for every litre you carry, plus food will be up to one kilo per day. It can be helpful to set up a spreadsheet listing every item in your pack and its weight so you can see where the grams are coming from. There's a saying that goes 'if you don't know what it weighs, it's too heavy'.

Gear checklist for multi-day hikes.

Make adjustments depending on the season or the destination.

- Plenty of food (*see* p. xvii)
- Plenty of water - minimum 2L per person per day (in warm weather or hilly terrain you will drink more)
- Water bottles or bladders
- Water purification system (filter or purification tablets)
- Tent
- Groundsheet to protect the base of your tent (a piece of Tyvek makes a tough and super lightweight alternative to a traditional groundsheet)
- Sleeping mat
- Sleeping bag or quilt
- Sleeping bag liner (adds extra warmth and keeps your sleeping bag clean)
- Inflatable pillow (some people stuff clothes in a dry bag to use as a pillow)
- Pack liner or plastic bin bag (see p. xvi)
- Stove and fuel

- Cooking pot (eat out of this and you won't need to carry a bowl)
- Cup
- Utensils and one sharp knife
- First-aid kit (*see* p. xii), emergency blanket, PLB (*see* p. xii)
- Insect repellent
- Sunscreen
- Hand sanitiser
- Toilet paper and trowel
- Mobile phone (loaded with navigation app and offline map of your route); power bank optional
- Paper map (*see* p. x)
- Whistle
- Headtorch
- Toiletries (*see* p. xvi)
- Rain jacket and pants
- Insulated jacket (down is lightweight and compact but doesn't like to get wet, synthetic is bulkier but hardier and more ethical)
- Clothes
  - 2 × pairs of socks/underwear (plus 1 × pair bed-socks)
  - 2 × short-sleeve thermal T-shirts
  - 1 × long-sleeve thermal top
  - 1 × fleece jacket
  - 1 × long pair pants
  - 1 × thermal leggings
  - 1 × shorts
  - beanie
- Camp shoes (lightweight and comfy)
- Gaiters (to keep dirt and sand out of shoes and/or provide some snake protection)
- Camera
- Walking poles
- Feel-good stuff (see p. xvi)

Notes on gear

- **Clothes:** Generally speaking, aim to wear one set of clothes and keep another set dry for evenings. Two sets of underwear should be enough - wash daily and rotate.

- **Packs:** Choose a pack that's comfortable for your torso size and have it properly fitted in-store if you can.

Hacks

- **Minimise packaging:** I used to use the stuff sacks that my sleeping bag, down jacket, sleeping mat, etc. came in, until I realised that the resulting 'cylinders' just created a lot of dead space in my pack. Removing stuff sacs can greatly reduce your pack volume. The same can be said for plastic containers. Roughly separate your gear by all means (food, clothes, for example), but use soft-sided bags and keep them loosely packed so they can find their own nooks and crannies inside your pack. When it comes to food, remove all unnecessary packaging before you head out on the trail to save weight and space, and to reduce the rubbish you need to carry home.

- **Keeping things dry:** You'll want to ensure that the contents of your pack stay bone-dry, regardless of the conditions. A pack-cover will shed the bulk of a downfall but lining your pack with a dedicated pack liner or plastic bin bag will give you ultimate security.

- **Toiletries:** It goes without saying that mini sizes are best when it comes to toothpaste, soap or deodorant. A loofah mitt (of the kind used to buff your skin smooth) is a great way to scrub your body squeaky clean at the end of a day with minimal soap and water. Also, a thick disposable dishcloth (e.g. Chux) works just as well as a travel towel and is a fraction of the weight and quick-drying.

- **Feel-good stuff:** It's amazing the morale-boosting power of small luxuries when you're living on the trail. Everyone's idea of a treat is different. Mine is a book to keep me entertained in camp, plus I also carry a tiny chunk of Lush massage bar. A little goes a long way and just a 5min rub of the feet, calves and thighs makes a massive difference to recovery.

Right Resting on Mount Oakleigh on Tasmania's Overland Track *Opposite* Walking east from Mount Sonder/Rutjupma on the Larapinta Trail, NT

FUELLING YOUR BODY

Drinking water

Ideally carry enough drinking water for your hike, rather than collecting en route. If you're doing a multi-day hike, most campsites will have either a water tank or a stream to top up. It's a good idea to filter, boil or chemically treat (with purification tablets) all water, even if it looks clean. With water tanks there is the chance of mosquito larvae wrigglers being in them; with rivers a risk of humans or animals upstream having contaminated the water. Getting diarrhoea or some long-lasting stomach bug like giardia is not pleasant, so it's best to be on the safe side.

Food

On a multi-day hike you'll need food that is lightweight, filling, non-perishable and ideally nutritious (particularly important on longer trips). Freeze-dried meals from a camping shop are a convenient albeit somewhat expensive option, however you can often do pretty well just stocking up from supermarket shelves.

Opt for choices like dried packet pasta meals (e.g. carbonara, tomato and bacon), ramen noodle soup, dehydrated mashed potato with flavoured tuna swirled through it (buy it in pouches rather than tins), flavoured couscous, rice noodles with soup mix, etc. It might not be haute cuisine but all food looks really appealing after a day on the trail. If you really want to get clever, dehydrate your own home-cooked meals. Leave tinned food at home – you'll regret the weight.

For lunch, you might want crackers or mountain bread wraps with your choice of filling (cheese, peanut butter, salami, etc). Breakfast options include porridge, muesli, dehydrated egg powder (yes, it's a thing) or oatcakes with spread. Energy-giving snacks include nuts, dried fruit, jerky or muesli bars. Chocolate is a great energy and morale booster.

Remove whatever packaging you can before you hit the trail to save weight and space. Zip-lock bags are great for storing things like muesli or nuts but seek out the growing array of reusable silicone bags to ensure you're not adding to the world's plastic problem.

FITNESS & TRAINING

No special training is required for a day outing, but if you're thinking about tackling one of the many longer hikes in this book then you'll enjoy it far more if you're physically and mentally prepared for it.

A strong and balanced body helps with any physical activity and, when it comes to hiking, core, glutes and knees will probably be your main focus. Whatever weaknesses you have will only be amplified once on the trail, so take care to address any niggles before you go.

Nothing prepares your body for walking quite like walking. Get your feet used to the regular impact – and make sure you wear your hiking shoes in. If you're not used to carrying a pack, carry one on training hikes, building up distance until you feel familiar and comfortable with it. It's quite possible that a little fine-tuning on the fit of your pack during training sessions will make a big difference to enjoyment when the main event arrives.

If you plan to hike in a group, go on some shorter walks together first to get a sense of how fit and prepared everyone is. Your group of friends might seem enthusiastic about a multi-day or strenuous hike, but not everyone will understand the reality of required fitness levels until you start.

One of the most valuable assets you've got is your mind and cultivating a positive can-do attitude will see you through most challenges. Multi-day hiking is not always a bed of roses but tough times rarely last.

THE EASIER PATH – TOURS

Nothing compares to the satisfaction and solitude of discovering a trail on your own, but if logistics or the thought of sourcing gear and carrying a heavy pack are deterring you, many of the longer hikes in this book are offered as part of a guided or self-guided tour. Check itineraries first as some walking companies offer an abridged version or a selection of trail highlights rather than the whole thing.

In every state and territory are local tour companies. Often they have an eco or environmental focus or a specific focus on First Nations' culture. Here are just a few of the many tour company options available:

Australian Walking Company
auswalkingco.com.au

Australian Walking Holidays
australianwalkingholidays.com.au

Auswalk
auswalk.com.au

Great Walks of Australia
greatwalksofaustralia.com.au

Life's An Adventure
lifesanadventure.com.au

Park Trek Walking Holidays Australia
parktrek.com.au

Trek Larapinta
treklarapinta.com.au

Tas Walking Company
taswalkingco.com.au

Trek Tours Australia
trektoursaustralia.com.au

Guided tours

There's very little preparation required for a guided multi-day hike, other than making sure your fitness is up to par. Guides will take care of all route-finding and are usually founts of knowledge on flora, fauna and history. While some operators use glamping tents, others will whisk you to a hotel at the end of each day and ply you with three-course meals, wine and foot spas. Luggage is transferred to your accommodation each night so all you need to carry is a daypack with your water, lunch, camera and a jacket. You'll have the security and also the social aspect that comes with walking in a group.

Self-guided tours

With self-guided you get the benefit of having logistics taken care of and no pack to carry, along with the flexibility of starting on any day that suits and not having to share the trail with anyone. Self-guided trips allow you to maintain that sense of discovery and provide the freedom to walk at your own pace. There's no one holding your hand along the way but you'll be given detailed walk notes, nightly accommodation in lodges or hotels, all meals including a packed lunch, and the tour company will transport your pack for you.

Top Walking the Jatbula Trail, NT

NO IMPACT WALKING

In the grand scheme of things, humans have made a substantial impact on the planet and out in the bush there is no one to tidy the place up after we've left. We share the space with other people and animals so keep a low profile and leave no trace.

Take only photos, leave only footprints

It's an oldie but a goodie. Avoid the temptation to pick wildflowers, don't walk on moss or other ground-dwelling plants (they take ages to grow), and definitely don't engrave your name on trees, rocks or huts. Carry all rubbish out with you, including organic matter like orange peel and eggshells.

Washing

When washing pots and bowls, do it well away from rivers and lakes, otherwise you'll end up tainting the water with grease and leftover two-minute noodles. Scoop up a pot of water and carry it at least 10m away to do the dishes. Likewise, wash your sweat/sunscreen/insect-repellent-covered body away from water sources. Keep soap to a minimum and ideally use a biodegradable variety. Don't spit toothpaste out right next to a water tank or in a prominent place. Scuff some dirt over it to cover it up.

Keep wildlife wild

It's tempting to want to connect with furry and feathered friends but you're not doing them any favours by sharing your food with them. Human food can make wild animals sick, deter them from foraging or hunting for their usual foods, and ultimately make them aggressive towards humans.

Music

If you want to listen to music, keep it stuffed in your ears rather than broadcast across the countryside.

Drones

Drones take amazing footage but can be annoying to anyone trying to enjoy a little serenity – and some people feel like they're an invasion of their privacy. Permits are required for drone use in many places so if you do want to use one, check the rules first and be considerate of other wanderers.

Say no to stone stacks

It's tempting to make a little stone stack work of art on a river bank or mountain top but stone beds stabilise environments and provide essential habitat for critters, even if you can't see them. Moving rocks can disturb or even kill them.

When nature calls

If you get caught out away from a loo when you need one, bury your efforts in a hole 15cm deep and at least 50m away from any watercourses. If you're lucky enough to find a long-drop toilet, remember that most require the seat lid to be closed after use to work effectively and break down the contents. There's nothing worse than seeing toilet paper discarded in the bush so take a bag to carry it out with you and dispose of it responsibly elsewhere.

Stick to the track

Shortcuts cause erosion, potentially destabilising a route or damaging flora and fauna. It's best to walk through puddles as constant deviations around them can widen the trail and damage the landscape.

City Walks

Sydney/Warrang

BONDI TO COOGEE

If you want to soak up some of Sydney's famous coastline, the Bondi to Coogee walk is 6km of impressive scenery. An easy footpath hugs the coast all the way, undulating around sculpted sandstone cliffs and headlands and dropping in at numerous divine beaches and ocean baths. Ocean gazing aside, highlights include Aboriginal rock engravings near Marks Park, the famously photogenic Bondi Icebergs ocean pool, Clovelly Bowling Club with its panoramic ocean backdrop and heritage-listed Waverley cemetery. If you want to press pause and take a swim, Gordons Bay underwater nature trail is fascinating (mask and snorkel required).

The walk might be short but by the time you factor in a few swims and cafe stops, it'll probably take a while. Public transport to either end is easy.

Resources
bonditocoogeewalk.com.

Left Spectacular coastal views from Bondi to Coogee
Opposite Capturing the views at the top of kunanyi/Mount Wellington in Hobart/nipaluna

Melbourne/Naarm

MAIN YARRA TRAIL

The Main Yarra Trail slips directly out of Melbourne's CBD to follow the Yarra River/Birrarung as it meanders north-east out of the city. While the whole trail is 35km, a super pretty section is Richmond to Fairfield, following a green corridor through the inner suburbs. This section takes in the historic Abbotsford Convent (now an arts precinct), Collingwood Children's Farm and Dights Falls. You'll finish at the historic Fairfield Boathouse, nestled amid the gum trees, where you can indulge in a cream tea or rent a rowboat (there's a fleet of hand-built replicas of British pleasure craft from the 1800s), or kayak to continue exploring this peaceful part of the river.

Allow a few hours for the walk, plus breaks. Trains and trams connect Richmond and Fairfield with the city.

Resources
walkingmaps.com.au/walk/4347.

Top Fairfield Boathouse

Adelaide/Tarndanya

MOUNT LOFTY

Mount Lofty is a magnet for Adelaide walkers and the steep 4km climb from Waterfall Gully forest to Lofty's 727m summit is literally the most popular trail in South Australia. It's a pretty hike through the forest, passing several waterfalls and maybe the odd koala and kangaroo, but if you don't fancy jostling with the lycra-clad crowd on a cardio workout there are plenty of less hectic ways to summit. The 3.8km Steub Trail is gentle and well-graded - great for families - and starts from Cleland Wildlife Park. Alternatively, try the energetic but still relatively crowd-free 15km route from Chambers Gully to the summit.

Whichever way you do it, anyone who reaches Mount Lofty's peak will be amply rewarded with expansive views over Adelaide and the distant ocean from a huge lookout and cafe complex.

Resources
Download the Cleland Conservation Park walking trails map from parks.sa.gov.au.

Top One of several trails to Mount Lofty's summit *Bottom* Enjoyng the view from Mount Lofty

Perth/Boorloo

KINGS PARK

You don't have to travel far for a great walk in Perth. On the south-western fringe of the CBD is the world's biggest inner-city park and two-thirds of it is bushland. Perched on the Mount Eliza escarpment and with stunning views over the Swan River and Perth skyline, Kings Park is crisscrossed with trails and one of the most scenic is the 2.5km Law Walk. It begins from the Karri Pavillion, launching onto a spectacular glass and steel walkway suspended 16m high in the tree canopy, before transitioning through the manicured Botanic Gardens to a natural bush track that is dotted with wildflowers in spring.

The entire loop takes about 45min but if you want to keep walking follow a 7km circuit around Kings Park, or just grab a bite at the Botanical Cafe and chillax in the extensive gardens.

Resources
bgpa.wa.gov.au/kings-park.

Top Exploring Kings Park *Bottom* Elevated walkway on the Law Walk

City Walks

Darwin / Garramilla

EAST POINT RESERVE

Just 6km north of the city, East Point Reserve was a significant military fortress during World War II, but now it's a popular recreation hangout for Darwin locals and visitors alike. Allow 2-3 hours for a roughly 7km loop around the point, with interpretive signage, passing mangrove habitat, remnant monsoon rainforest, coastal lookouts and the remains of military infrastructure, including an observation tower. Efforts are being made to regenerate the land and it's home to wildlife, including wallabies, monitor lizards, orange-footed scrubfowl and migrating birds.

Pause to drop in at the Darwin Military Museum or grab a meal or a drink at the classy Pee Wees at the Point, overlooking the sea. Afterwards, cool off with a swim in Lake Alexander.

Resources
darwin.nt.gov.au.

East Point Reserve's rainforest trails

Brisbane/Meanjin

MOUNT COOT-THA FOREST

At 5km west of the city of Brisbane, Mount Coot-tha Forest is the closest place for a dose of the bush and it's riddled with scores of trails for hikers and mountain bikers. They're short, ranging from 300m to 3km in length, but you can piece together any number of them to create a walk that suits as you traverse this eucalypt forest popping with bellbirds. The Summit Track is the flagship trail, a steady 1.9km/30min climb from JC Slaughter Falls picnic area to Mount Coot-tha Lookout, with its sweeping views across Brisbane's CBD, Moreton Bay and the surrounding peaks of Mount Barney, Flinders Peak and the Tweed Volcano.

If you need to blow out the cobwebs, try the wickedly steep Kokoda Track, or immerse yourself in the spring wildflowers that proliferate around Simpson Falls Track.

Resources
Download the Mount Coot-tha Forest Track map from brisbane.qld.gov.au.

City Walks

Mount Coot-tha Lookout

Hobart/nipaluna

KUNANYI/MOUNT WELLINGTON

You can't miss the impressive and often snow-capped bulk of kunanyi/Mount Wellington, rising 1271m behind the island state's capital city. Catch a metro bus or the Mount Wellington Explorer Bus to access the mountain and numerous trails that vary in length and puff factor. An easy 1.4km route across the summit plateau showcases a wonderland of dolerite boulders, small pools and sturdy alpine plants, and the expansive views over Hobart and the Derwent River are utterly epic. Another popular option is the 3hr return hike to the Organ Pipes where a wall of hexagonal dolerite pillars rise up to 120m.

There's plenty more to explore but if conditions are too gnarly for hiking - trails and roads can be closed due to inclement weather and snow - simply retreat to the summit's glass-fronted observation shelter and soak up the views.

Resources
Download the Bushwalking Information Sheet and map from wellingtonpark.org.au.

Top Commanding views from kunanyi/Mount Wellington

New South Wales

Australia's most populous state offers diverse hiking, from the highest mountain peak to outback and a spectacular coastline.

Walk around one of the world's most spectacular harbours, passing secluded coves, cliff-tops, and multi-million dollar houses.

Bondi to Manly Walk

This walk is on <u>Eora Country</u>.

WHY IT'S SPECIAL

The Bondi to Manly – also called the B2M – might essentially be an urban hike but this coastal meander around the dazzling headlands and inlets of Sydney Harbour, between the two famous beaches of Bondi and Manly, provides a glimpse into sides of Sydney/Warrang that you wouldn't otherwise come across. Stretches of bush peeking through to emerald coves sprinkled with yachts, are interspersed with residential pockets whose architecture is just as spectacular. The entire Bondi to Manly route rarely strays from the coast so be prepared to get distracted by regular swimming opportunities in hidden coves and ocean pools, as well as al fresco cafes with water views.

Traversing the coast on foot gives a far deeper understanding of Sydney than can be gained any other way. You travel slow enough to smell the flowers, dip your toes in the many alluring bays, meet the locals, and understand the layers of history that tell the story behind one of the world's greatest harbours.

WALK IT

You could allow anything from three to seven days for this one, travelling light and fast or taking time to linger for a swim, see the sights en route and have a few leisurely lunches. If you're not up for the full distance, pick a section such as the popular 9km/3.5hr leg from The Spit to Manly.

One of the delights of this walk is that you don't need to carry much. Leave the tent at home and stay in hotels along the way (*see* p. 15), and if you can't find something to fit your budget at day's end, catching a bus to and from the trail is pretty easy. Water filling stations are plentiful so you rarely need to carry more than a bottle with you, and there are loads of cafes to keep the belly stoked. Though track signage is minimal, following the course on the trail's app makes staying on route a piece of cake.

 Trail talk
- Distance: 78km
- Time: 3 days
- Rating: Easy-moderate
- Technicality: It's mostly sealed surfaces and well-defined bush track with a sprinkling of beaches.
- Puff factor: Though it follows the coast, be ready for numerous short climbs and steps peppered throughout.
- Watch out for: Sun exposure. Good sun protection is a must.

 When to go
Summer offers long days and warm seas but can make for hot walking. Winter is drier and cooler and there's the chance of spotting whales but the sea will be colder.

 Resources
Visit bonditomanly.com for suggested itineraries, printable maps and trail notes. Download the Bondi to Manly app for easy navigation.

The Bondi to Manly Walk: the Definitive Guidebook by Tara Wells gives detailed interpretive information and suggestions on the many places to break your journey and find a bed and a meal.

Opposite Skirting the cliff-tops around Vaucluse *Previous* Main Range Track

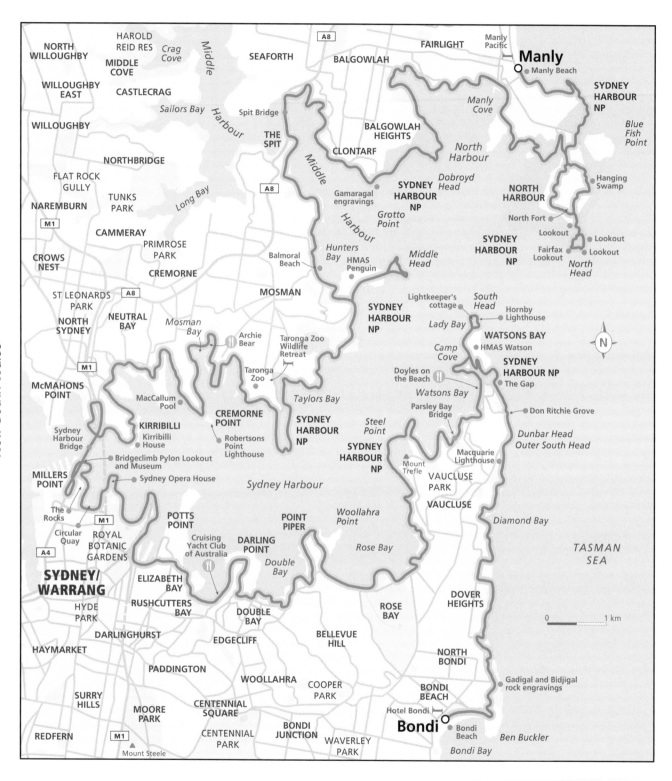

New South Wales

NORTH WILLOUGHBY
HAROLD REID RES
Crag Cove
MIDDLE COVE
SEAFORTH
A8
FAIRLIGHT
Manly Pacific
Manly
BALGOWLAH
Manly Beach

WILLOUGHBY EAST
CASTLECRAG
Sailors Bay
Spit Bridge
Manly Cove
SYDNEY HARBOUR NP

WILLOUGHBY
Middle Harbour
THE SPIT
BALGOWLAH HEIGHTS
North Harbour
Blue Fish Point

NORTHBRIDGE
A8
CLONTARF
Dobroyd Head
NORTH HARBOUR
Hanging Swamp

FLAT ROCK GULLY
Long Bay
Gamaragal engravings
SYDNEY HARBOUR NP
North Fort
Lookout

NAREMBURN
M1
TUNKS PARK
Grotto Point
Lookout
Lookout

CAMMERAY
Balmoral Beach
Hunters Bay
HMAS Penguin
Middle Head
Fairfax Lookout
SYDNEY HARBOUR NP
North Head

CROWS NEST
PRIMROSE PARK
CREMORNE
MOSMAN
Lightkeeper's cottage
South Head
Hornby Lighthouse

ST LEONARDS PARK
A8
SYDNEY HARBOUR NP
Lady Bay
WATSONS BAY

NORTH SYDNEY
NEUTRAL BAY
Mosman Bay
Archie Bear
Taronga Zoo Wildlife Retreat
Camp Cove
HMAS Watson
SYDNEY HARBOUR NP

McMAHONS POINT
MacCallum Pool
Taronga Zoo
Taylors Bay
Doyles on the Beach
The Gap
Watsons Bay

Sydney Harbour Bridge
KIRRIBILLI
Kirribilli House
CREMORNE POINT
SYDNEY HARBOUR NP
Steel Point
Parsley Bay Bridge
Don Ritchie Grove

MILLERS POINT
Bridgeclimb Pylon Lookout and Museum
Robertsons Point Lighthouse
SYDNEY HARBOUR NP
Dunbar Head Outer South Head
Macquarie Lighthouse

The Rocks
Sydney Opera House
Mount Trefle
VAUCLUSE PARK
Diamond Bay

Circular Quay
M1
ROYAL BOTANIC GARDENS
POTTS POINT
POINT PIPER
Woollahra Point
VAUCLUSE
TASMAN SEA

A4
SYDNEY/ WARRANG
Cruising Yacht Club of Australia
DARLING POINT
Double Bay
Rose Bay
DOVER HEIGHTS

HYDE PARK
ELIZABETH BAY
ROSE BAY

DARLINGHURST
RUSHCUTTERS BAY
DOUBLE BAY

HAYMARKET
PADDINGTON
WOOLLAHRA
BELLEVUE HILL
NORTH BONDI
Gadigal and Bidjigal rock engravings

SURRY HILLS
MOORE PARK
CENTENNIAL SQUARE
COOPER PARK
BONDI BEACH
Hotel Bondi
Bondi

REDFERN
M1
Mount Steele
CENTENNIAL PARK
BONDI JUNCTION
WAVERLEY PARK
Bondi Beach
Ben Buckler
Bondi Bay

0   1 km

N

LOCAL SNAPSHOT

The land around Sydney Harbour has long been hot property. It is the Traditional Land of about 29 clan groups of the Eora Nation and Gadigal and Bidigal Peoples' rock engravings are passed on this walk (day 1). When European settlers arrived from 1788, private estates began securing waterfront real estate, and public access for leisure activities such as swimming, fishing and picnics became more difficult. However, from the late 1800s onwards, community movements, protests and organisations, such as the Harbour Foreshores Vigilance Committee, sought to turn the tide. From the 1960s, the state government began buying up foreshore for public green space and in 1975 Sydney Harbour National Park was gazetted, preserving 392ha of discontinuous harbourside foreshore. It's pockets such as these that often provide some of the highlights of walking the B2M.

Top Snack break at Camp Cove

ITINERARY

DAY 1
Bondi to Rushcutters Bay, 24km, 8hr

Bondi Beach is a hive of activity when I start at 7am on a summer's morning. It feels like an early start for me but the locals are already pumping out ocean swims and working buff bodies on the open-air gym equipment, leaving me feeling decidedly unattractive in comparison.

As the walk heads north through Dover Heights and Watsons Bay, it squeezes between the ocean and the first of many impressive water-view homes, along strips of grassy cliff-top parkland wriggling with dogs and stretches of boardwalk, with views of the pounding ocean below.

Rock engravings in the cliff-top sandstone by the Gadigal and Bidjigal Peoples would be hard to find without the trail's handy app flagging them. Unfenced and with only a small plaque acknowledging them, the engravings are at risk of weathering away. Already, the council did a little DIY regrooving in 1964 – the success of which is debatable. Other areas of interest flagged on the app include Macquarie Lighthouse (the site of Australia's first lighthouse) and Don Ritchie Grove, a tribute to a local resident who talked at least 160 people out of suicide at the notorious cliff-top, The Gap.

Old gun emplacements, a lighthouse and lightkeeper's cottage dot South Head, and from here the route turns west into the Harbour where I'm immediately tempted to buy a snack I don't need at a tiny kiosk strung with bags of oranges set at one end of a sheltered arc of golden sand. Sat under a thatched umbrella at Camp Cove and sucking on fresh OJ, I could be somewhere in the Med yet, surreally, I'm in a major capital city with views of the city across the water.

It's in the discovery of such gems as this that the B2M excels, taking you off the standard tourist trail and showcasing places you wouldn't come across unless you're a local. Parsley Bay is another treat. A historic suspension footbridge spans its clear emerald waters and then the walk flits between beaches, unsealed coastal trails and the back streets of Double Bay and surrounds, where the houses are so flash that even some car garages have windows with Harbour Bridge views.

I spend a night at a motel a 5min walk from the Cruising Yacht Club of Australia and share a few drinks with the crew of a yacht preparing for an imminent Sydney to Hobart Race.

DAY 2
Rushcutters Bay to The Spit, 32km, 10hr

In the still morning, the yachts of Rushcutters Bay glow in the early sun. I leave them behind to wind through the narrow streets and steps of Potts Point with its Art Deco apartment buildings. The middle part of this walk is unavoidably urban as it passes through the city but, with up-close looks at the Harbour Bridge and Opera House, I am not complaining. Beyond the Royal Botanic Gardens I make my way around Circular Quay and The Rocks and then cross the Harbour Bridge. The pedestrian walkway along its eastern side is caged for safety but still offers fabulous views of the Harbour. If you're serious about getting the ultimate panorama, catch the lift up to the Bridgeclimb Pylon Lookout and Museum, or harness up and traverse the Bridge's iconic steel arches on a guided tour (bridgeclimb.com).

Architecture is different on the northern side but it's as equally jaw-dropping. After pressing my nose against the gates of Kirribilli House (the Prime Minister's residence), I follow paved trails with fragrant gardens on one side and fresh views of the Harbour on the other. Cremorne Point is renowned for its Federation-style homes, hung with greenery and tiered into the sandstone as it slopes towards sea. Winding in and out of sleepy coves, I pass MacCallum Pool (a 1920s seawater pool overlooking the Harbour), the deep green waters of Mosman Bay and a small white lighthouse clinging to Cremorne Point.

Beyond the tall fences of Taronga Zoo are a good three hours of excellent dirt track, where peeling Sydney red gums offer shade and Eastern water dragons regularly laze mid-path. Ever present is the Harbour, peeking through the bushes and showing off its litter of vessels from fishing boats to super yachts. A well-earned swim in Taylors Bay washes away the sweat and revives my aching feet in readiness for the final leg for today, past the heritage-listed military fortifications at Middle Head and the expansive Balmoral Beach with its Art Deco bathers pavilion. With no convenient accommodation nearby, I catch an easy 10min bus to Manly and check into the same place I'll stay after the walk; it also means I can offload my belongings for the final day's hike.

DAY 3
The Spit to Manly and North Head, 22km, 7hr

Spit Bridge is raised several times daily for boats to pass through but at 6am all is quiet and it's just me, a lone pelican and a cormorant swimming in the clear water below like an odd-looking fish. The stretch from Spit to Manly has long been a popular hike and for good reason. This is a proper bushwalk, winding through lush pockets of strangler figs, moss-covered rocks and bracken fern, then drier sections of coastal heath, grass trees and wildflowers. You get the obligatory swimming opportunities in sleepy coves, plus extras like the Hanging Swamp where pooling water in the sandstone has created a peaty swampy wetland.

At Dobroyd Head is Grotto Point, featuring 1000-year-old Gamaragal People's sandstone engravings of fish, kangaroos and boomerangs. Such engravings are an important record of the Eora Nation's occupation and though there would have been a number of similar sites around the Harbour, many have been lost or damaged in Sydney's development.

The first clear look at the finish line comes at Dobroyd Head with expansive views across to Manly, but while the walk ends there the route first passes through Manly and continues out the other side to round North Head. Like South Head and Middle Head before it, this detour takes in more defence reminders with a barracks and parade ground, a Memorial Walk commemorating Australia's war history, quarantine cemetery and optional guided tours to explore the underground tunnels of North Fort. War history aside, North Head also has some dramatic cliff-top lookouts and the return back to Manly picks up a few more beaches for one last dip.

BEST EATS

- **Doyles on the Beach:** It's a Sydney seafood institution that's been going since 1885 with hard-to-resist al fresco dining right on the waterfront. You might have trouble cranking up the muscles after a leisurely lunch but hey, you're here to enjoy yourself! 11 Marine Pde, Watsons Bay; (02) 9337 2007; doyles.com.au.
- **Cruising Yacht Club of Australia:** Outdoors on the huge deck, overlooking Rushcutters Bay and surrounded by yachts, is the place to enjoy a few drinks and great pub food. 1 New Beach Rd, Darling Point; (02) 8292 7800; cyca.com.au.
- **Archie Bear:** This casual diner at the historic Mosman Rowers Club is perched right over the water at picturesque Mosman Bay. Great for breakfast, lunch, coffee or a cool drink. 3 Centenary Dr, Mosman; (02) 8006 8880; birdandbear.com.au.

———

BEST SLEEPS

Depending on where you want to break your walk each night, there are plentiful options. Here are a few recommendations:

- **Hotel Bondi:** Packing in loads of character, this renovated heritage hotel (1919) is located right across the road from the park and Bondi Beach. With a bistro, bar and beer garden onsite, it's location, location, location. 178 Campbell Pde, Bondi Beach; (02) 9130 3271; maloneyhotels.com.au.
- **Taronga Zoo Wildlife Retreat:** It's more than just a bed for the night. Add another dimension to your walk by spending a night overlooking a sanctuary that's home to koalas, platypus and echidnas. The deal includes guided wildlife tours, dinner, breakfast and entry to the zoo. Taronga Zoo, Bradleys Head Rd, Sydney; (02) 9969 2777; taronga.org.au.
- **Manly Pacific:** Recently renovated with light and cool coastal décor, this is a great choice to be right in the thick of the action and overlooking Manly Beach. 55 North Steyne, Manly; (02) 6190 1206; manlypacific.com.au.

Opposite top Whale markers are found along the walk
Opposite bottom Taylors Bay is one of many idyllic swimming opportunities

Palm forests, waterfalls, remote beaches and epic cliff-top hiking in the world's second-oldest national park.

Royal Coast Track

This walk is on <u>Dharawal Country</u>.

WHY IT'S SPECIAL

It might be a mere 1hr south of Sydney/Warrang by public transport but this coastal route in Royal National Park is a tour through some stunning and diverse terrain, making it a locals' favourite. We're talking sheer cliff-tops overlooking a pounding ocean, lush palm jungles, sandstone outcrops with swirling colours like neopolitan ice-cream, and a waterfall flowing directly into the ocean (reputedly one of only three in Australia), to name just a few highlights. Sprinkle in some wildflowers, lyrebirds and the possibility of spotting a whale or two and it's a real treat. Pack your swimming gear because there are beaches, creeks and waterfalls to swim at along the way. Australia's first national park certainly earned its place.

WALK IT

This is a one-way hike between Otford and Bundeena (either way is good but hiking north means you'll avoid finishing with a big climb up to the escarpment), so if you're not up for a car shuffle, public transport from Sydney offers an easy alternative. From Otford train station it's a 15min walk to the southern trailhead, and from the northern trailhead catch a ferry between Bundeena and Cronulla and an onward train. Hiking north to south means finishing with a decent climb up to Otford, plus the trains back to Sydney can be infrequent. There's car access to several points en route so dropping in for an out-and-back walk at places like Garie Beach or Wattamolla Falls allows for a shorter walk, or use the Park Connections bus (weekends only, parkconnections.com.au) to hop-on, hop-off at various points en route.

If you want to take your time, hike it over two days and camp at North Era Beach. It's only 8km from the southern trailhead however, which means you'll have one short day and one long one. If you've got the fitness, travelling light and fast and hiking the whole thing in a day might be preferable (if you skip the loop around Jibbon Head at the northern end, you can make it a 6–9 hour hike over 27km).

Trail talk
- Distance: 31km
- Time: 1 long day
- Rating: Moderate
- Technicality: Mostly straightforward dirt track, boardwalk and steps with a little rock hopping.
- Puff factor: With over 1000m of elevation to tackle, it can be a tad tiring.
- Watch out for: The route is often exposed to the elements. Care is required around the many unfenced cliffs and on river crossings; be extra careful after heavy rain.

When to go
Any time is good. Spring sees a burst of wildflowers on the heath. Whales may be spotted from the cliffs between June and Aug.

Resources
Visit nationalparks.nsw.gov.au for more details and wildwalks.com for detailed track notes. If you begin your walk from outside the park (i.e. Bundeena and Otford), then no National Parks Pass is required. If you drive to access points mid route, the cost is $12 per day.

Opposite A waterfall dropping into the ocean makes for a spectacular sight

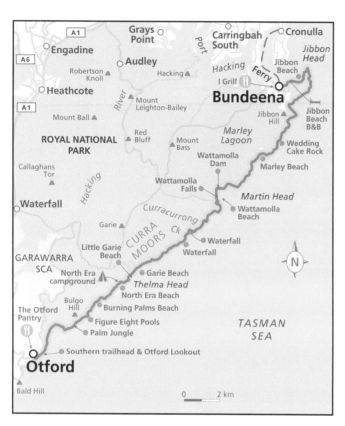

Map legend (labels on map):

Grays Point
Carringbah South
Cronulla
A1
Engadine
A6
Audley
Robertson Knoll
Hacking
Hacking
Jibbon Head
Jibbon Beach
I Grill
Ferry
Heathcote
Bundeena
A1
Mount Leighton-Bailey
Jibbon Hill
Jibbon Beach B&B
River
Mount Ball
Red Bluff
Mount Bass
Marley Lagoon
Wedding Cake Rock
ROYAL NATIONAL PARK
Wattamolla Dam
Marley Beach
Callaghans Tor
Wattamolla Falls
Martin Head
Wattamolla Beach
Hacking
Curracurrong
Waterfall
Garie
CURRA MOORS Ck
Waterfall
Waterfall
GARAWARRA SCA
Little Garie Beach
N
North Era campground
Garie Beach
Thelma Head
North Era Beach
Bulgo Hill
Burning Palms Beach
The Otford Pantry
Figure Eight Pools
Palm Jungle
TASMAN SEA
Southern trailhead & Otford Lookout
Otford
Bald Hill
0   2 km

◉ LOCAL SNAPSHOT

In the 1920s and Depression years of the '30s, things were tough. On private farms (later incorporated into Royal National Park), out-of-work men lived off the land, catching rabbits and fish and growing vegetables to feed their families. They built little cabins from local materials and 140 of these now heritage-listed shacks still scatter the coast around Little Garie, Era and Burning Palms beaches. The only access is on foot and there's no power or water, but families have passed these huts down through the generations and still use them as retreats today. A number of them are passed on this walk.

Bottom Walking across swirling sandstone cliffs
Opposite The Palm Jungle

ITINERARY

Look at any map of this route and you'll see the long string of enticing features drizzled along its length, but even the first steps out of Otford drop me in a peaceful forest layered with bracken ferns, banksia and the twisted rust-coloured boughs of Sydney red gums. Within an hour I'm deep in the Palm Jungle, an oasis of towering palms, hanging vines, strangler figs and rocks flocked in green moss. Green fronds clatter as I pass, the fallen ones creating a soft bed underfoot, and lyrebird song only adds to the magic (you'll hear one before you see it; keep an ear open for a super clear voice and a medley of different birdcalls).

When the trail emerges onto boardwalk over open grassland, I'm hit with expansive views across the ocean. A side-track leads down to the appropriately-named Figure Eight Pools, one of Sydney's most Instagrammable locations, where perfectly rounded plunge pools are worn into rock platforms – extreme care should be taken if you choose to have a look as large waves often crash over them. Only attempt access at low tide and in calm conditions.

Rising and falling, the route dips down to remote beaches and passes some of the many heritage-listed shacks built in the first half of the 1900s that scatter the coast. If you've planned to spend a night on the trail, North Era campground (see p. 20) is where you'll pitch a tent, about a 2.5hr walk from the southern trailhead. It's a simple grassy clearing behind the dunes of North Era Beach, unpatrolled and popular with surfers who hike in. It's a decent climb around Thelma Head to reach Little Garie Beach, from where the trail squeezes between a steep grassy slope and the polished rocks lining the ocean's edge. Further on, Garie Beach, about 45min from North Era campground, is accessible by car and has toilets and water. On weekends, the kiosk is open and the surf beach is patrolled.

After the hills of the southern end, the easy snaking boardwalk across the Curra Moors makes a welcome change. Low heath is punctuated by the stalks of gymea lilies and kangaroo tail grasstrees, and then it's up onto the exposed cliff-tops for some truly spectacular views down the coast. Here, the region's sandstone is on full display, sheering off in vertical walls that fall to frothy seas and swirling in shades of cream and caramel underfoot. I get really excited about a half-metre-wide flow of water spilling over the cliff-edge in a tiny spout, only to walk a little further to discover several proper waterfalls gushing 82m from the cliffs into the ocean. Located at about the halfway point, Curracurrong Creek, above the falls, seems like a good place to peel off my runners and soak my feet. It's also idyllic for a swim, having shallow and sheltered pools.

Wattamolla really deserves a few hours of attention but since I'm gunning for a day walk, I can only gaze longingly at this sheltered inlet with its wide sandy beach and the lucky people swimming beneath a waterfall that spills from a sheer and curving wall of rock 9m high (jumping from it is prohibited and many people have died trying). Beyond the rock hop over Wattamolla Dam the trail emerges on the ocean cliff-tops again, across sweeping rock platforms. I brace my legs wide before risking a peek over the cliff-edge, then realise I'm on the wrong side of a very big crack in the rock. No minor matter considering that (at time of writing) Wedding Cake Rock (which is smooth like marzipan) further on, is fenced off due to its predicted imminent collapse into the sea.

The trail feels quieter at its northern end, crossing Marley Beach and rounding Jibbon Head which features Dharawal engravings of whales, kangaroos, a stingray and spirit figure in sandstone slabs. They're some of the best-preserved carvings in the Sydney metropolitan area and a new viewing platform provides an elevated vantage point from which to appreciate and respect them. Such images are made by first 'pecking' the rock in a series of dots, which are then 'rubbed' to create a continuous groove in the sandstone about 2cm wide and 1cm deep. Grooves are prone to being filled by sand or lichen growth and senior men in the Dharawal community maintain the carvings.

By the time I flop into the sea at Jibbon Beach in Bundeena for a refreshing swim, my feet are aching and my mind spinning at everything I've seen in one day.

BEST EATS

- **The Otford Pantry:** This ocean-view, family-owned bakery is a great place for a pre-hike pie or empanada, or to grab a packed lunch for the hike. The coffee is good too and there is an extensive array of cakes. 22 Lady Wakehurst Dve, Otford; (02) 4294 1243.
- **I Grill:** With a Mediterranean edge, this popular place dishes up falafel, Greek gyros and Lebanese shish kebabs, alongside steak, seafood and burgers. 42 Brighton St, Bundeena; 0407 245 288; igrill.com.au.

BEST SLEEPS

- **North Era Campground:** This basic grassy campsite, located behind the dunes at North Era Beach, is located on the track, about 8km from the southern trailhead. It has a drop-toilet but no drinking water so you'll need to carry enough to see you through. Bookings are required through NSW National Parks, 1300 072 757. You'll also need to have a National Parks Pass.
- **Helensburgh Hotel:** You'll get classic pub-style accommodation at this heritage corner hotel, located just 5km from the southern trailhead. Rooms are basic (shared bathroom) but clean and recently renovated, and having a bar and bistro onsite is super handy. 112 Parkes St, Helensburgh; (02) 4294 1005; helensburghhotel.com.au.
- **Jibbon Beach B&B:** If you want to stay the night in sleepy Bundeena, you're best looking at a holiday rental such as this one (there are no hotels). It's right on the beach with fabulous sea views, and just a short walk from Royal National Park and the Bundeena Ferry. 1 Neil St, Bundeena; (02) 8521 7041; stayz.com.au.

Endless ocean views

Skirt around the inside of a lush canyon via rock ledges, ferns and waterfalls.

Grand Canyon Track

This walk is on <u>Dharug</u> and <u>Gundungurra Country</u>.

WHY IT'S SPECIAL

Over a million hectares of sandstone plateaus, escarpments, gorges and forest earned the Blue Mountains UNESCO World Heritage status in 2000, and of all the many gorgeous walking tracks that crisscross it, this one is especially awesome. It descends through moss-covered rainforest to follow Greaves Creek and the swirling walls of a canyon it has cut over millennia. In a feat of engineering – the track was cut in 1907 – the trail often sidles around the canyon's interior on narrow rock ledges and beneath overhangs that drip with ferns and waterfalls. A rock hop alongside the creek on the canyon floor is followed by a climb back out to Evans Lookout and a commanding view across the Grose Valley.

WALK IT

This loop walk is in the Blackheath area of the Blue Mountains. You can park at Neates Glen carpark or Evans Lookout but walking anti-clockwise from Neates is my preference, allowing you to start descending immediately into the action and return via a gentle climb back out of the canyon. Saving the short roadside section for the very end makes for a nice cool down.

If you're not averse to cold water, pack some swimwear for a dip in the pools along the canyon floor. It's best not to fill up drink bottles here – carry in what you'll need. It's also handy to carry a torch or your phone (if it has a torch) for one short rock-tunnel stretch mid-walk.

 Trail talk
- Distance: 6.3km loop
- Time: 3-3.5hr
- Rating: Moderate-hard
- Technicality: Dirt track, lots of steps and some rock hopping.
- Puff factor: There are a few steps in and out of the gorge but you'll be pausing so often to admire the scenery there'll be plenty of time to catch your breath.
- Watch out for: Surfaces can be slippery in both wet and dry conditions. Be especially careful near the edge of the canyon.

 When to go
It's good year-round and is particularly appealing for a cool escape on hot days. Rug up in winter because it can get extra cold down there. Avoid after heavy rain when the creek may be in flood.

 Resources
Visit nationalparks.nsw.gov.au for more info or wildwalks.com to download a detailed map and trail notes.

👁 LOCAL SNAPSHOT

When Europeans started creating walking tracks across the Blue Mountains from the 1820s, it began a growing movement and by the 1880s (about a decade after railway lines were introduced), tourism was booming. Towns like Katoomba, Leura, Wentworth Falls and Blackheath competed against each other to develop trails that drew the crowds and it was thought a path through the Grand Canyon might be nice. Hotel operator and Blackheath Railway stationmaster Tomas Rodrigues invited tenders for its construction but most builders thought the task impossible. All, that is, except for Thomas Williams (builder of the Govetts Leap track), who eventually picked up the gauntlet, and on 16 Feb 1907 the 'Blackheath Grand Canyon' Track was officially opened.

Opposite Stepping stones guide walkers through the forest

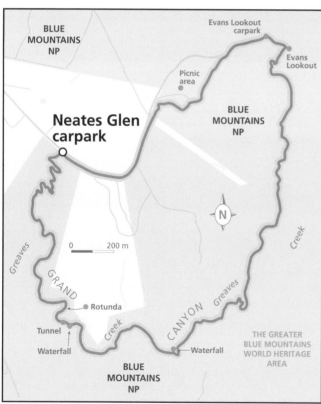

BLUE
MOUNTAINS
NP

Evans Lookout
carpark

Evans
Lookout

Picnic
area

**Neates Glen
carpark**

BLUE
MOUNTAINS
NP

Greaves

N

Creek

0   200 m

GRAND

Creek

Rotunda

CANYON   Greaves

Tunnel

Waterfall

Waterfall

THE GREATER
BLUE MOUNTAINS
WORLD HERITAGE
AREA

BLUE
MOUNTAINS
NP

Top Soaking up the views at Evans Lookout *Opposite* Sunlight
streaming through the canopy

ITINERARY

It doesn't take long for the fun to get started on this one. From Neates Glen carpark, I zig-zag with the trail, descending from dry and sandy terrain into an increasingly lush one peppered with tree ferns, as it sinks to Greaves Creek. The route seems to flow like the water that created this canyon, sweeping left and right, and carving a winding passage through the sandstone, its sides smooth and carpeted in moss. Little pools of water reflect dappled light on the underside of rock overhangs.

The route opens up briefly, offering a chance to get my bearings with a wide-angle view of the canyon's orange and black walls rising above the forest in striated layers and overhangs. Within minutes I'm diving back into the greenery, descending steep steps beneath the canyon walls to reunite with the creek and a decent-sized rock overhang with sandy floor referred to as the 'Rotunda', which was once used as a shelter by Traditional Owners. There's even a 'rain shower' at the far end, cascading off a rock wall.

The track winds through the forest, suddenly disappearing into a black hole and a tiny curving tunnel. It's only short but I still need the torch on my phone to light the way and avoid the trickle of water falling through the ceiling. Emerging on the other side is like entering Wonderland, a canyon so beautiful it's as though it's been landscaped for a theme park. The path sneaks behind a waterfall spraying from the top of a curved rock wall, then continues skirting around the inside of the canyon via narrow rock ledges beneath overhangs. It's incredible to think such a route was hand-cut simply with shovels, crowbars and a bit of dynamite.

The sound of water is everywhere and occasionally I'm sprayed in mist. The walls gather closer, squeezing around tenacious trees and shelves of ferns clinging to the rock in hanging gardens, until the creek disappears into the dark depths. This is the point where canyoners abseil between slick curves to explore parts of the canyon impossible without ropes. It's super slippery here so take care; thankfully most of the path is fringed by a guardrail.

Birds flocks to the few snippets of dry forest of banksia and grass trees but mostly this walk revels in a damp and cool world. When I cross a bridge over a slot and past another waterfall, the presence of canyoners is given away by a few shrieks (something about freezing water).

Following the creek along the canyon floor feels like wandering Eden. Thin streams of water spill into pebble-lined pools, enclosed by ferns and giant moss-covered boulders, and half a dozen creek crossings are tackled via sturdy stepping stones, which in normal flows are well above the water. I feel small here but in a good way. It's a soothing place that beckons me to slow down and soak it up. A few picnickers perch on boulders.

It's an inevitable law of hiking that what goes down must go back up, and after a steady climb back through the cliffs, the track eventually emerges at Evans Lookout, overlooking the Grose Valley. It's a perfect vantage point to appreciate how water has shaped the land. Govetts Creek is just a thin line cutting through tiny trees far below, and the plateau's rim is fringed in sheer walls lit orange in the late afternoon sun. It's a short walk along a roadside path to return to Neates Glen carpark.

The Grose Valley

BEST EATS

- **Altitude Delicatessen:** This place is renowned for its generously-sized sandwiches (perfect for a packed lunch) and great coffee. 20 Govetts Leap Rd, Blackheath; (02) 4787 6199.
- **Cinnabar:** 'Travel the world in one night' is the concept of this hugely popular restaurant run by two ladies with long pedigrees in hatted restaurants. Expect dishes such as Ethiopian berbere spiced chicken or sizzling Jamaican prawn pot with blackened lime. 246 Great Western Hwy, Blackheath; (02) 4787 7269; cinnabar.kitchen.

BEST SLEEPS

- **Secrets Hideaway:** These cosy self-contained suites are tucked away within sprawling mountain gardens and are only a kilometre from the trailhead. Breakfast hampers, complete with homemade bread, will keep you going all day. 173 Evans Lookout Rd, Blackheath; (02) 4787 8453; secretshideawayblackheath.com.au.
- **Kyah Boutique Hotel:** This remodelled 1970s motel is super cool with Palm Springs-inspired design and reputedly the oldest cherry blossom tree in the southern hemisphere. There's no need to wander far for dinner, with in-house restaurant Blaq offering a fancy night in. 13-17 Brightlands Ave, Blackheath; (02) 4787 8108; thekyah.com.au.

WHILE YOU'RE HERE

- **Blue Mountains Adventure Company:** Take your exploration of the Grand Canyon next level by joining a canyoning tour. You'll don a wetsuit and helmet and dive into the thick of things. It's a literally immersive experience, involving scrambling over rocks, swimming and abseiling through waterfalls but you're guaranteed to see parts of the canyon most don't get to witness. 84a Bathurst Rd, Katoomba; (02) 4782 1271; bmac.com.au.
- **Blue Mountains Cultural Centre:** Comprising an interactive exhibition on the Blue Mountains and one of Australia's leading regional art galleries, this state-of-the-art facility is a great place to spend an hour or two and it also offers occasional workshops and free creative sessions for teenagers. 30 Parke St, Katoomba; (02) 4780 5410; bluemountainsculturalcentre.com.au.

Skirt the rim of the Jamison Valley, between Katoomba Falls and the Three Sisters, for a string of epic views.

Prince Henry Cliff Walk (Federal Pass return option)

This walk is on <u>Dharug</u> and <u>Gundungurra Country</u>.

New South Wales

WHY IT'S SPECIAL

It's the blue-ish haze, caused by airbound eucalyptus oil, that gave rise to the name Blue Mountains. This vast UNESCO World Heritage Area of forest, sandstone escarpments and gorges is a playground for hikers but to get an understanding of what the Blue Mountains are all about you first need to stand somewhere high and gaze out over them. This cliff-top trail on the edge of the Jamison Valley is perfect. Ample lookouts show off expansive views of a vast treed valley rimmed by sheer orange cliffs, plus you get to take in the impressive Katoomba Falls, Katoomba Cascades and iconic Three Sisters.

Follow the cliff-top out and back from Katoomba Falls or, if you're feeling energetic, descend into a thick rainforested valley and return via the base of the cliffs for a whole new viewpoint.

WALK IT

The route described here spans Katoomba Falls and Echo Point (Three Sisters lookout) along the cliff-top. That part is easy but if you don't feel like retracing your steps, descend the rather more energetic yet hugely impressive Giant Stairway to the Federal Pass track (rated hard) and return along the bottom of the cliff. To get back up to Katoomba Falls Reserve carpark you'll need to scale the Furber Steps or, alternatively, catch the world's steepest passenger railway (52°) operated by Scenic World (note, the last ride up is at 4.50pm, scenicworld.com.au).

Parking is expensive at Echo Point so it's preferable to leave the car at the Katoomba Falls end.

 Trail talk

- Distance: 3km return (5km via Federal Pass loop)
- Time: 2hr return (3.5-4hr via Federal Pass loop)
- Rating: Easy (hard via Federal Pass loop)
- Technicality: Sealed and unsealed track and a few steps.
- Puff factor: Pretty mild unless you return via Federal Pass, in which case there are about 900 steps to descend the cliffs and plenty more to get back up again.
- Watch out for: The Giant Stairway involves a lot of very narrow and steep stone steps that can be a tad awkward for big feet, plus they can be slippery.

 When to go

It's good year-round but spring and autumn are best (not too hot, not too cold). Midweek is a little less busy.

Resources

Visit nationalparks.nsw.gov.au for more info or wildwalks.com to download detailed maps and trail notes.

Opposite Katoomba Cascades

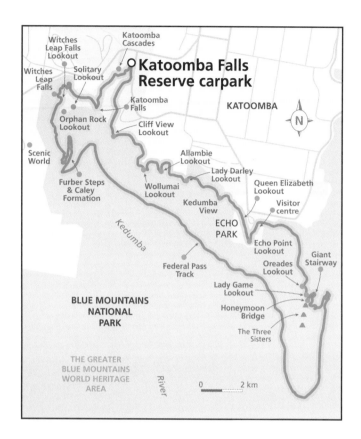

◉ LOCAL SNAPSHOT

The Blue Mountains have their origins in layers of sediment dumped by rivers, tidal lakes and lagoons as far back as 400 million years ago. It formed a plateau, later cut by streams and rivers to create the deep and sprawling valleys of today. As water infiltrated vertical fault lines, it eroded into layers of sandstone, claystone, shale and coal. The fact that soft claystone erodes fastest allowed unsupported rock above it to collapse, and has resulted in the vertical cliffs so characteristic of the Blue Mountains.

Since different soils support different plants - and therefore different animals and birds - the resulting cross-section of habitats that walkers experience as they descend into these valleys offers a tonne of variety, from the Dwarf Mountain Pine trees and Smooth Bush-pea flowers of the upper regions to the lush and cool temperate rainforest lower down.

Katoomba Falls spilling off the plateau

ITINERARY

There's a rainbow in the middle of Katoomba Falls when I spy it from a lookout a few minutes into the trail. As waterfalls go, it's impressive, pouring off the cliff-rim in several drops like a wide flat ribbon, past sheer walls and bursts of greenery. At night it's floodlit, part of a 1.3km 'Night-lit Walk' that explores a rabbit warren of paths at this end of the cliff that dash out to views such as Orphan Rock Lookout, Solitary Lookout and Witches Leap Falls Lookout. Solitary Lookout gazes out over the Jamison Valley and the tabletop Mount Solitary, and my view briefly includes a cable car from Scenic World out on a ride spanning the cliffs.

The first half of the cliff-top track is paved and there is a 20min return section that is accessible. It passes through lush forest dotted with tree ferns, and every lookout offers another aspect of the cliffs as they curve around the valley. Stepping stones hop across the shallow pool at the base of Katoomba Cascades, an ideal place to cool off, and not long after the track turns to dirt, undulating through thick forest peppered with the tall white trunks of gum trees.

I spend the next hour dodging rain showers but a large rock overhang and the visitor centre at Echo Point offer a few convenient shelters. From its size and elaborate layout, it's clear Echo Point lookout cops a lot of visitors, which is unsurprising, considering it's prime vantage point for the Three Sisters, those striking rock stacks that reach out into the Jamison Valley. A view like this can hold the attention for ages and it's worth coming back for sunset when the low sun sets the rock aglow.

The Prince Henry Cliff Walk continues all the way to Leura but it's here that I begin the detour down the cliffs towards Federal Pass, soon coming across a lookout peering directly over the stone stacks that are the most iconic sight in the Blue Mountains. Vertical jointing in the sandstone has allowed the elements to wear away at the cliffs, creating the beautiful Three Sisters formation. A sidestep over Honeymoon Bridge lets me stand on a rock ledge half way up one of the formations before I backtrack to descend down the Giant Stairway.

There's no rest for the knees on this stretch. The steps seem endless, sometimes metal and sometimes sandstone so worn that they dip in the middle from erosion and the millions of feet that have passed over them since construction finished in 1927. It's super pretty though, down the side of sheer rock cliffs and into lushly thick rainforest with the songs of lyrebirds, and the easy track that winds along the base of the cliffs offers a welcome breather.

I'm too late in the day to catch the world's steepest train back up to Reids Plateau but the climb up the Furber Steps gives me a chance to have a good look at the layers of shale and sandstone of the Caley Formation, and to appreciate the Hanging Swamps that form when seeds germinate in waterlogged layers of clay in the cliffs.

With height, I begin to catch new views out towards the Three Sisters and a 10min side trip gets me right up close with Katoomba Falls at their midway point. Witches Leap is a small waterfall just before the last haul up to the plateau and Katoomba Falls carpark to complete the loop.

BEST EATS

- **Red Door Cafe:** A Leura favourite with a menu that caters well for vegans and gluten-free needs. Sit indoors or in the leafy courtyard. 134 Leura Mall, Leura; (02) 4784 1328.
- **The Bootlegger Smokehouse and Bar:** It's all about slow cooking and Southern barbecue-style smoked meat at this cool venue located in the historic Niagra building (circa 1905). An extensive cocktail list complements the usual bar offerings. 92 Bathurst Rd, Katoomba; (02) 4782 6368; bootlegger.com.au.

BEST SLEEPS

- **14 Lovel St:** This 100-year old guesthouse feels like a home away from home. Television is shirked in favour of a cosy lounge and a long and leafy verandah, keeping the vibe peaceful, and there's a communal kitchen if you want to make your own food. Choose from dorms or private queen rooms. 14 Lovel St, Katoomba; (02) 4782 7104; 14lovelst.com.
- **The Carrington Hotel:** This heritage-listed manor (circa 1883), right on the main street in Katoomba is bursting with period charm and elegance. Indulge in a high tea if you're there on a Sunday afternoon. 15-47 Katoomba St, Katoomba; (02) 4782 1111; thecarrington.com.au.

WHILE YOU'RE HERE

- **Leuralla Toy & Railway Museum:** Take a blast through the past at the southern hemisphere's largest collection of 20th-century toys, trains and memorabilia. It's set within a historic mansion with 5ha of award-winning gardens to roam. 36 Olympian Pde, Leura; (02) 4784 1169; toyandrailwaymuseum.com.au.
- **Blue Mountains Adventure Company:** With so many excellent rock walls around, it would be remiss not to explore them up close by abseiling or rock climbing. Blue Mountains Adventure Company run guided forays for complete beginners through to intermediates. 84a Bathurst Rd, Katoomba; (02) 4782 1271; bmac.com.au.

Right Katoomba Falls *Opposite* Ample lookouts provide views over the valley

Wander a rugged coastline of red cliffs and secluded bays, while keeping an eye out for whales along the sparkling Sapphire Coast.

Light to Light Walk

This walk is on <u>Yuin Country</u>.

WHY IT'S SPECIAL

Perhaps the most striking aspect of this walk is the brick-red siltstone and sandstone that dominates this part of the coast, appearing in expansive rock platforms underfoot and coastal cliffs that contrast dramatically against the sapphire ocean and green interior. Stretching between Boyds Tower – originally designed to be a lighthouse, but ultimately used as a whale-spotting tower – and Green Cape Lighthouse, the trail winds through Ben Boyd National Park. At the time of writing is in the process of being renamed to recognise the significance of the area to the Yuin People, and due to Ben Boyd's role in what is known as the 'Blackbirding' slave trade. The walk alternates between groves of tea tree, heath plains and woodland, and passes three excellent beaches. Wildflowers sprinkle extra colour in winter and whales splash offshore in spring.

If you're into rock, this is an interesting patch of ground. Sediments here were laid down between 345 and 410 million years ago, compressing into red, brown and green shale, sandstone and siltstone, and their compressed and folded curves and arches are often visible on the trail. Conglomerates and quartzites are seen in the boulders and stones littered along the waterfront. Venture further afield after your hike and you'll discover more interesting formations, such as eroded orange- and white-banded cliffs at The Pinnacles, north of Eden.

WALK IT

This is a walk undergoing change. The land was impacted by bushfires over the summer of 2019/2020, however the landscape is regenerating well. At the time of writing, proposals were in place to make the Light to Light a 3-day hut-to-hut walk (overnighting at Mowarry Point and Hegartys Bay), but still retaining the option of hiking it as a fully independent pack-camper and staying in existing campsites (Mowarry Point, Saltwater Creek and Bittangabee Bay). Some parts of the track are also flagged for realignment and improvement. Whatever happens though, and whichever way you walk it, this is a cracking piece of coastline that will not disappoint.

Opposite Boyds Tower atop the region's famously red cliffs

 Trail talk
- Distance: 30km
- Time: 2 days
- Rating: Moderate
- Technicality: Fairly straightforward track with a few steps and some rock hopping. Three creek crossings require care.
- Puff factor: Though there are no major climbs, persistent undulations in the northern section can be a little bit tiring.
- Watch out for: Aim for a low tide crossing of Saltwater Creek and Woodburn Creek when water levels are usually ankle deep. At high tide it's knee-deep and after heavy rain it can swell to chest-deep so check conditions prior to setting out (NSW Parks Merimbula, ph: (02) 6495 5000). Keep food well secured against prying goannas and possums.

 When to go
Summer is ideal for swimming, autumn is when lyrebirds display, winter brings wildflowers and spring is prime whale-viewing season.

 Resources
Visit nationalparks.nsw.gov.au for more info and to book campsites. For detailed track notes, visit wildwalks.com. National Park entry fees apply ($8 per vehicle per day).

Arrange transport from Eden to and from the trailhead with local operators such as: lighttolighttransfers.com.au.

You can walk it in either direction but it's nice to finish with a stay at the Green Cape Lightstation at the southern end (*see* p. 39). There is road access to Saltwater Creek and Bittangabee Bay, giving the option to just walk a shorter section if preferred. At present the trail is fairly well marked, however care is required when crossing beaches and long rocky sections to spot markers for the onward route; this is likely to get easier with proposed track improvements.

It's a one-way walk, so park the car at one end and enlist the services of a local operator to transfer you to the other. Alternatively, catch public transport to Eden and organise your transfers from there.

The itinerary outlined here allows for two days of walking with an overnight at Saltwater Creek. Both Saltwater and Bittangabee Bay are set up for car campers and have toilets, shelters and gas barbecues; bookings are required (costs $24pn for two people). If you opt for a three-day itinerary you could choose to add in a night at the quieter walk-in only camp at Mowarry Point which is free but has no facilities.

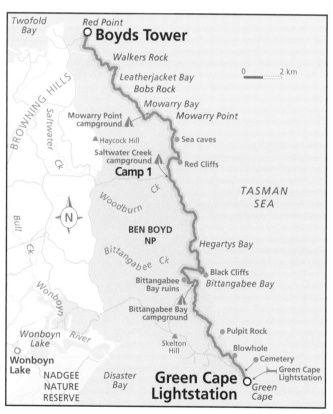

◉ LOCAL SNAPSHOT

The harbour of Twofold Bay, at the trail's northern end, was once a convenient hunting ground for migrating humpback, southern right, minke and blue whales. Killer whales (actually large dolphins) have been herding them into its waters for centuries, driving them into the shallows and attacking en masse to overcome their larger quarry. Rumour has it that between 1840s and 1930s, the killer whales worked in cooperation with European whalers, tail-flopping to attract prey, driving them towards the more efficient hunters and then sharing the spoils - killer whales feasting on lips and tongues, and humans taking the rest. Even earlier, the Yuin People say killer whales were ancestral spirits who provided food for the Yuin when the whales beached themselves in an effort to escape their predators. Records from early Europeans talk of witnessing ceremonies where the Yuin would 'call' the killer whales to drive the whales to shore. By 1929 the killer whales were rarely seen, the numbers of whales having plummeted so greatly.

Top Flowering heath *Opposite* Tunnels of tea tree

ITINERARY

DAY 1
Ben Boyds Tower to Saltwater Creek, 13km, 5hr

The adventure starts at Boyds Tower, a 20m-high turret-like sandstone building perched on the cliff-tops at the entrance to Twofold Bay where it meets the Pacific Ocean. Built by Scottish slave trader Ben Boyd, in 1847, it was intended as a lighthouse but the Crown didn't think it appropriate for the job, so it was repurposed as a spotting tower for whalers. A corner of its turret is missing following a lightning strike.

It might be the shorter of the two days but persistent minor undulations between the cliff-ridge and the water's edge can make it a little tiring. The track hugs the coast, regularly alternating between pockets of tea tree, banksia woodland and eucalypt forest, with regular peeks across the shimmering ocean and up and down the rocky coastline. Within a few kilometres, the trail gets up close with the region's famously red landscape, dipping to a bay to hop across red rocks, boulders and the red gravel left by those pulverised by the elements. Close to the water's edge, the rock looks at times blood-red against the blue waves and, in contrast, beautifully polished green and grey stones glisten with water.

Back in melaleuca and banksia woodland, sandy trails are littered with leaves and are easy underfoot. Though the summer bushfires of 2019/20 definitely took their toll, fluffy green regrowth is accelerating and, although the land has been impacted, the dazzling coastline itself remains unchanged. Rock dominates it and while there are three notable arcs of sand on the route, beaches are often rock fields.

After 4.5km the cosy Leather Jacket Bay appears – part sandy, part rocky. About 8km in, the trail reaches Mowarry Bay and it's probably the most treasured by hikers, having a stunning and sheltered sandy beach that is only accessible on foot. There are no facilities here but it's a popular choice to camp for the night if you're looking to make this a 3-day walk. Pitch a tent on the beach or on the grassy headlands on either side. Water can be collected from the creek that intersects the trail at the bay's northern end, but ensure you boil or filter it.

After a stretch through casuarina and eucalypt forest dotted with bracken fern, the route trails across several more sections of red rock, in striking coastal platforms, at times so expansive it's like a sea of red, and then atop the Red Cliffs with commanding views over the ocean.

At low tide, it's an ankle-deep wade across Saltwater Creek to reach camp for the night and another seriously good beach. This long and wide sweep of sand is hemmed in by two creeks, Saltwater at the northern end and Woodburn at the south, both of which pool into treacle-coloured lagoons stained by tree tannins before flowing out to the ocean that are ideal for a sheltered swim. Saltwater Creek has 14 campsites tucked in apple gum woodland behind the beach and, accessible by car, it's likely to be busier than your average hike-in campsite but you do get all the mod-cons of fire-pits, gas barbecues, toilets, water tanks and shelters. You'll probably share it with a few kangaroos too.

DAY 2
Saltwater Creek to Green Cape Lightstation, 17km, 5–6hr

The day begins with a wander down the beach and a wade across the sandy-bottomed Woodburn Creek, before climbing through the tea tree to emerge onto open grass and heathland. The trail alternates back and forth between open heath cut by narrow sandy trails and shaded woodland, offering regular views of the ocean.

The route descends to cross coastal rock platforms sandwiched between ocean and trees and it's an uneven rock hop at times, before arriving at Hegartys Bay. The bay itself is devoid of sand but the colours in the rock platforms and boulders that spill into the sea are photogenic.

There's more alternating between woodland sprinkled with ferns and open heathland across the cliff-tops to reach the coast again atop the Black Cliffs. Marker poles indicate the route across what is an extensive section of rock platforms, rippled like elephant hide in places, dotted with rockpools and offering prime views across the ocean and of the swirling and smashing waves below. It's a great vantage point for ocean gazing and whale spotting but the dark rock sucks up the sun so if it's a hot day you may not want to linger.

Where the rock descends to water level again, the trail dives into tunnels of tea tree, more open heath and then tall eucalypt forest sprinkled in ferns. Bittangabee Creek is the third creek crossing requiring care on the route – usually a dry-boot rock hop in good conditions – before a forested path leads hikers to Bittangabee Bay camping area, the second overnight stop popular with those on a three-day itinerary. There's only a small beach here but the car-accessible camping area offers toilets, shelters and gas barbecues. Keep an eye out for lyrebirds in the surrounding woodland.

In 1844, the Imlay brothers had their eyes on this area as a base for grazing and whaling, and the foundations of their house remain. There is also the roofless remains of a stone storehouse on the waterfront built in 1881 by Albert Aspinall, though never completed.

South of Bittangabee Bay, the trail currently moves inland but if the proposed realignments go ahead, the track will hug the coastline from here all the way to Green Cape. For now, walkers pass through more banksia, melaleuca forest and grass trees, before emerging back onto coastal heath with views of the lighthouse in the distance. At present it's a 1.5km detour to Pulpit Rock, following a staircase down to more rock platforms buffering the sea, but a new alignment would see the trail pass it directly.

The final few kilometres to Green Cape pass across more of the low coastal heath – a significant habitat for vulnerable and endangered species, such as the eastern ground parrot and southern brown bandicoots – and pockets of woodland, banksia and grass trees. A cemetery tucked in the melaleuca, just 300m from the trail's end, is the resting place of 71 victims of the *Ly-ee-moon*, shipwrecked on Green Cape in 1886.

On a flat grassy perch atop the pointed finger of Green Cape is the lightstation that marks the end of the walk. It comprises a 29m high white lighthouse (1883), plus tidy lightkeeper's cottages and a telegraph station (both now converted into accommodation). A 1hr tour run by NSW Parks will fill you in on the history. Spending a night at Green Cape (*see* p. 40) gives the opportunity to soak up the wild coastline and maybe spot some wildlife, such as fur seals, sea eagles, gannets, albatross, whales and dolphins. Wombats too may be seen around the lighthouse. It's a suitably impressive ending to this walk.

Opposite Saltwater Creek Beach

BEST EATS

- **Sprout Eden:** Part cafe, part produce store, this place focuses on supporting local farmers and offers a quality menu. The food is fresh and tasty with interesting options like banana and fig muffins, mushroom burgers or salmon gravlax bruschetta. The fish chowder is renowned. 134 Imlay St, Eden; (02) 6496 1511; sprouteden.com.au.
- **Ollie Masons Bistro:** Winner of the 2022 Australian Good Food Guide's Reader's Choice award, this cafe and wine bar is a great choice for lunch through to dinner or afternoon tapas. An inspiring menu includes dishes like finger lime and caviar oysters or kingfish ceviche. 126 Imlay St, Eden; 0490 240 288.

BEST SLEEPS

- **Green Cape Lightstation:** Walk straight off the trail and into your accommodation at this 1883 lightstation perched above the ocean at the trail's southern end. Choose from one of the restored nautical-themed lightkeeper's cottages or rest in a bunk bed in the old Telegraph Station. A tour of the lightstation is included in the price. 2086 Green Cape Lighthouse Rd, Green Cape; 1300 072 757; nationalparks.nsw.gov.au.
- **Twofold Bay Motor Inn:** Within walking distance of the beach, restaurants and the sights of Eden, this place is a favourite for visitors to the region. All rooms are clean, comfortable and spacious, but deluxe and executive rooms have also had a modern makeover. 164-166 Imlay St, Eden; (02) 6496 3111; twofoldbaymotorinn.com.au.
- **Seahorse Inn:** Set on expansive lawns right on the shores of Twofold Bay, this award-winning property dates back to 1843 and combines contemporary luxury and old-world charm. The brasserie and bar here is definitely worth a visit. Boydtown Park Rd, Eden; (02) 6496 1361; seahorseinnhotel.com.au.

WHILE YOU'RE HERE

- **Eden Killer Whale Museum:** Whaling was big around these parts from the 1840s to 1930s and this museum explains its fascinating history. Exhibits include wooden whaling boats and the skeleton of 'Old Tom', one of the pod of killer whales reputed to have assisted whalers in their hunting forays. 184 Imlay St, Eden; (02) 6496 2094; killerwhalemuseum.com.au.
- **Beach hopping:** The Sapphire Coast glitters with a string of inviting beaches and gin-clear bays. Bermagui's famous Blue Pool is a natural rockpool regularly flushed by the ocean, yet sheltered enough to enjoy swimming and snorkelling. Mimosa Rocks National Park's Nelson Lagoon is ideal for birdwatching and fishing, while Merimbula's Bar Beach lies on the channel of Merimbula Lake and offers sheltered waters. Between Bermagui, Tathra, Merimbula and Pambula, there are dozens more idyllic beaches to explore; sapphirecoast.com.au/beaches.
- **Hit the Oyster trail:** The estuaries and lakes of the Sapphire Coast represent one of the biggest oyster-producing regions in Australia and there are plenty of ways to partake. Visit farm gates, tour the oyster leases by boat, learn how to shuck and prepare oysters or simply kick back at a waterside restaurant and indulge in the freshest produce; sapphirecoast.com.au/oysters.

Ocean views are a regular treat

*Wander a moving feast of scenery through the
Berowra Creek valley.*

Thornleigh to Cowan (part of the Great North Walk)

This walk is on <u>Kuring-gai Country</u>.

WHY IT'S SPECIAL

If you've got two weeks up your sleeve, you might want to consider launching yourself on the epic 250km Great North Walk stretching between Sydney/Warrang and Newcastle/Muluubinba. If you don't, try this two-day taster through Berowra Valley National Park instead. Spanning Thornleigh and Cowan, it covers a huge variety of terrain, from mossy forests to saltmarsh, dry rock gardens peppered with grass trees and peaceful riverside. Its proximity to Sydney (half an hour north) and easy access via train makes it a logistical piece of cake, plus there's the option of a leisurely lunch in a waterfront restaurant at Berowra Waters on the second day.

WALK IT

There's not really any part of this route that I'd want to miss out on but if you're not up for two fairly big days, it's easy to snip off bits or tackle it in sections. Train access to Thornleigh and Cowan is super easy but if you want to drop in or out at Hornsby Heights, Crosslands Reserve or Berowra Waters you might need to do a car shuffle or enlist a friend to help with a pick up.

Crosslands Reserve is the midway point, a spacious riverside camping area with toilets, gas barbecues and drinking water (bookings required through hornsby.nsw.gov.au). It's accessible by car, so if you don't fancy carrying all your camping gear there's an option to sweet talk a 'support team' to meet you there with beer and sausages.

→ Trail talk
- Distance: 36km
- Time: 2 days
- Rating: Hard
- Technicality: Mostly well-formed with some rock hopping and a few sections aided by metal rungs. A few places require care to stay on course.
- Puff factor: There are a few climbs to tackle (although none are too long), plus the sheer length of the walk can sap some energy.
- Watch out for: Take care on creek crossings and occasional slippery boulders. Berowra Creek is susceptible to contamination and swimming isn't recommended.

When to go
Late autumn, winter and spring are best. Avoid peak summer when high temperatures can be a challenge and bushfire risk increases.

Resources
Download map and detailed track notes from wildwalks.com. Check out nationalparks.nsw.gov.au for further info on Berowra Valley National Park, the Benowie Track and Great North Walk.

Opposite top Boardwalk across mangroves and estuarine wetland *Opposite bottom* Morning mist over Berowra Creek

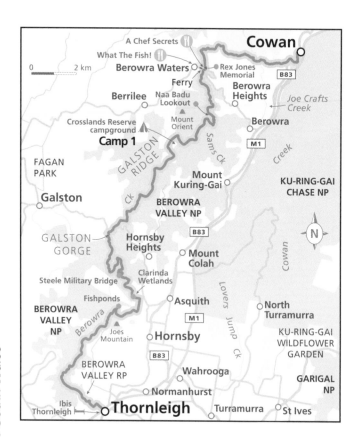

Considering the Hawkesbury River and its tributaries are a mecca for boats, it's perhaps unsurprising that Berowra Waters is reputed to be home of Australia's first motorboat hire boat fleet. It all began with young Rex Jones who returned from World War I to start a business renting out rowboats in 1925 and motorboats two years later. Tragically, Rex drowned in 1936, entangled in a rope off his own boat, later to be discovered by his 15-year old son who went to the vessel with the intention of using it to search for his dad. There's a memorial for Rex on the trail, just after crossing Berowra Waters Rd.

Bottom Descending to Galston Gorge *Opposite* Berowra Creek from Naa Badu Lookout

ITINERARY

DAY 1
Thornleigh to Crosslands, 22km, 7–8hr

It's very convenient that within just a few streets of Thornleigh train station you can slip from suburbia straight into the forest of Berowra Valley Regional Park. The track soon meets the Berowra Creek that leads the way for this walk, carving through peeling gum trees, bracken fern, grass trees and rocks flocked in green moss. Amid the early morning birdsong I hear the unmistakably clear tone of a lyrebird, then moments later see its flamboyant tail feathers passing through the underbrush.

A big appeal of this track is the frequently changing terrain. One minute I'm on sandy trails through a sandstone boulder garden sprinkled with banksia and grass trees, the next I'm passing through open woodland or rock hopping a lush gorge smeared in moss. Small tributaries occasionally intersect the trail as they feed into Berowra Creek and one crossing takes me over a rock platform tinged in green and pocked like Swiss cheese from water erosion over millennia. For a while I follow the gorge, past giant boulders and dark pools overhung with greenery – a 2min detour leads to Fishponds, a particularly large waterhole – before the trail climbs out of the gorge for a short stint through the sleepy streets skirting Hornsby Heights.

Where I rejoin the track is at Clarinda Wetlands, created in 2001 to help filter stormwater flowing into Berowra Creek and now home to birds, frogs and other native animals. It's a pleasant jaunt through the forest on wide management roads, over the historic Steele Military Bridge (1964) and alongside outcrops of sandstone. I spot a large goanna slowly spiraling up a tree and the air rings with cicadas and lyrebirds. The fact that one mimics a car alarm gives away this trail's close proximity to civilisation but, on the whole, you wouldn't know it.

I descend into Galston Gorge with the help of a few metal rungs bolted into the rock, slipping beneath Galston Gorge Road, and on the other side there's a beautiful stretch through boulders and grass trees. Closer to Crosslands the river starts to widen. Fish hang in the shallow current, blending in with the leaves alongside them, and it's a super peaceful riverside walk beneath a canopy of trees all the way to camp at Crosslands Reserve (*see* p. 47).

DAY 2
Crosslands to Cowan, 14km, 6–7hr

Beyond Crosslands, Berowra Creek really blooms in size – it eventually flows into the mighty Hawkesbury River and out to sea – and intruding salinity means that a boardwalk section crosses a saltmarsh and mangroves.

The creek is mirror-like calm in the early morning and a low fog hangs over the trees growing right to its edge. Sams Creek crossing is a jumble of super-slippery rocks capped in moss, and overhung with a jungle-like tangle of trees, but once I'm across, the route zigzags to climb to Naa Badu Lookout with a commanding view over Berowra Creek. It's proper river width now and from this height looks like a sapphire streak sunk into the treed valley, with a few pleasure boats trailing lines of wash behind. Naa Badu means 'see water' in Dharug language, and the creek is believed to have been a natural boundary between coastal and western clans.

The sandstone that lines the river valley wears into undercuts in places, revealing delicious swirls of caramel and cream in the rock. It's a really pretty walk following the river all the way into Berowra Waters, a tiny settlement that seems more based on water than land. Scores of houseboats, motorboats and yachts moor in peaceful silence and a 250m cable-ferry provides access between the eastern and western shores. There are just a couple of waterfront restaurants (*see* p. 47) that would make a handy lunch stop but check opening times before you skip your packed lunch. Neither the ferry nor the restaurant on the eastern shore were operating during my visit (yay for the egg and bacon roll stashed in my pack).

After dangling my legs in the water to cool off, I begin the climb out of the river valley via the sandstone cliffs, aided by another smattering of metal rungs, and from here the track heads east, leaving Berowra Creek behind. In 30°C heat it's a hot and fairly exposed track, but a soak in Joe Crafts Creek at the midway point revives me for the finish into Cowan.

Creek crossing

BEST EATS

- **A Chef Secrets:** It's the only option on Berowra Creek's eastern shore (i.e. the side the trail is on), but note that it's only open for lunch Wed-Sun or dinner Fri-Sat. Located in a historic 1898 boatshed right on the waterfront, the views and authentic Italian food are divine. Lot 466 Berowra Waters Rd, Berowra Waters; (02) 9456 6614; achefsecrets.com.
- **What The Fish!:** Relax on the large over-water decks with a seafood platter or regular cafe fare, or takeaway fish and chips, burgers and salads. It's just a quick ferry ride across the creek to the western shore. 199 Bay Road, Berowra Waters; (02) 9456 4665; whatthefish.com.au.

BEST SLEEPS

- **Crosslands Reserve:** This spacious grassy camping area is right on the shores of Berowra Creek at the trail's midway point and has toilets, gas barbecues and drinking water. It's accessible by car should you want family or friends to meet you here for the night. Bookings required; hornsby.nsw.gov.au.
- **Ibis Thornleigh:** Just a kilometre from the southern trailhead, this hotel makes a handy budget option before hitting the trail. 200-212 Pennant Hills Rd, Thornleigh; (02) 9481 7500; all.accor.com.
- **Berowra Waters Holidays:** Most accommodation at Berowra Waters is only accessible by boat but book a studio, lodge or house here and you get a tinny thrown in as well so you can explore the river. They also have houseboats. 0405 565 256; berowrawatersholidays.com.au.

A circuit walk crowning the roof of Australia.

Main Range Walk

This walk is on <u>Ngarigo Country</u>.

WHY IT'S SPECIAL

There's something pretty cool about knowing you're one of the highest people in the entire country, and this circuit walk scoops up the summit of Mount Kosciuszko (2228m) on its way around the Main Range. The route is nearly entirely above the tree line, following undulations atop the range, which means nearly constant 360-degree mountain views. Add some granite outcrops, glacial tarns, wildflowers and maybe a few dollops of snow and it's a truly epic hike that befits the roof of Australia.

An alternative route from the top of the Thredbo chairlift fast tracks to Mount Kosciuszko's summit and back in 3hr, although this isn't a landscape you want to rush.

WALK IT

The adventure starts at Charlotte Pass, a tiny ski resort village at the end of Kosciuszko Rd, 42km from Jindabyne. Anticlockwise is the way to go. The route stays above 1800m the entire time with zero shelter from the elements (unless you count the underground bunker-like toilets at Rawsons Pass), so cooperative weather is required. Alpine environments are prone to sudden and drastic changes in weather so carry warm and waterproof clothes in all seasons. Note that icy temperatures or blustery winds can send 'feels like' temperatures plummeting, even with glorious blue skies.

 LOCAL SNAPSHOT

The Ngarigo/Monaro People are the Traditional Owners and they lived on the peaks of the Snowy Mountains for thousands of years, for trade, ceremonies and to feast on the thousands of bogong moths that flock here in summer to escape the summer heat. The moths were a major seasonal food source, collected from caves and rock crevices, roasted and then ground down into 'moth meat' (reputed to have a nutty flavour).

It was Polish explorer Paul Edmund Strzelecki - he summited in 1840 - who gave the highest peak its current name, after Polish freedom fighter Tadeusz Kosciuszko.

Trail talk
- Distance: 22km loop
- Time: 7-9hr
- Rating: Moderate-hard
- Technicality: Mostly well-formed dirt, gravel and rock 'paving', with some long stretches of boardwalk.
- Puff factor: After the initial haul up to Blue Lake, the undulations are more gradual. Still, expect around 800m of climbing.
- Watch out for: Check the forecast before you go and always carry warm and waterproof clothes as alpine conditions change suddenly. At this altitude sunscreen is a must. March flies can be annoying if the wind is low.

When to go
The region is blanketed in snow in winter and early spring (June to Oct), so spring to autumn is best. Wildflowers in spring and early summer are spectacular.

Resources
Visit nationalparks.nsw.gov.au for more details. A Kosciuszko National Parks pass is required, available on entry.

Opposite top Lake Albina *Opposite bottom* On the side trip to Blue Lake

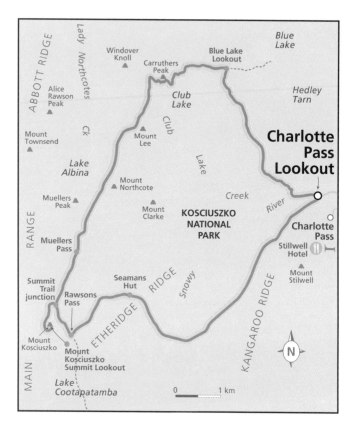

ITINERARY

From Charlotte Pass Lookout, Australia's highest mountain looks like just one of many other modest undulations that roll across the skyline. Between 10,000 and 30,000 years ago, snow and ice were a permanent fixture here, and glaciers scoured the mountains down to their current size and shape.

It's -1°C on a sunny spring morning when I set out, rock-hopping across the Snowy River before a solid climb to Blue Lake convinces me that stripping down to a T-shirt is a good idea. The 10min detour to the glacial cirque and its surrounding Ramsar-listed wetlands is well worth it, before rejoining the main trail heading south-west towards Mount Kosciusko atop the Main Range.

I'm soon staggering in the wind, the layers back on and the storm-hood of my jacket zippered up to my nose. Spectacular views wrap around 360 degrees and it's hard to know where to look. Snow sits like pools of spilt milk in grassy green curves, Club Lake dives deeply off to the left, and further on the infinity pool of Lake Albina drains from its high valley. Long stretches of rusted metal boardwalk hover over a surprisingly fragile ground and, though I'm a smidge too early for the wildflowers that carpet the area in early summer, the leaves of the silver snow daisy still tint the ground blue-grey.

It's a persistent climb to the Summit Trail junction, where things get significantly busier with walkers from Thredbo joining the short side trip to stand on Australia's highest point.

The summit itself is marked by a stone pillar and there's a queue to stand on it for the obligatory photo, so I opt to join others draping themselves over the jumble of lichen-covered granite boulders instead. Kosciuszko is more plateau than pointed peak but the views are beautiful – a panorama across bare rolling mountains littered with rocky nubs. On a Saturday it's a busy place, but I've been here mid-winter too during a cross-country ski trip, when the ranges are carpeted in snow and ice, and it's an entirely different world.

I descend to Rawsons Pass, home to Australia's highest loos, and from here it's an easy 7.5km downhill cruise all the way along what was once the Old Kosciuszko Road, linking Charlotte Pass to Australia's tippy top. It closed to cars in 1976 to preserve the environment and now walkers share the wide gravel track with mountain bikers, passing the historic stone Seamans Hut, built in 1929, and across open plains.

The embrace of twisted snow gums welcomes walkers back to Charlotte Pass.

BEST EATS

- **Stillwell Hotel:** Recharge on burrito bowls, nachos and pizza, either indoors or on the mountain-facing sundeck. Charlotte Adams Way, Charlotte Pass, stillwellhotel.com.au.
- **Cafe Darya:** This authentic Persian restaurant has been a Jindabyne favourite for decades. Snowy Mountains Plaza, 3 Kosciuszko Rd, Jindabyne; cafedarya.com.au.

BEST SLEEPS

- **Stillwell Hotel:** Sleep at Australia's highest hotel, within 'cooee' of the start of this walk. Rooms are fairly basic but clean and tidy, and almost all have mountain views. Charlotte Adams Way, Charlotte Pass; (02) 6450 4030; stillwellhotel.com.au.
- **Alpine Resort Motel:** The lake views alone are reason enough to stay here, either from your room or the rooftop deck, plus it's just a 2min drive from the bright lights of Jindabyne. 1 Nettin Circuit, Jindabyne; (02) 6456 2522; alpineresortmotel.com.au.

WHILE YOU'RE HERE

- **Thredbo:** Visit the ski village of Thredbo for some of the best cross-country and downhill mountain biking in the country. There's also an exhilarating bobsled track, scenic chairlift rides, bike skills parks and swimming in the Thredbo River; thredbo.com.au.
- **Wildbrumby Distillery:** Combine award-winning tipples and good food with art at Australia's highest distillery. Gin and schnapps are made from pristine alpine water, organic fruit and botanicals with flavours like sour apple, butterscotch and elderflower. Enjoy a long lunch indoors or out in the garden, surrounded by sculptures. Alpine Way and Wollondibby Rd, Crackenback; (02) 6457 1447; wildbrumby.com.

Top In places, a rusted steel boardwalk drapes over the Main Range *Opposite* The final stretch to the summit

A spectacular landscape of volcanic spires, blades and bluffs.

Breadknife & Grand High Tops

This walk is on <u>Gamilaroi</u>, <u>Wiradjuri</u> and <u>Weilwan Country</u>.

WHY IT'S SPECIAL

Warrumbungle is a Gamilaroi word meaning 'crooked mountain' and the occasional oozing and erupting of Warrumbungle Volcano around 17 million years ago has left a landscape punctuated by volcanic plugs, lava domes, flows and dykes. Walking amongst these dramatic formations makes for arguably one of Australia's most spectacular one-day walks. It starts amongst the trees and climbs to an open rocky ridgeline with an epic 360-degree panorama. You can return the same way or add a few more kilometres to make it a circuit.

Photographers will have a field day here, not only with changing sunlight on the rock formations but with long-exposure cartwheels of stars in the park's famously clear night skies. It is the only Dark Sky Park in Australia (*see* p. 57), so camping here is a special experience.

Unsurprisingly, such a dramatic and powerful landscape has made the Warrumbungles a highly cultural place for Gamilaroi, Wiradjuri and Weilwan Custodians for at least 20,000 years.

WALK IT

It's a 30km drive from Coonabarabran, the closest town, so carry in all the food and supplies you'll need. The visitor centre inside the park has only limited groceries and snacks.

If you're serious about capturing the perfect photo, consider bunking down for the night at trailside Balor Hut (bookings required through nationalparks.nsw.gov.au, click on the 'Camping and accommodation' heading). It's adjacent to the 90m-high blade of rock called the Breadknife, which turns the colour of burnt butter at dawn, and also positions you ideally for a quick hike to the Grand High Tops summit or Bluff Mountain for sunset and sunrise panos.

Whatever you do, don't rush off. There are a dozen other walks in the national park, taking in such features as the trachyte dome of Belougery Split Rock and Tara Cave, a significant First Nations site.

 Trail talk
- Distance: 12.5km return (or 14.5km to make it a circuit)
- Time: 4-5hr (5-6 for the circuit)
- Rating: Moderate-hard
- Technicality: A mix of well-defined track, lots of steps and a little rock hopping.
- Puff factor: It's uphill a good portion of the way to the Grand High Tops but the views are guaranteed to take your mind off the effort.
- Watch out for: Take your time on rocky sections.

 When to go
It can be very cold in winter and too hot to hike in peak summer. Spring is ideal for wildflower season, in particular golden wattle.

 Resources
Visit nationalparks.nsw.gov.au for more details. A NSW National Parks pass is required, available online or at any Parks office.

Opposite Looking out towards Crater Bluff and Tonduron Spire from the Grand High Tops

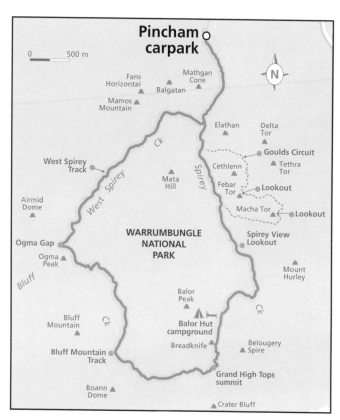

LOCAL SNAPSHOT

Warrumbungle National Park is Australia's first Dark Sky Park, an international status given to areas of exceptionally starry skies and where measures are taken to protect them. Neighbouring Coonabarabran is the astronomy capital of Australia, with a massive research facility at Sliding Spring Observatory (*see p. 57*) and Australia's biggest telescope. Animals love the dark here too. Nearly all Australia's native mammals are nocturnal and the artificial light that spills from cities (where night skies can be hundreds or even thousands of times brighter) has a huge negative impact on both predators and prey.

Pausing for spectacular views over the Breadknife

ITINERARY

The majority of visitors here simply hike out and back to the Grand High Tops but there are a few side trips off this route that are way too tempting, so I set out from Pincham carpark not long after dawn with plans to tick off as many as I can. In the early hour, I disturb a mob of eastern grey kangaroos in the middle of a foot-thumping, barking match, calling for a cautious side-step of a huge male bracing his ripped pecs like a bodybuilder.

Goulds Circuit can be tackled as a separate hike but if you don't want to double up on the first few kilometres that connect it to the carpark, plan to scoop it up on your way. The views from Febar Tor and Macha Tor involve a short rock scramble but offer the first of many epic views for the day.

What starts from the carpark as a wide and flattish track soon becomes steeper and riddled with steps but there are ample rest points to pause and blame it on the steadily increasing views. On the left, Belougery Spire, a volcanic plug, thrusts from the greenery and, on the right is the Breadknife, a narrow fin of rock (a dyke, in geologist speak) barely a few metres thick, 90m high and over 40m long.

With little warning, I'm suddenly right beside the Breadknife, feeling heat emanate off its orange flank. Once upon a time it was liquid magma rising through a vertical crack in the sandstone but now it's hard, fractured and streaked in black. Further on, a short unmarked scramble to the right peers over the top of it and gives me a spectacular view.

From the Grand High Tops the outlook is 360-degrees of jaw-dropping amazingness that warrants a decent snack break. Warrumbungle Volcano once spread across 50km and its ancient crater is now a rippling mass of trees and rocky protrusions. Apart from the views that have chased me to the summit, I can now see south as well, towards Crater Bluff – a massive plug of trachyte that looks like a 200m-long loaf of bread standing on its end – and Tonduron Spire, peeking out from behind it, 5km away.

I avoid retracing my steps in favour of the circuit route via West Spirey Track, which passes a side trip to Bluff Mountain. It's an energetic detour but so worth it to stand on the highest peak in the Warrumbungles, where views extend across the extinct volcano to the flat plains beyond. From here, the park's features are less random rocky spires and more part of clearly visible lines of rock.

Bluff Mountain is a lava dome and as the track descends to Ogma Gap it follows a ridgeline around it, revealing a striking near-vertical 250m wall. The trail then sinks back into the forest to amble along West Spirey Creek, usually bone dry yet lined with greenery, to return to Pincham carpark.

BEST EATS

- **Feathers Cafe:** Serving home-cooked food and with eclectic décor, Feathers also sells a few local crafts and produce to take away. 66 Cassilis St, Coonabarabran; (02) 6842 1141.
- **The Black Cockatoo:** This one offers yum burgers and pizzas alongside more adventurous options such as szechuan kangaroo and coconut rice. 13 John St, Coonabarabran; 0487 468 490.

BEST SLEEPS

- **Camp Blackman and Camp Wambelong:** Located inside Warrumbungle National Park, Blackman has space for powered and unpowered campsites dotted across several large camping areas, with showers, toilets and barbecues provided. Wambelong is a little quieter and more basic (no showers). Bookings required: nationalparks.nsw.gov.au, click on the 'Camping and accommodation' heading.
- **Balor Hut:** Roll out a sleeping bag on one of the slab bunks in this historic hut (circa 1958-62) or camp outside. It's located mid-trail, half a kilometre away from the Breadknife. Bookings required: nationalparks.nsw.gov.au, click on the 'Camping and accommodation' heading.
- **Acacia Motor Lodge:** Acacia offers modern and spacious rooms, slap bang in the middle of town. The pool and onsite bistro are handy. 10 John St, Coonabarabran; (02) 6842 1922; acaciamotorlodge.com.au.

WHILE YOU'RE HERE

- **Star Gazing: Sliding Spring Observatory** is a research facility, open to visitors during daylight only. Observatory Rd, Coonabarabran; (02) 6842 6363; slidingspringobservatory.com.au. Alternatively, explore distant galaxies, nebulae and planets yourself through powerful telescopes with Peter Starr (yes, really) at **Warrumbungle Observatory**. 841 Timor Rd, Coonabarabran; 0488 425 112; tenbyobservatory.com.
- **Pilliga National Park:** Take a short walk to the spectacular Sandstone Caves, featuring Gamilaroi rock engravings. It's not signposted (as requested by Elders), so you need to check in at the **Pilliga Forest Discovery Centre** at Baradine to get instructions and info. 50-58 Wellington St, Baradine; (02) 6843 4011; nationalparks.nsw.gov.au.
- **Sculptures in the Scrub:** This 3km (1.5-2.5hr) return walking track in Timmallallie National Park is dotted with sculptures that tell stories of the Gamilaroi People's history and culture. Start walking from the Sculptures in the Scrub picnic area and campground; nationalparks.nsw.gov.au.
- **Crystal Kingdom:** Get an understanding of the region's geology, plus see a huge array of fossils, minerals and crystals. Newell Highway, Coonabarabran; crystalkingdom.com.au.

Top Climbing past the base of the Breadknife *Opposite* The Warrumbungles are full of volcanic spires, blades and bluffs

Victoria

Compact in size, Victoria packs in a huge amount of variety,
from alpine to coast and everything in between.

Wander rainforest and a granite coastline cradling aqua bays and powder-white beaches.

Wilsons Promontory Southern Circuit & Lighthouse

This walk is on <u>Boonwurrung Country</u>.

Victoria

WHY IT'S SPECIAL

'The Prom', as it's fondly referred to, is hugely popular with Victorians and justly so, but hit this four-day trail and you'll leave the crowds behind. This striking granite promontory sprawls over 505sqkm, bubbling with giant boulders and headlands that cradle coves of powder-white sand and blue gin water. Rainforest, fern gullies and woodland are home to tons of wildlife – this is one of the most reliable places in Victoria to spot a wombat – plus you can drop in at the 1859 lighthouse or take a side trip to witness the blustery beauty of mainland Australia's southernmost tip. Come for a world-class walk, for the variety in terrain, and to savour the joy of having remote and perfect beaches all to yourself.

WALK IT

Trails crisscross the southern half of The Prom and there are more campsites than are listed in this walk, so the options are numerous. While the route suggested here takes in most of the highlights, if you're pushed for time (or have trouble booking space at your chosen campsite) take a shortcut or make up your own route (*see* Options below).

Consider the tides when choosing dates so you can plan to cross Sealers Creek (Day 3) at low water. Campsites have drop-toilets and drinking water but if you fancy a night of comfort, book to stay in the cosy cottages at the Lightstation (foot access only; *see* p. 67).

Avoid driving to Tidal River at dusk and after when the access road is heaving with wildlife.

OPTIONS

Telegraph Saddle / Roaring Meg / Little Waterloo Bay via Lightstation / Sealers Cove – Telegraph Saddle – 53km, 4 days.

Telegraph Saddle / Sealers Cove / Telegraph Saddle – 20.4km, 1–2 days.

Telegraph Saddle to Lightstation via inland route / Lighthouse to Telegraph Saddle via Waterloo Bay (no tent required) – 38.7km, 2 big days.

Telegraph Saddle / Little Waterloo Bay / Sealers Cove / Telegraph Saddle – 35.7km, 3 days.

 Trail talk
- Distance: 53km
- Time: 4 days
- Rating: Moderate-hard (make it easier by adding in extra camps to shorten your days).
- Technicality: Generally well-formed trail with just one creek crossing (shin-deep at low tide).
- Puff factor: There are quite a few steady undulations and a dash of beach walking to slow you down.
- Watch out for: Aim for low tide for Sealers Creek crossing. Keep food secure as wildlife here is very savvy to opportunities.

 When to go
It's great year-round but spring and autumn are a good bet weather-wise while avoiding peak summer crowds. If you can wangle a midweek visit, even better.

 Resources
Visit parks.vic.gov.au for more information and to download the Southern Circuit map and guide, and Wilsons Promontory Visitor Guide. Campsites need to be booked in advance.

Opposite On the final stretch to Telegraph Saddle *Previous* High on the Grampians Peaks Trail

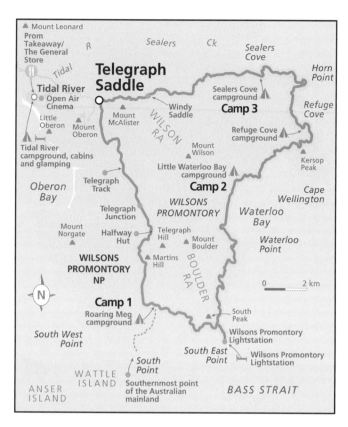

◉ LOCAL SNAPSHOT

Parts of Wilsons Promontory have been preserved as
national park since 1905, but it wasn't until 1939 that a
decent road was built to Tidal River on the south-west coast,
the Prom's only settlement, 30km from the park entrance. Its
namesake is tannin stained and lined with reeds and granite
boulders, and the boardwalk that shadows it to the sea is a
good spot from which to throw in a fishing line. Walking trails
around Tidal River are a good bet for wombat spotting but
if you visit the Open Air Cinema here (open during summer
and all school holidays), you're almost guaranteed to see
one or two hoovering up popcorn while movies run.

ITINERARY

DAY 1
Telegraph Saddle to Roaring Meg campground, 12km, 4hr

I walk the Prom every few years and every time I'm reminded just how damn impressive it is. My route varies but this time I'm starting from the inland carpark at Telegraph Saddle.

A telegraph line once connected Foster – a small town 60km north – with the Lightstation at the Prom's South East Point and the first day of walking follows its route via the Telegraph Track. It starts as wide gravel 4WD track through forest, eventually melting into singletrack south of Telegraph Junction. The open heathland here is chockers with wildflowers in spring which can really slow you down if you're prone to taking the odd photo, as I am. Harder to capture is the large flock of yellow-tailed black cockatoos I spot, moving from tree to tree, crunching their way through nuts and seeds. The stone Halfway Hut makes a good rest stop before the final push to Roaring Meg camp, tucked in forest next to a tinkling stream.

If you want to stand at the southernmost point of the Australian mainland, the 2hr return hike from here through lush forest to South Point is well worth the effort. The entire Prom is literally made of granite – once liquid magma 3km below the surface that cooled slowly, only coming to light when the surrounding earth weathered away. Granite slabs, boulders and tors are prominent everywhere, poking through the greenery and eroding into silica white beaches and clean blue water, however this huge belt of rock actually continues from this point all the way to eastern Tasmania. Standing on this southern tip can be a wild and blowy experience but there are a few rocks to shelter behind.

Top left Idyllic Refuge Bay *Top right* Wildlife is plentiful at The Prom

DAY 2
Roaring Meg campground to Little Waterloo Bay campground, 17km, 5.5hr

It takes me about two hours to hike from Roaring Meg campsite to the lightstation, through fern-filled forest and on to a drier, rockier landscape peppered with grass trees and coarse-grain boulders. Offshore, Wattle Island looks like a sea-bound pyramid and in the distance the Wilsons Promontory Lightstation, built in 1859, comes into view, perched bravely on the tip of South East Point as it reaches into Bass Strait.

To check out the lightstation up close involves deviating off the main circuit walk on a side-trail. It's a short yet viciously steep descent and climb but it's got to be done. For such a remote outpost, the lightstation is exceedingly tidy with manicured lawns, flower-lined dry-stone walls, and a complex of white-washed cottages. Unsurprisingly, the outlook is stunning and for those who want to stay the night there are three cottages with kitchen facilities (*see* p. 67). The lighthouse is now something of a museum, with memorabilia including a flag collection and radio communications equipment.

After retracing my steps to the main trail, the Southern Circuit continues around the coast, past granite tors and rock slabs, with epic views across the shimmering ocean that just beg for a snack break. The track then dives through pockets of coastal forest carpeted with bracken ferns and dotted with the odd tree fern-filled gully, until you pop out at a view of drool-worthy Waterloo Bay. Greenery rolls off the flanks of Mount Wilson, slowing down to a flat valley meeting white sand and baby blue, crystal-clear water. It's impossibly beautiful yet entirely empty, being a 4hr walk from the nearest carpark. I down my pack to wander its glorious length only to spy, from a distance, two black ravens raiding my pack of its precious nectarine and bag of nuts, prompting a completely futile 'run' back across the soft sand while waving my arms.

Half an hour further, Little Waterloo Bay camp is tucked in the trees next to a creek and the beach, and it's one of my favourites. The sand is as soft as talcum powder and blobs of granite dot it like giant limpets. On dusk, I'm visited by a wallaby and wombat who come to munch grass around my tent.

DAY 3
Little Waterloo Bay campground to Sealers Cove campground, 13.6km, 4.5hr

Continuing around the coast in the morning sun, I look back on Waterloo Bay to see the beach glowing like a light saber. The day is a mix of tall forest, tree fern gullies, and sandy coastal trails flanked by boulders, and the ocean is a regular companion. Kersop Peak is a worthy short side-trip for views inland and seaward.

The first peek into Refuge Cove reveals a bay far different to others here. It's almost opalescent, mottled in green, blue and yellow from the toffee-coloured sand lining it, and on each side of its small beach, slabs of orange granite slide into the water. Refuge is popular with yachts and behind the beach is a little homage to those who have visited, a wooden fence carved with vessel names and hung with buoys and a few whale ribs. There's a pretty campsite tucked in the paperbarks which makes a nice option but I skip it and push on to Sealers Cove, 6.4km further.

I trade blue ocean for a sea of green, wandering through rainforest, ferns and eucalyptus to reach Sealers Cove. It feels like paradise with a long golden beach and a sheltered bay for swimming – it's warmer than other bays too. You can easily pass hours roaming the beach and exploring the treacle coloured Sealers Creek with its sandy ripples and pools, or sitting in the forest with rosellas and cockatoos for company. This camp can be busier than the others on the circuit due to its popularity with overnight hikers from Telegraph Saddle.

DAY 4
Sealers Cove campground to Telegraph Saddle, 10.2km, 3hr

First on the agenda today is crossing Sealers Creek and at high tide it's a swim, so timing is everything here. I manage to catch it at ankle height. Beyond the beach walk the route dives into the bush to begin the return west to Telegraph Saddle, starting with boardwalk through tall grassy reeds, then past swampy areas and lush mossy rainforest peppered with tree ferns. It's a steady climb to Windy Saddle, a grassy clearing at 300m with a few picnic seats, which marks the transition to drier and rockier terrain for the gentle descent to Telegraph Saddle.

Opposite Waterloo Bay is a picture of perfection *Overleaf* Sealers Creek is best crossed at low tide

BEST EATS

- **Fish Creek Hotel:** You'll pass this Art Deco icon with a massive fish resting on its roof on the way to the Prom. Drop in for a drink and great pub food. 1 Old Waratah Rd, Fish Creek; (03) 5683 2404; fishcreekhotel.com.au.
- **Prom Takeaway/The General Store:** The food offering at Tidal River's takeaway and General Store varies but if you need nosh inside the national park, this is your only option. 2 Ring Rd, Tidal River; (03) 5680 8520.

BEST SLEEPS

- **Tidal River campground, cabins and glamping:** Parks Victoria runs a huge complex with 484 camping and caravan sites, plus cabins, units, huts and safari-style glamping tents spanning beach and riverside. It's all hugely popular so book well in advance over peak holiday periods. 13 1963; parkstay.vic.gov.au.
- **Wilsons Promontory Lightstation:** Live like a lighthouse keeper and sleep perched 100m above the wild Bass Strait. You can book Lightstation Banks Cottage with your group or the Lightstation Shared Cottage with other walkers. Bookings are for one- or two-night stays; parkstay. vic.gov.au/lightstation-shared-cottage-accommodation.

WHILE YOU'RE HERE

- **Wilsons Promontory Cruises:** You'll get a totally different perspective of this rugged coastline and its offshore islands from a boat. The humungous granite monolith of Skull Rock is a highlight but you'll also see dolphins, fur seals, sea birds and maybe whales too. Wilsons Promontory Cruises, Tidal River, Wilsons Promontory; 0428 400 155; promcruises.com.au.
- **Keep walking:** There are a few dozen short walks on the Prom, from 30min to 3hr in length, showcasing its huge variety. Wander the expansive sand dunes of the Big Drift, summit the park's highest point at Mount Oberon for epic 360-degree views, or check out the bird lovers' paradise of Millers Landing wetlands.
- **Touring routes:** This corner of Gippsland is filled with quaint little country towns offering boutique shops, wineries, distilleries and gastronomic offerings. A few notable options include the Loch Brewery & Distillery, eclectic vintage clothes and goods at Merchants in Korumburra, and the traditional Italian fare at Meeniyan's Trulli. Check touring route suggestions at visitpromcountry.com.au/drives.

An epic traverse of Grampians (Gariwerd) National Park, featuring spectacular mountains, sheer escarpments, wildflowers and waterfalls.

Grampians Peaks Trail

This walk is on <u>Djab Wurrung</u> and <u>Jardwadjali Country</u>.

WHY IT'S SPECIAL

The opening of this long-distance trail across one of Victoria's most popular outdoor playgrounds in 2021 created quite a buzz. Stretching from Mount Zero in the north to Dunkeld in the south, the route links up many of Grampians (Gariwerd) National Park's most famous highlights – The Pinnacle, Mount Difficult, and the Major Mitchell Plateau, to name a few – as well as 100km of previously untracked terrain.

The Grampians/Gariwerd mountains look like crested waves washing eastwards across the Wimmera Plains. Essentially they're a long system of tilted sandstone ranges with near vertical escarpments on one side and gently sloping down to the plains on the other. Geologists call them cuestas. Hikers simply call them stunningly beautiful. Trailing up, over and through this string of rocky ridges and peaks doesn't make for the easiest walk but it does deliver plenty of 'wow' moments.

WALK IT

Don't underestimate the challenge. While daily distances are short, the terrain is tough and slow going (2kph is about the average), and if you hike the whole thing you'll nearly climb the height of Everest! It's full on so if you're anything less than hardcore, try tackling it in sections rather than locking in for the entire epic. Regular entry and exit points mean you can pick anything from a day hike to two days and upwards to the whole shebang; for example, just a few days in the northern section will give you an impressive taster.

The trail is walked from north to south. It's a 90min drive between Mount Zero and Dunkeld and while you could organise your own car shuffle and food drops along the way (using car access points en route), an easier option is to enlist the services of Grampians Peaks Walking Company (*see* Resources), who arrange transfers at numerous points along the trail, and also food drops so you don't need to carry more than a few days' worth at a time.

 Trail talk
- Distance: 164km
- Time: 13 days
- Rating: Hard
- Technicality: A good portion of the trail involves rock hopping, off-camber traverses and the occasional scrambling and exposure.
- Puff factor: It's big-time puffy with over 8000m of elevation. Pack calorific food because you're going to need it!
- Watch out for: Check the forecast before you go as many sections are high and exposed to the elements. Take care in the wet when rocks become slippery, and keep a keen eye for navigational markers, particularly on rocky sections where there is no defined ground trail to follow.

 When to go
Sep-Dec or Apr-May are best. Wildflowers in late winter and spring are spectacular. Avoid Jan-Mar when bushfire risk is high, and winter when icy winds and snow are a possibility.

 Resources
Visit parks.vic.gov.au for more details, suggested itineraries and to book campsites. Trail transfers, food drops and official maps can be organised through Grampians Peaks Walking Company (grampianspeaks.com.au).

Opposite Following the yellow triangles

All campsites have toilets, water tanks and USB charging points and most have a communal shelter. Camps at Gar and Werdug (in the northern section) also have 4-bunk private huts available to those on guided tours. Be sure to check water tank levels via parks.vic.gov.au prior to heading out so you don't run out of precious water. You may need to top up supplies before reaching some camps, using additional water tanks dotted en route near road junctions (these are monitored and filled as required.)

👁 LOCAL SNAPSHOT

Gariwerd has long held great cultural and spiritual significance for the Djab Wurrung and Jardwadjali Traditional Owners. Its mountains offer abundant food, water and shelter in the caves worn into sandstone overhangs, and over 80 per cent of all rock-art sites discovered in Victoria have been found here, dating occupation as far back as 20,000 years at least. Over 120 sites have been discovered so far, with new ones being found all the time. Only five are open to the public, including the hand-stencils at Manja Shelter and a painting of Bunjil, the Great Ancestor Spirit who created Gariwerd, at Bunjil Shelter. For the Djab Wurrung and Jardwadjali People, the mountains' pointed profiles looked nose-like (translating to Gariwerd), but when explorer Major Thomas Mitchell visited in 1836 they reminded him of the Grampians Mountains in his native Scotland.

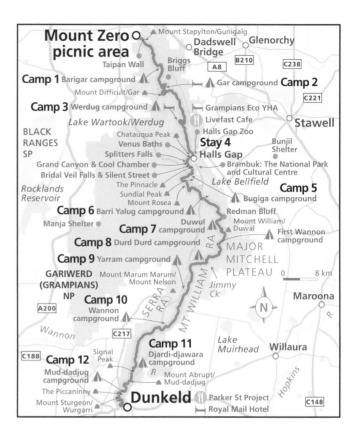

Right An echidna hunting ants around Wannon camp *Opposite* Rugged walking in the Northern section *Overleaf* A meadow filled with wildflowers near Durd Durd camp

ITINERARY

DAYS 1–2
NORTH
Mount Zero to Barigar, 12.1km, 6hr
Barigar to Gar, 11.3km, 6hr

Summiting Mount Zero is not strictly part of the GPT (the trail starts at Mount Zero Picnic Area at its base) but if you want to tick off all the highest peaks linking the route, this one-hour side trip from the picnic area, before launching on the GPT, is a must. From its summit I take in the terrain ahead. I've given a handful of the 1672sqkm park's highlights plenty of attention in the past but the prospect of exploring new frontiers is exciting.

There's no easing into things on this first day. Gariwerd is dominated by sandstone mountains and it's a fact you're constantly reminded of. Day 1 sees me inching up vast rock slabs before sinking into the Mount Stapylton Amphitheatre towered over by the Taipan Wall, a sheer orange cliff streaked in black and white from algae and bird poo. A 30min return side trip leads to Mount Stapylton Viewpoint with expansive views across what is a particularly gnarly and impressive part of Gariwerd.

In a spectacular lightshow, dark clouds mingle with the late golden sun as I rock hop an exposed and unformed route towards Briggs Bluff, along ridgelines sprouting channels of wildflowers and low scrub. The track descends for three creek crossings, finally passing a small waterfall just a few hundred metres from Barigar Camp. Tent pads are tucked in the trees, surrounded by mountains and cliffs, and an architecturally-designed rusted iron shelter contains a few picnic tables and solar-powered USB charging points – a luxury that leans more towards necessity on a trail this long.

Day 2 involves lots of rock hopping and is almost entirely uphill, rising 576m in elevation, and it becomes clear this trail will be no cake walk. To make it even more interesting, I cop wind, rain, hail and sun, but somehow the elements only add to the drama of the landscape. Little yellow triangles guide me along narrow ridgelines, past waterfalls, through vast open valleys, and across sloping rock slabs crinkled like elephant hide. I decide to skip the 1hr return side trip to Briggs Bluff (I've done it before and its exposed rock slabs and sheer cliffs are no place to be in strong winds).

A spectacular climb through serrations of tilted sandstone leads up to Gar, probably the most impressive camp of the entire route and perched just metres from a cliff-edge. I down my pack for the day, pull on a down jacket and settle on one of the timber sun lounges bolted onto the escarpment rim, letting the late afternoon sun 'warm' my face while I soak up the million-dollar views. Though it's mid November, the temperature dives below zero overnight and I'm grateful for the super-cool charred-timber communal shelter with soaring glass frontage in which to cook dinner and hide from the icy winds.

All campsites have traditional names and Gar – 'pointed mountain' – refers to nearby Mount Difficult. Apparently the 1km side-trip to its summit (starts 300m south of camp) is epic at sunrise but in the early hours it's a whiteout and blowing a gale and I'm forced to sleep in instead.

DAYS 3–4
NORTH
Gar to Werdug, 14km, 6–7hr
Werdug to Halls Gap, 13km, 5–6hr

On Day 3, it's rock, rock, rock all the way from Gar camp to Werdug camp, over undulations that require giving up any notions of keeping a good pace. Aside from a few pockets of trees dotted with wildflowers and orchids, much of the route is exposed and the views spread far, including my first look at sprawling Lake Wartook/Werdug, an important water collection point for towns north of the park. The trail skirts spectacularly close to the rim of a sheer escarpment, before arriving at Werdug camp situated on a high knoll at 750m. I get there just in time to retreat inside the enclosed communal shelter before the heavens open, leaving the trees drooping under the weight of fresh rain. Tent pads are tucked in the trees but at the far end of camp (near the guided-walker huts) is a spectacular outlook over distant Lake Wartook (140m lower) which shimmers golden in the setting sun.

On Day 4, the air is finally still and I can hear the birds. For the first time, the route is more defined track than vague rock hopping. The 500m descent to the small town of Halls Gap showcases how plant life changes with altitude and soil type, taking me from exposed sub-alpine rock slabs to colourful wildflower gardens, spindly trees furry with moss and lichen, and finally a lush forest filled with bracken ferns, orchids and the screech of cockatoos. The 30min side-trip to Chatauqua Peak is a worthy scramble if you have the energy and don't mind a little exposure.

The region's main centre, Halls Gap, is a one-street affair but there's enough good food and comfy beds here to recharge and refresh for the onward section.

DAYS 5–6
CENTRAL
Halls Gap to Bugiga, 8.5km, 5hr
Bugiga to Barri Yalug, 15.2km, 6hr

It might only be 8km from Halls Gap to Bugiga camp but much of it is a relentless slog up 500m of elevation. Thankfully it's via some of the most well known and jaw-dropping attractions the Grampians/Gariwerd has, and I'm barely 5min into it when I'm lured to soak my feet in the smooth rock cascades of Venus Baths. Splitters Falls comes next, then the maze of surreal rock formations and passageways of the Wonderland Range. Gariwerd's rock has a signature texture (layered and wrinkled) and here it has eroded into remarkable forms. The trail passes through Grand Canyon, a deep chasm whose lumpy grey walls tower over those walking its base. A creek flows through it and it can really pump after rain, but I miss the whole thing since the upper exit is closed for works during my visit, and I'm forced to take a detour around the canyon, rejoining the GPT just where a steel staircase climbs out of it.

I pass Cool Chamber, a large rock overhang and keep climbing before rock hopping a creek at Bridal Veil Falls. A metal staircase descends into the next canyon, Silent Street. It's long, straight and narrow, just a tight squeeze at its highest end. I walk the bed of rock that passes through it and then up onto the escarpment, finally reaching The Pinnacle which juts out from the cliff and gives epic views over Halls Gap and Lake Bellfield. This is the most visited part of the Grampians/Gariwerd – many day walkers flock here from Halls Gap or the higher Wonderland carpark – but in the late afternoon it's all mine.

A 3.6km side trip to Sundial Peak reputedly has some of the most impressive views from the Wonderland Range, across to Mount William Range, the Fyans Valley and Mount Rosea, but I'm too knackered to add another hour to my day; I finish instead with a peaceful walk through wildflowers and forest to Bugiga camp. The only shelter here is a semicircular 'wind tunnel' of rusted iron lined by two long bench seats. Circular timber tent pads radiate off an elevated walkway and there are fabulous views of the line of sheer cliffs topping Mount Rosea opposite. As I cook dinner, I'm joined by grazing wallabies and koalas growling in the trees.

Humans dissipate the further south I move from Halls Gap, and on Day 6 the sense of solitude and remoteness quickly amplifies. It's a long climb towards the ridgeline of Mount Rosea over vast rock slabs cascading like lava flows. A scramble through mossy crags has me on my knees at times but as

the route hugs the escarpment edge, the sight of sheer and impossibly high rock faces blows me away. Nothing is fenced here so keep well away from the edge. A 10min side trip leads to the summit of Mount Rosea at 1009m, offering endless views in good weather.

The change in colour palette as I descend from grey rocky terrain and blue skies into a green fern-filled forest dotted with crimson rosellas is striking, and rustles in the undergrowth alert me to a fat echidna snuffling out ants. I set up my tent at Barri Yalug camp which peeks through the trees to distant Lake Bellfield, and while there's no enclosed shelter here, a 'gathering place' offers a few picnic tables for preparing dinner.

DAYS 7–9
CENTRAL
Barri Yalug to Duwul, 13.2km, 8–9hr
Duwul to Durd Durd, 14.5km, 7–8hr
Durd Durd to Yarram, 11.9km, 4–5hr

Barri Yalug to Duwul is the longest and toughest stretch of the entire route, an 8hr epic involving the greatest elevation change on the GPT. The 700m climb starts on rock slabs dotted with explosions of lichen, and through a maze of emerald moss and pink flowers. The remains of a long rusted halfpipe of water fluming, part of the Stawell water supply scheme in the 1800s, shadows the route at times. I keep climbing, following the rim of the Seven Dials Escarpment, ignoring the sheer drops to one side and focusing instead on scrambling through the jumble of giant rocks. I need to take my pack off for one squeeze but at least the trail's technicality keeps my mind off the effort required.

There are about half a dozen false summits to drag myself over, before I triumphantly summit Redman Bluff at 1017m to be hit with some of the finest 360-degree views of the trail, stretching to the mountains where I've come from and the many more leading to Dunkeld in the far south. It's both satisfying and a tad demoralising.

I follow the eastern escarpment, passing a pretty pond surrounded by tea tree and heath, before gratefully reaching Duwul camp. I've earned a rest but it's hard to even get my tent up in the gale-force winds that gust at 70kph (I know this because I'm right next to Mount William, the highest point of the entire trail at 1167m and topped with a weather observation tower). This is one of the few campsites without an enclosed shelter.

On Day 8, I climb through montane forest on dirt track and sealed management road to summit Mount William but thick fog swallows any views. When I veer east to descend through a saddle, the wind becomes visible in whirlpools of white mist. I dip through the forested Boundary Gap and pass First Wannon camp, an informal area with only a drop-toilet, before climbing steep stone steps to top the Major Mitchell Plateau. By now the weather has cleared and I bask in the epic views over a sheer escarpment on one side and a long rippling fin of rock rising from the adjacent Serra Range (from the word 'serrated') on the other. Today the plateau's flat, easy and open walking couldn't be more welcome but in poor weather this plateau can be a challenge. Snow can occur between May and Oct; in July the average temperature rarely rises above 5°C and 170mm of rain is the norm. Durd Durd is the modest summit of this high plateau. Its name means 'stars' and no doubt you'd see a gazillion of them from here at night.

I descend down a ridgeline that slips into blessedly flat forest, then finish the day roaming a glorious open meadow littered with alpine daisies and grazing wallabies. Durd Durd is another hiker camp with only a gathering place of picnic tables plus tent pads tucked in the trees, but a timber platform lookout frames epic views of the Serra Range opposite.

The terrain changes on Day 9, the final leg of the central section. As I descend over 500m in elevation, tracking over honey-coloured gravel through banksia and grass trees to Jimmy Creek, spectacular background views stretch all the way down the William and Serra Ranges. It's a good spot for wildflowers; flame grevillia bloom from Apr to Nov.

I climb again, traversing slopes that dissolve into a tiring rock hop to Yarram camp, tucked at the top of a steep forested gully facing. The steep and compact nature of this site necessitates some clever design and tent pads are tiered like resort balconies which, along with the enclosed communal shelter, have great views across to Mount Marum Marum/Mount Nelson.

DAYS 10–11
SOUTH
Yarram to Wannon, 11.1km, 4–5hr
Wannon to Djardi-djawara, 16.3km, 6hr

The days get a smidge easier south of Yarram and though the notes for Day 10 describe a trail that 'undulates like a rollercoaster', it's at least a fairly gentle one. From a knife-edge ridge, the snaking Serra Range alongside me looks velvety green and punctuated by a backbone of rock. In the distance the distinct outlines of Signal Peak and Mount Abrupt/Mud-dadjug, which overlook the finish line at Dunkeld, begin to grow encouragingly larger.

I spy the large grassy meadow of Wannon camp long before reaching it – an ideal grazing ground for echidnas and kangaroos at dusk. Once my tent is up, I relish a rare lazy afternoon, kicking back with a book on one of the timber sun lounges set on the high point of a slope.

On Day 11, I notice a significant change of habitat south of Wannon. In the gap between the Mount William and the Serra ranges, I wander a vague route across grassland littered with fallen trees and flighty kangaroos, then bracken-filled forest to cross the Wannon River. Swampy river flats flitting with birds and butterflies merge into sandy trails, past Austral grass trees, red grevillia and blue tinsel-lilies. The thick heath here is important habitat for small mammals – the long-nosed potoroo, southern brown bandicoot and heath mouse, to name a few – and Parks Victoria follow elements of traditional burning methods to create the mix of vegetation, food and shelter that these animals can thrive in.

It's a long climb up gravel tracks and stone steps into the Serra Range, from where I follow its undulating ridgeline. Every saddle is clustered with stringybarks and shrubs – a haven for wildlife. I side-step a snake, then witness the rare sight of a wedge-tailed eagle soaring through the trees, following by an emu crashing through sparse woodland. That they can run at all on these steep and rocky slopes without breaking a long leg is a marvel.

I descend to Djardi-djawara camp, backed by open heathy forest and facing out over the spectacular serrations of the Serra Range. An enclosed shelter complements the tent pads tucked lower down, between the trees.

DAYS 12–13
SOUTH
Djardi-djawara to Mud-dadjug, 7.9km, 4–5hr
Mud-dadjug to Dunkeld, 14.7km, 5hr

The elevation profile for Day 12, as printed on the bottom of the map, shows two steeply pointed peaks on the agenda. It's 400m of elevation to scale Signal Peak and another few hundred more for Mount Abrupt/Mud-dadjug but formed rock steps, in blushing pink and orange, make the going a little easier than climbs earlier in the trail. Views are glorious and unimpeded for most of the day and I pass bushes of white wildflowers buzzing with bees.

It's a steep descent from Mount Abrupt/Mud-dadjug through messmates and tea tree to reach Mud-dadjug camp perched on a rocky outcrop at 500m. I arrive in time for lunch and it's a long and hot afternoon with little shade, but by dinnertime

Djardi-djawara camp

I'm hit by the mother of all storms. It's a job to hang onto my tent against the onslaught of wind and torrential rain while thunder and lightning cracks overhead, but when it eventually passes I'm rewarded with possibly the most dramatic sunset I've laid eyes on. Low cloud washes over neighbouring Mount Sturgeon/Wurgarri, like dry ice, and mandarin light pierces the dark clouds to cast the land in an other-worldly glow. Sunrise is almost as dazzling, lighting up the rocky prows of Mount Sturgeon/Wurgarri and Mount Abrupt/Mud-dadjug, and beaming through the low mist on the plains below where tiny trees cast long shadows.

After nearly two weeks of non-stop hiking, it's a satisfying moment to sit atop Mount Sturgeon/Wurgarri on Day 13, the last of the hills behind me. Finally the mountains have run out, replaced by a pale green patchwork of farming plains. The small hump of The Piccaninny, en route to it, is a 30min return side trip and apparently great for orchid spotting in winter and spring, but I've had enough of climbing and skip it.

It's always hard returning to civilisation after a long walk but the GPT provides a gentle transition, dripping off the back of the ranges and into the back garden of the Royal Mail Hotel (aka Mount Sturgeon Biodiversity Reserve), where open grassland and woodland is scattered with gnarled red gums, kangaroos and emus. The transition is complete when I wash off days of stink and grime in one of the Royal Mail's rooms and, in a surreal change of pace, within two hours of finishing my hike I'm sipping fine wines in the cellar. Bliss.

BEST EATS

- **Livefast Cafe:** Come here for coffee and nourishing food. You'll get anything from kale and quinoa salads to pork belly burgers. 5/97 Grampians Rd, Halls Gap; (03) 5356 4400; livefast.com.au.
- **Parker St Project:** The Royal Mail Hotel calls this its casual diner but the fare is well above your average, with much of the produce pulled from the kitchen garden. Tuck into dishes like confit chicken oysters with hay hollandaise or broccoli risotto with poached quail eggs and parmesan crisp. 98 Parker St, Dunkeld; (03) 5577 2241; royalmail.com.au.

BEST SLEEPS

- **Grampians Eco YHA:** This hostel is way cooler than most with funky design, cosy lounges with wood-fire heaters, plus guests are welcome to help themselves to home-grown fruit and veg and free-range eggs. Stay in 4-share dorms, private doubles or family rooms. 14-16 Grampians Rd, Halls Gap; (03) 5356 4544; yha.com.au/hostels/vic.
- **Royal Mail Hotel:** This is a treat you'll definitely have earned by trail's end. Sink into quality rooms with views of Mount Sturgeon/Wurgarri, and replenish at its super-yum diner or the award-winning, two-hatted Wickens Restaurant. 98 Parker St, Dunkeld; (03) 5577 2241; royalmail.com.au.

WHILE YOU'RE HERE

- **Brambuk: The National Park and Culture Centre:** Renovations were ongoing at the time of research but it's worth checking ahead to see if this award-winning cultural centre is open; visitgrampians.com.au/products/brambuk--the-national-park-cultural-centre.
- **Grampians Helicopters:** Take to the skies for a bird's eye view of the rippling mountains and forests that the GPT passes through. Opt for anything from a 10min blast to a 60min loop covering the entire Grampians (Gariwerd) National Park. Flights depart from Stawell Airport; 0438 981 438; grampianshelicopters.com.au.
- **Halls Gap Zoo:** Victoria's largest regional zoo has over 160 species, from American bison and giraffe to close encounters with dingoes, meerkats and red pandas. 4061 Ararat-Halls Gap Rd, Halls Gap; (03) 5356 4668; hallsgapzoo.com.au.

The trail skirts many sheer cliffs

Rock hop around a granite peak in the You Yangs, rising from volcanic plains, before climbing to its summit.

East West Walk & Flinders Peak/Wurdi Youang

This walk is on Wadawurrung Country.

WHY IT'S SPECIAL

Though the You Yang Ranges began life as liquid hot magma, they never actually made it to volcano status, instead oozing and pushing their way into sedimentary rock around 350 million years ago, before solidifying well below the surface. Over millions of years, the surrounding rock eroded away, leaving huge granite tors and boulders that make for a walker's playground. It's all just an hour's drive south-west of Melbourne or half an hour north-east from the regional city of Geelong. Carving around the flanks of Flinders Peak/Wurdi Youang, this trail negotiates sloping granite slabs and winds past giant marbles and rock walls, with near-constant views across the surrounding Western Plains that stretch all the way to Melbourne. At 340m, Flinders Peak/Wurdi Youang is not exactly a cloud piercer however, but sitting on the world's third largest basalt plain, it feels pretty impressive. The scenery is exciting for all ages but kids in particular will get a kick out of exploring here.

The walk gets bonus points for being dog-friendly, though dogs must be on lead.

WALK IT

This hike combines two tracks: the East West Walk, circumnavigating Flinders Peak/Wurdi Youang, and a return hike to its summit. Do one or both, depending on time and energy levels.

Parking is at the Turntable carpark but if that's full (and it does get busy on weekends) there are lower carparks situated next to half a dozen super scenic picnic areas with gas barbecues.

The You Yangs are a bit of an adventure playground with a network of purpose-built mountain-bike trails (*see* p. 83), plus areas for rock climbing, abseiling and even horse riding. After you've finished this walk, check out other trails to Big Rock or into the Northern Range.

 Trail talk
- Distance: 4.5km circuit + 3.2km for the peak
- Time: 2hr circuit + 1hr for the peak
- Rating: Moderate
- Technicality: Quite a bit of rock hopping on the East West Walk; well-graded track with 450 steps up to Flinders Peak/Wurdi Youang.
- Puff factor: Between rocky terrain and a steady climb, you'll get the heart rate going on this one.
- Watch out for: Rocks are extra slippery in the wet.

 When to go
Autumn to spring is best. The trail is often exposed and can get hot in summer. Midweek is less busy.

 Resources
Download a visitor guide and map from parks.vic.gov.au.

Opposite There's plenty of fun rock-scrambling in the You Yangs

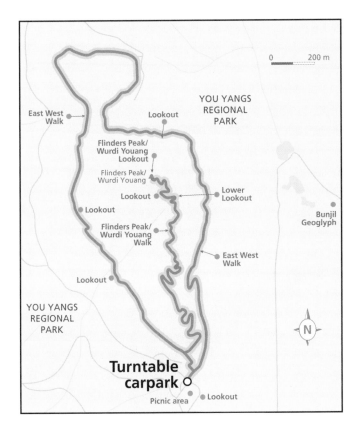

Map labels:
- East West Walk
- YOU YANGS REGIONAL PARK
- Lookout
- Flinders Peak/ Wurdi Youang Lookout
- Flinders Peak/ Wurdi Youang
- Lower Lookout
- Lookout
- Lookout
- Bunjil Geoglyph
- Flinders Peak/ Wurdi Youang Walk
- East West Walk
- Lookout
- YOU YANGS REGIONAL PARK
- N
- Turntable carpark
- Picnic area
- Lookout
- 0   200 m

👁 LOCAL SNAPSHOT

If you've heard the phrase: 'you've got two chances, Buckley's and none', then you've had an introduction to William Buckley. In 1803 he arrived at Sullivans Bay Penal Settlement (aka Sorrento, on the Mornington Peninsula) at age 23, soon escaping to eventually join the Wathaurong People with whom he lived for 32 years. The You Yangs is one of six sites flagged on the William Buckley Discovery Trail and is identified as a place where he once searched for food, though found none. He ended up spending most of his time around Geelong and surrounds, learning the language and ways of the Wathaurong People, before eventually being discovered by the authorities in 1835 and given a pardon. His slim chance of survival is at the root of the Aussie phrase: 'Buckley's chance'.

Opposite top Regular views look out over the Western Plains
Opposite bottom There are scenic picnic areas in the park, perfect for a pre- or post-walk meal

ITINERARY

It's a rare hiking trail in Australia that welcomes dogs – national parks don't allow pets – but the You Yangs is one such place. It's good news for the miniature schnoodle and poodle that I'm walking with who stamp their furry little feet in excitement on arrival at the trailhead. Though mid winter, we've scored a gloriously sunny day, perhaps helped by the fact that the You Yang Ranges are the driest part of Victoria south of the Great Dividing Range, thanks to the rain shadow cast by the lush Otway Range to the west.

We're doing the East West Walk first – it's a nice warm up for the climb later – skirting around the lower flanks of Flinders Peak/Wurdi Youang. Views across the surrounding plains are a steady companion on this hike and with no obstructions they reach far. Heading anticlockwise we notice first the blue slick of Port Philip and even the skyline of Melbourne, 50km away.

The path climbs gently, regularly interrupted by knobs of granite. It's a bit of a scramble at times as the track traces over rocks and decent slabs of granite. If you're with a pooch, a long lead is recommended if you want to give them their head and avoid being yanked down a boulder-filled route faster than your own legs can manage.

Looking east you can't miss the splayed wings of a giant wedge-tailed eagle, 100m across, in the treed valley below. This stone geoglyph of Bunjil, the creator spirit of the Wathaurong People, was created by artist Andrew Rogers to commemorate the Melbourne 2006 Commonwealth Games. In nearby Little River is a Wathaurong rock arrangement, possibly 10,000 years old, called Wurdi Youang. The egg-shaped positioning of basalt rocks, 151m in circumference, is believed to have been aligned precisely to map the sun.

Wind whistles through needles of casuarina and there's a smattering of eucalpytus, but mostly the vegetation is shrub-like with patches of mint bush and cassinia. Granite bubbles up into giant marbles and there are dozens of rock slabs with expansive views, ideal for lingering. As the trail moves to the western side of the circuit you score views of bayside Geelong, the state's second biggest city. One steel platform lookout hovers over a popular rock-climbing area.

With the circuit almost complete, the turn-off to Flinders Peak/Wurdi Youang appears, and while there are no tricky rocks to negotiate on this track, there are 450 steps rising 200m in elevation, albeit well spaced out. It's a steady climb that begins to tire my schnoodle's little legs towards the top, but it's nothing that a summit picnic won't fix.

There's a well-earned 360-degree view to be had from the steel-platform lookout at the top and plenty of space to laze about on huge granite slabs. Matthew Flinders was the first European to summit here in 1802, calling it 'Station Peak', and a decade later it was changed to Flinders Peak in his honour. But it will always be the You Yangs, the Wadawurrung name for this 'big hill in the middle of a plain'.

BEST EATS

- **Millars Lara:** This is the best and closest cafe for bites such as paninis, burgers, fish tacos or nourish bowls. Takeaway is also available. 80 Westlakes Blvd, Lara; 0438 369 301; millarslara.com.au.
- **del Rios Winery & Restaurant:** Sit outdoors or inside where soaring windows look out over the vineyard and surrounding hills. The menu is tapas-style and uses local produce including Angus beef and lamb farmed onsite. 2290 Ballan Rd, Anakie; 1300 171 259; delrios.com.au.

BEST SLEEPS

- **Lara Lodge:** These studio and 2-bedroom cabins sit on a quiet 40 acres of horse agistment, a mere 7min drive from the trailhead and with views of the You Yangs. They're simple on the outside but fitted out with new and quality furnishings. 325 Forest Rd, North Lara; 0418 106 982; laralodge.com.au.
- **Geelong:** The You Yangs is only a 30min drive from Geelong where there are plentiful accommodation options to suit all budgets.

WHILE YOU'RE HERE

- **Mountain biking:** There are over 50km of trails, graded green to black, across two purpose-built mountain-biking areas in the You Yangs. Kurrajong is best for beginners and intermediates, while Stockyards will suit intermediate to advanced. Download trail maps from parks.vic.gov.au.
- **Werribee Open Range Zoo:** Join a safari on the 225ha of open savannah at Werribee Zoo and you'll get a real African Plains experience, seeing giraffe, zebra, lions, cheetahs, hippos, African wild dogs, gorillas and plenty more. Overnight sleepovers are something special. K Road, Werribee South; 1300 966 784; zoo.org.au/werribee.
- **Werribee Park:** This grand estate incorporates Werribee Park Mansion, a 60-room property built in 1877 by early pastoralists, and the manicured gardens and 5000 odd blooms of the Victoria State Rose Garden. Take a tour of the opulent mansion, picnic in the grounds or stay a night at the Mansion Hotel. K Road, Gate 2, Werribee Park, Werribee; 13 1963; parks.vic.gov.au.

Top A lookout perched above a popular rock climbing area

Walk cliff-tops, remote beaches and koala-filled forests on Victoria's most famous stretch of coastline.

Great Ocean Walk

This walk is on <u>Gadubanud</u> and <u>Girai wurrung Country</u>.

WHY IT'S SPECIAL

With its string of stunning beaches and striking cliff formations, the Great Ocean Road is one of Victoria's most treasured attractions and this walk offers a backstage pass. On foot you get a far deeper understanding and appreciation of the coastline than you do with quick peeks from designated lookout points (as most car-based visitors experience it), plus you'll do it without the crowds.

Between Apollo Bay and the Twelve Apostles, walkers get to enjoy a steady buffet of remote beaches, winding cliff-top paths, shipwreck remains, eucalypt forests filled with koalas and Australia's oldest working lighthouse at Cape Otway. The grand finale is the giant sea-bound limestone stacks of the Twelve Apostles. Migrating whales between June and Oct are a bonus.

WALK IT

Campsites are well done on this walk with three-sided shelters, picnic tables, long drop-toilets and water tanks, but if you want cushy options you can have them too. There are plenty of entry points where someone with wheels can collect you at day's end and whisk you off to somewhere with wine and a hot tub. Another option is to just explore a section of the trail, for anything from one day to two days or upwards to the whole experience.

The walk is done one way, heading west from Apollo Bay to finish at the Twelve Apostles. It's a pretty wild coastline with rips and strong currents, and swimming is not recommended on unpatrolled beaches (*see* beachsafe.org.au or download the Beachsafe app). You'll also want to consult the tide times before locking in your dates to ensure low tide beach walks coincide with a convenient time of day (some parts of the track are inaccessible at high tide).

 Trail talk
- Distance: 100km
- Time: 6-8 days
- Rating: Easy-hard
- Technicality: A mix of well-defined track and beaches. Three river crossings require care.
- Puff factor: Steady undulations (some quite steep) and a bit of beach walking make for a reasonably puffy walk.
- Watch out for: Check the tide times to be safe on beach walking sections. River crossings are usually easy peasy but heavy rain and hide tides can change that.

 When to go
It's doable year-round but spring to autumn is best. Check the fire danger rating before you set out (emergency.vic.gov.au or download the VicEmergency app).

 Resources
Visit greatoceanwalk.com.au for planning advice, trail suggestions, accommodation and transfer options, and suggested day and multi-day walks for anything from 2-8 days. Buy the official Great Ocean Walk Information Guide and Map from Parks Victoria and Visitor Info Centres. Campsites need to be pre-booked via parks.vic.gov.au/stay.

Opposite On the home stretch towards the Twelve Apostles

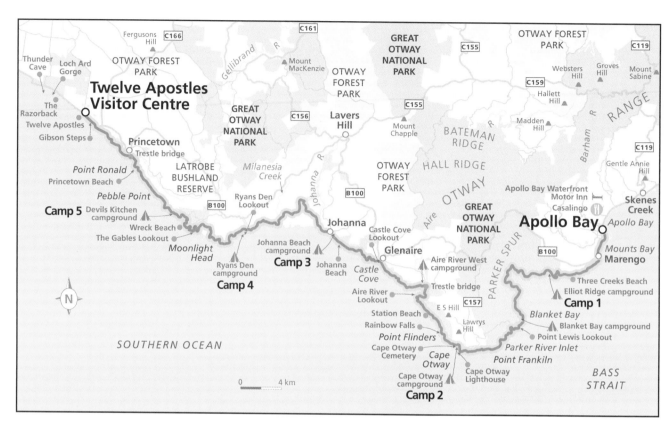

Camp 5
Camp 4
Camp 3
Camp 2
Camp 1

SOUTHERN OCEAN

BASS STRAIT

LOCAL SNAPSHOT

West of Cape Otway stretches a gnarly coastline that has claimed hundreds of lives in shipwrecks since people started sailing here in the 1600s. Figures vary but it's estimated around 600-700 shipwrecks came to grief on its reefs and rocks, though only about a third have been discovered and documented. From wooden sailing ships navigating by stars and incomplete charts, to cargo and passenger ships blown off course in storms, their remains - a few of which are seen on this walk - now scatter what is referred to as the Shipwreck Coast.

Right Koalas are plentiful *Opposite* Wreck Beach *Overleaf* Walking the forests of Great Otway National Park

ITINERARY

DAY 1
Apollo Bay to Elliot Ridge campground, 10km, 3.5hr

It's convenient that a train and bus combo can transport hikers from Melbourne to the trailhead, but after an hour of winding scenic roads – during which I come awfully close to filling the plastic bag in my seatback pocket – the fresh ocean air comes not a moment too soon. The Great Ocean Road lives up to its name, hugging the coast as it winds through the towns of Anglesea, Aireys Inlet, Lorne, Wye River, Kennett River, Skenes Creek and eventually depositing me at the fishing and holiday town of Apollo Bay.

The walk starts from the Visitor Centre which is conveniently where the bus drops me off. Beyond the streets of Apollo Bay, the full grandeur of the Southern Ocean becomes apparent. Coastal rock platforms lead to grassy paths climbing over headlands, with views that offer an introduction to the coastline ahead. Forested ranges pour into rocky bays. A short stretch on Three Creeks Beach leads into eucalypt forest and I round a corner to suddenly see a fluffy-eared koala sitting in the middle of the track. Unfussed by my presence, it crawls a few steps into the ferns and stays there as I pass. Numbers are in decline and in Feb 2022 koalas were declared endangered in NSW and Qld, but Great Otway National Park is a koala hotspot and the last time I hiked here I saw two in the first three hours.

If you've never heard a koala before you likely will at Elliot Ridge camp and it can be alarming – imagine a cross between a pig snort and lion growl. All night I hear them in noisy arguments with the possums.

DAY 2
Elliot Ridge campground to Blanket Bay, 12km, 4.5hr
Blanket Bay to Cape Otway campground, 11km, 3.5hr

I opt to combine a couple of short sections into one big day and the first leg takes the trail's biggest deviation inland, deep into Great Otway National Park, yet still kilometres away from the busy Great Ocean Road that shadows it further inland. Wide tracks slice through tall forests of mountain ash, the tallest flowering tree in the world, reaching heights of over 110m. In the mid 1800s, these trees were favoured by loggers and occasionally the telltale springboard holes, used by workmen to climb above the buttresses and make sawing easier, can be seen in trailside trunks. This section of trail can get pretty muddy after rain but the undulations are gentle, allowing plenty of opportunity to gaze up and around at this lush forest sprinkled with ferns. When the route finally returns to the coast, it's at Blanket Bay where a hiker's camp straddles forest and beach.

The trail climbs gently to pass Point Lewis Lookout, then dives back into woodland where beautifully formed tracks wind between the roughened grey trunks of gum trees, and another koala suddenly springs up a tree only a few metres away. If it

hadn't crashed through the ferns beforehand I'd never have known it was there, prompting me to wonder how many others I've missed.

The track descends steeply to cross Parker River Inlet, a meandering tannin-stained waterway that shifts with the sands. It's one of three rivers to be crossed on the whole route and while they're mostly ankle- to shin-deep, they can swell with rain or high tides, so care is required. The tiny remote beach on the other side is a worthy spot for a break, before climbing back to the cliff-tops for some epic ocean views.

Cape Otway lighthouse looks out from the cliff-tops, 90m above the ocean. It was built in 1848 to try and curb growing numbers of shipwrecks and you can take a tour of the lighthouse (GOW hikers get 50 per cent discount on entry; lightstation.com), telegraph station, World War II bunker or even splash out on a night in one of the lightkeeper's cottages. I opt to set up my tent in the designated walker's camping area, tucked in the trees about 500m from the lighthouse.

DAY 3
Cape Otway campground to Aire River, 10km, 3.5hr
Aire River to Johanna Beach campground, 14km, 5.5hr

I head off by headlight half an hour before dawn to avoid a later river crossing and beach traverse at high tide. In the dark I pass the tiny Cape Otway Cemetery, a resting place for lighthouse families and shipwreck victims, before reaching the cliff-tops where the transition through sunrise is stunning. Golden light spills across green shrubs and a calm ocean and in the distance I spot the breach and misty exhalations of a whale. At Station Beach the GOW offers two options: to traipse north on the sand for several kilometres before rejoining the main trail, or continue north via the inland route. Parks Victoria encourages going inland with its panoramic ocean views and firm track (it gets my vote), but if the tide is low there is an option to deviate south off Station Beach to visit Rainbow Falls (a 3km round-trip). The falls flow over colourful algae on a rock face that meets the coastal rock platform beneath.

A stunning viewpoint overlooks the sizeable Aire River as it slides between vegetated dunes and emerald ranges on its way out to sea, and hikers cross it via a wooden trestle bridge. Beyond it, the trail stays high with steady ocean views before descending through shrubs tumbling steeply to rocky beaches. I skirt beneath limestone cliffs pocked with holes, while birds of prey circle on the updraft, and the scene is so unfamiliar to me I have to remind myself where I am – despite having visited this coastline a dozen times. It's a sudden surprise

when I round a bend and see the tarmac of the Great Ocean Road lightly brushing my track where they meet at Castle Cove lookout.

While the main road heads inland again, the GOW stays close to the coast, undulating through coastal scrub and beautiful bracken fern forest, later giving way to a far drier landscape of grass trees and banksia. The path descends steeply to cross Browns Creek (usually dry) and onto Johanna Beach for 2km of sand, narrow enough in one short section for the feisty surf to pin me to within a metre of steep dunes. The sizeable Johanna River cuts the beach at its midway point, named after a schooner that washed up here in rough weather in 1843. I arrive not a moment too soon, rolling up my pants for an icy knee-deep crossing before the final push to Johanna camp, perched high above the sand dunes.

Views from Johanna Beach campground are epic, stretching far down the beach and taking in frothing waves dotted with surfers. The ocean is a distant roar all night.

DAY 4
Johanna Beach campground to Ryans Den campground, 14km, 5hr

One of the most rugged and remote sections of the track starts off in vivid green along steeply rolling farmland, where dozens of grey kangaroos blend in with random tufts of tussock grass. It's a gradual climb up around 180m of elevation before the trail begins its descent to the coast again at Milanesia Creek.

It's another crossing that can swell with the tides or rain, though it's a trickle on my shift. At low tide, keep an eye out for the ancient spherical rocks, from marble to cannonball size, embedded in the cliffs along the beach.

The sense of wildness on this stretch is powerful. There are plenty of steps and steep undulations, as the track alternates between fern-filled woodland and skirting around the cliffs of a rugged and untouched piece of coastline.

Ryans Den is a gem of a campsite, tucked in the trees with an awesome lookout over the ocean, and is a prime spot to witness sunset and a billion twinkling stars.

DAY 5
Ryans Den campground to Devils Kitchen campground, 13km, 5hr

Today follows another wild route through coastal forest, in which I cross paths with an echidna, to blustery cliff-top paths with panoramic sea views. The Gables lookout gazes out from a perch 130m above the ocean towards Moonlight Head and the reefs that have foiled so many ships over the centuries.

Considered one of the more difficult sections of trail, there are a few hills to tackle on this leg but they're mostly finished by the time you arrive at Wreck Beach, and although there is a high tide alternative around it, this is one beach walk you don't want to miss. Low water is a must so I pass an indulgent few hours in the sun with my boots off, waiting for the tide to recede. When it does, long rock platforms carved with smooth round holes like Swiss cheese and carpeted in neon green weed are revealed. In one rockpool rests the rusted anchor from French sailing ship *Marie Gabrielle* (1869), while others are like deep fishbowls. I walk the beach, sandwiched between tall cliffs and ocean, and pass a rusted anchor from the *Fiji* (1891) propped upright in the sand – a memorial to the sailing ship that now rests 7m offshore.

Devils Kitchen camp is one of the best and has a loo with a view across the ocean.

DAY 6
Devils Kitchen campground to Twelve Apostles, 16km, 5hr

Following the narrow rise between the Gellibrand River and coast, the views grow increasingly impressive as the trail draws closer to the estuary mouth and the orange cliffs of Point Ronald, rising on the far shore. It's worth the short deviation to Princetown Beach, where a brown tannin-stained estuary collides with blue ocean and fishermen cast lines into the surf.

Beyond the trestle bridge crossing of the Gellibrand, I'm on the home stretch across open cliff-top tracks. The pièce de résistance comes into view long before reaching it. Rising an impressive 45m from the churning Southern Ocean is a string of twisted rock stacks – the Twelve Apostles. Completely ocean-bound, these soft limestone pillars are slowly being claimed by the ocean, and there are actually only seven remaining, but they're utterly captivating, especially at sunset when the golden rock ripens. Before reaching them, the route passes one more highlight – the Gibson Steps, where 89 steps lead down to a beach flanked by a 70m-high vertical cliff that looks as though it's been cut with a cookie cutter.

Arriving at the Twelve Apostles Visitor Centre, thronging with cars and tour buses, is a reminder of just how lucky I've been to see parts of the coastline few see – and without the crowds.

BEST EATS

- **Casalingo:** With homemade pasta, wood-fired pizza and more, this stylish Italian restaurant makes for an ideal pre-hike stoke up. 1 Moore St, Apollo Bay; (03) 5237 7613; casalingoapollobay.com.au.
- **Forage on the Foreshore:** As the name suggests, this beachfront cafe, a 10min drive further west of the Twelve Apostles in Port Campbell, uses ingredients foraged, grown or produced locally with a menu that ranges from abalone salad to rock lobster risotto. 32 Cairns St, Port Campbell; (02) 5598 6202; forageontheforeshore.com.au.

BEST SLEEPS

- **Apollo Bay Waterfront Motor Inn:** Just a stone's throw from the ocean and within walking distance to shops and restaurants, this tidy motel is a popular choice. 173 Great Ocean Rd, Apollo Bay; (03) 5237 7333; apollobaywaterfront.com.au.
- **The Port O Call:** In the tiny coastal village of Port Campbell, a 10min drive from the end of the trail, is this stylish motel with cool nautical-theme decor. It's just a short amble to the fishing jetty. 35-37 Lord St, Port Campbell; (03) 5598 6206; theportocall.com.au.

WHILE YOU'RE HERE

- **Drive the Great Ocean Road:** While the trail ends at the Twelve Apostles, this is just the start of another spectacular piece of coastline heading west and littered with exceptional lookouts and short walks showcasing sheer limestone cliffs, ocean-bound rock stacks, sheltered bays and smashing waves. There's enough to keep you busy for a day but highlights include Loch Ard Gorge, London Bridge, Thunder Cave and the Razorback. Download the Port Campbell National Park and Bay of Islands Coastal Park Visitor Guide; parks.vic.gov.au.
- **Live Wire Park:** Whiz through the trees by zipline or tackle a high-ropes course in the canopy at this off-grid adventure park. 180 Erskine Falls Road, Lorne; 1300 5483 9473; livewirepark.com.au.

Opposite Rock hopping coastal platforms at the trail's eastern end

Circumnavigate a hidden lake encircled by tree ferns and towering mountain ash.

Lake Elizabeth

This walk is on <u>Gadubanud Country</u>.

WHY IT'S SPECIAL

If you need a reminder of Earth's dynamic nature, witness Lake Elizabeth. When a landslide sheered off the steep valley walls of the Otway Range, one wet June in 1952, it dammed the Barwon River East Branch and within a few months a new lake had formed. Lake Elizabeth nestles in the folds of a long forested valley, and its most prominent feature is the grey spires of dead tree trunks that rise from its still waters. It's eerily beautiful, peaceful and home to tonnes of birds and the old platypus. Wander to the lake at night and you'll see glowworms too. Dogs on lead are welcome here.

The lake is just a short drive from the picturesque town of Forrest, known for its mountain-biking scene and craft brewery.

WALK IT

Take care driving the final few kilometres from Forrest to the lake's carpark as the road is unsealed and can get a little slippery in wet conditions. It takes around 20min to walk to the lake from the carpark, from where a loop track skirts the perimeter.

If you're keen to see glowworms, head in after dark and scan the dark and mossy banks, beneath overhangs, and on tree roots and fallen logs along the trail edge. Keep voices quiet and torches directed at the ground rather than the glowworms as any disturbance causes them to switch off their bioluminescence for up to 15min. Not only will you not see anything but the glowworms will lose valuable feeding time. Platypus are sensitive to noise and movement too, so sit quietly at the water's edge when on a stakeout.

Trail talk

- Distance: 4km
- Time: 2hr
- Rating: Easy
- Technicality: Well-formed dirt trail.
- Puff factor: Only a few gentle undulations with the odd short sharp climb.
- Watch out for: Be careful not to trip on the long shards of bark that litter the track. Mud gets slippery in the wet.

When to go

Anytime of year is beautiful. Very early in the morning is best for spotting platypus or linger on dusk at the end of your walk.

Resources

Check out parks.vic.gov.au and visitotways.com for more information.

Opposite The Otways are a lush, fern-filled wonderland

Victoria

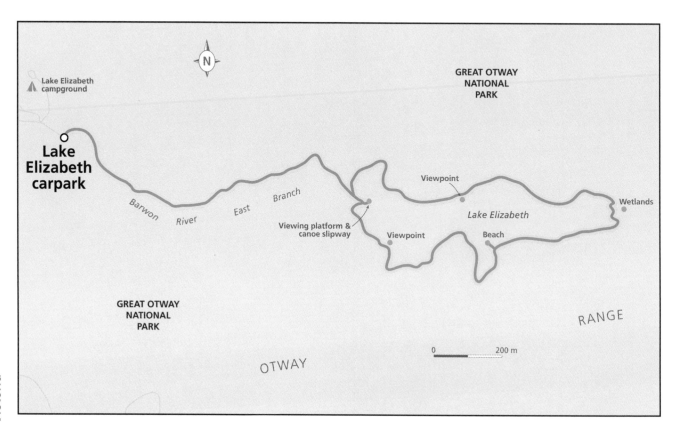

👁 LOCAL SNAPSHOT

Some of the highest rainfall in Victoria has resulted in the cool temperate rainforest and abundant waterfalls that dominate the Otway Range. The rain feeds rivers and dozens of waterfalls (perhaps hundreds, if you include the unmapped), that have carved cool gullies bursting with giant eucalypts, ferns, moss and fungi. Every waterfall has its own character. You can visit one or more before or after your walk. Near to Lorne, Erskine Falls is one of the most popular, cascading 30m over a high ledge to polished boulders below, while Lower Kalimna Falls washes over a large rock chamber overhang, allowing walkers to picnic behind it. Triplet Falls, nearer to the little towns of Lavers Hill and Beech Forest, features three distinct cascades, and Hopetoun is a spectacular 30m plunge waterfall. Then there's Sheoak Falls, Beachamp, Galliebarinda, Sabine and more. Stevensons Falls is one of the closest waterfalls to the town of Forrest, about a 10km drive, and only a short walk from the waterfall's carpark. So many waterfalls, so little time.

ITINERARY

Step out of the car at the Lake Elizabeth carpark and the urge to inhale deeply at the clean air and smell of tree oils and rich earth is almost a reflex action. It's cool, even in summer, and background birdcalls are a constant.

I set off into the greenery along a charcoal-coloured dirt track, following the trickling Barwon River East Branch as it climbs gently upstream towards the lake. Contrasting against the medley of greens are the pale trunks of mountain ash, also referred to as stringy gum on account of their long threads of bark that peel from lower flanks to create a messy tangle on the forest floor. The whole place feels rich with life, and moss and tiny parasols of fungi creep over fallen trees – also a perfect habitat for glowworms.

If you've ever had the urge to recreate *Dirty Dancing*'s memorable 'dancing on a log' scene, you're in luck because the trail passes a pond with a massive fallen tree trunk hovering horizontal over the water. It's extremely photogenic too, with a profusion of tree ferns and arrow-straight mountain ash backing it, creating perfect mirror reflections in the water.

The track meets Lake Elizabeth at its western end, the water stretching away from me like a long dark finger. A few scattered tree trunks rise like spears from its midst, mirrored in the depths of still water and in the still-living specimens that punctuate the greenery sliding down the valley to the water's edge. A small platform here is where platypus-spotting canoe tours launch (*see* p. 97).

I head anti-clockwise around the lake. The aspect shifts as you walk further, through tunnels of ferns and trees with regular peeks at the water. A few bench seats offer opportunities to linger and listen to the medley of cicadas and birdsong. Birdwatching is popular here, with satin bowerbirds, superb fairy wrens and eastern yellow robins common.

A quarter of the way around, a short sidetrack leads to a small sandy beach at the water's edge. At half way, a boardwalk trails through a patch of open wetland, thick with reeds and wildflowers and with views back down the lake. Here the ghostly tree skeletons creep from water to land – no doubt reclaimed by the lake in high flows. Skirting the northern edge of the lake, the track is crowded by tree ferns.

There's something magical about Lake Elizabeth. It's beautiful, exceptionally peaceful and the path is gentle (even my 82-year-old mother has walked around it). It has the feeling of being a hidden secret – and had a party of people not been dispatched in 1952 to investigate why the river had stopped flowing, it might have remained that way. The word is out now but this lake retains the power to still and quieten those who visit.

Top Leafy trails make for easy walking *Opposite* The lake is prime platypus habitat

BEST EATS

- **Forrest General Store:** This place is a magnet for locals and visitors who flock for healthy homemade fare, from pies to soups and salads, sourdough and cakes. Pick up local produce and boutique gifts while you're there. 33 Grant St, Forrest; (03) 5236 6496; forestgeneralstore.com.au.
- **Forrest Brewing Company:** Grab a tasting paddle of pale ales, lagers and stouts brewed onsite using pure Otways water, or sit down in the dining hall for charcuterie boards and burgers. 26 Grant St, Forrest; (03) 5236 6170; forrestbrewing.com.au.

BEST SLEEPS

- **Lake Elizabeth Campground:** There are 20 basic campsites nestled in the forest near the trailhead, offering toilets, picnic tables and fireplaces. Book ahead; parks.vic.gov.au.
- **Cabin retreats:** The Otways is cosy cabin central, whether tucked in the woods or within inhalation reach of salty air. Browse endless options in Forrest and surrounding coastal towns; forrestvictoria.com, visitotways.com.

WHILE YOU'RE HERE

- **Otway Eco Tours:** Gliding around Lake Elizabeth by canoe in the misty calm of dawn or the magic light of dusk gives a whole new perspective, plus there's a very good chance of spotting platypus; 0419 670 985; platypustours.net.au
- **Forrest Mountain Bike Trails:** Around 65km of cross-country trails, graded beginner through to advanced, weave through eucalpyt forests, scrub and fern gullies around the tiny town of Forrest. Download a trail map; forrestvictoria.com.
- **Otway Fly Treetop Adventures:** Get a different view of the Otways on elevated walkways through the rainforest canopy, 25-30m above the ground. For an even more exhilarating experience, try ziplining. 360 Phillips Track Beech Forest, Weeaproinah; (03) 5235 9200; otwayfly.com.au.

Lake Elizabeth was formed by a flooded river valley

*Endless panoramas from an undulating alpine ridge,
plus a summit of Victoria's second highest peak.*

The Razorback Walk

This walk is on <u>Taungurung</u> and
<u>Gunaikurnai Country</u>.

WHY IT'S SPECIAL

There's something about a view that lifts the soul, and they don't get much more vast and unimpeded than on the Razorback, a high alpine ridge linking Mount Hotham and Mount Feathertop in Alpine National Park. Visible far into the distance, the track trails like a line of string over the rocky spine as it undulates – pretty gently for a mountain route – towards Mount Feathertop, the state's second highest peak at 1922m. This walk starts from just below Mount Hotham Village (Hotham Heights) to the summit of Mount Feathertop and returns via the same track.

For much of this walk you'll be surrounded by rippling mountains as far as the eye can see. Throw in a sprinkling of snowgums, wildflowers and maybe a few dollops of snow and this is a standout hike.

WALK IT

The easiest way to tackle it is as an out-and-back walk from Diamantina Hut, located on the Great Alpine Road just below Mount Hotham village (Hotham Heights), but if you're averse to retracing your steps, another option is to do a car shuffle between Hotham and Harrietville (40min one way) and descend via Bungalow Spur Track to Harrietville instead.

Getting to Feathertop and back is a big day out but even just an hour or two spent walking along the Razorback rewards with stunning alpine views, making it possible to tailor-make your hike to suit all ages and fitness levels.

Sunset from the top of Mount Feathertop is pretty special, so another option is to spread the walk over two days (as I do here in this itinerary), carrying camping gear and setting up for the night amongst the snow gums at Federation Hut, half an hour beneath the summit.

Trail talk
- Distance: 22km return
- Time: 7-8hr
- Rating: Moderate
- Technicality: Largely well-packed trail, though a little loose and rocky in places.
- Puff factor: Steady undulations and a few short, sharp climbs. The last push up Mount Feathertop is a decent haul of nearly 200m.
- Watch out for: This is an exposed alpine trail so check the forecast before you go and always carry warm clothes, a rain jacket and supplies.

When to go
Spring through to autumn is best. In winter it's covered in snow.

Resources
Use a mapping app or pack a topographic map (Rooftop's 'Mount Feathertop - Hotham') to maintain your bearings.

Opposite top and bottom Ridgeline walking offers constant views

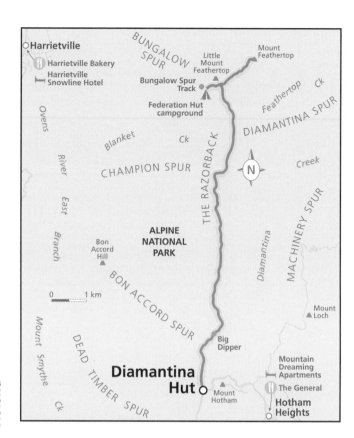

⊙ LOCAL SNAPSHOT

Though relatively untouched now, in the early 1900s
Mount Feathertop was flagged to be a major ski resort.
Interest for the sport was on the rise and in 1923, 150 people
slogged up from Harrietville with packhorses for a snow
carnival and ski race. The construction of the 32-bed
Feathertop Bungalow (a commercial ski lodge) in 1925 was
the first step in an ambitious plan to develop a 300-bed
chalet, ski runs, walking track and an international standard
ski jump. Struggles to secure a decent land lease, combined
with objections from the owners of a competing lodge at
Mount Buffalo, meant plans never came to fruition, and in
1939 Feathertop Bungalow closed and the mountain's ski
industry plans faded along with it.

For an alpine walk, the trail is fairly gentle

ITINERARY

One of my first-ever overnight hikes was on the Razorback and though I've done it numerous times since, it never gets old. From the first steps off the Great Alpine Road, the views are epic with nothing to interrupt the line of sight across waves of distant mountains mottled green and grey from hardy shrubs and snow grass. This time I'm tackling it with a small group of friends, with plans to camp at Federation Hut and soak up the serenity.

Embarking on the Razorback is like boarding a rollercoaster, albeit a mellow one. There's even a section early on flagged on the map as the 'Big Dipper'. The path drapes itself over the top of the ridgeline, as it breathes in and out, alternating between knife-edges and brief grassy plateaus, sidling around hillocks and cresting ridges, with endless 360-degree views.

It's early summer and we're in luck with fine weather – no small bonus considering how exposed the route is and how changeable alpine weather can be. On previous jaunts I've been sizzled by relentless sun one day, only to be lashed by freezing rain and 50kph winds the next. The occasional copse of twisted snow gums provide a few snatches of shelter – a favourite with red rosellas – but for the most part we're sitting (or standing) ducks for whatever the elements decide to throw at us.

In places, surrounding ranges are covered in snow gum skeletons (casualties of the 2003 bushfires) rising above a rolling green of new growth like greying whisker stubble. Mount Feathertop grows in size with every kilometre passed and it's a good-looking peak – chunky, imposing, and gouged by steep gullies that often hold snow long into summer. Midway to it, I start catching glimpses of the distant Federation Hut, in a grassy clearing at the top of the Bungalow Spur.

We pass dozens of hikers along the way but it's a big mountain range with plenty of space to spread out, so it never seems crowded. Added to that, many walkers deviate down various spurs that radiate from the Razorback towards other trails and camps.

After around 3hr of walking, a junction points left to Federation Hut and right towards Mount Feathertop. It's only a 5min walk to the cosy campsites tucked between the snow gums where we'll stay the night, and a water tank and toilet, so we drop our packs here before heading for Mount Feathertop. The 1.5km climb to the summit is a fairly steep haul but it's infinitely easier without packs – so much so that we do the summit once in the afternoon and again on sunset.

The views from the summit at 1922m befit its position as Victoria's second highest mountain and, unlike many mountains around these parts, Feathertop has a satisfyingly pointed ridgeline peak for that 'on top of the world' feeling. Sunset is a 360-degree lightshow, sending a golden glow and long shadows across the mountains. It's a hard view to leave but the next day we peel ourselves away to return back along the Razorback to Diamantina Hut on the Great Alpine Road. The footprint is the same but things look different when you turn 180-degrees and we savour the trail anew.

Views from the top of Mount Feathertop are captivating

BEST EATS

- **The General:** This pub/bar/general store is a Mount Hotham hub year-round for locals and visitors alike. Enjoy a great vibe and food and epic mountain views from the back deck, particularly at sunset when the lightshow is one of the best you'll see anywhere. 96 Great Alpine Road, Mount Hotham; (03) 5759 3523; thegeneral.com.au.
- **Harrietville Bakery:** Renowned for hearty homemade pies, vanilla slices and more, this Swiss bakery is super cosy with a rustic and electic décor. General Store, 219 Great Alpine Road, Harrietville; 0421 063 066.

BEST SLEEPS

- **Mountain Dreaming Apartments:** Tucked behind The General, these luxurious studio and 2-bedroom apartments are beautifully fitted out and have epic mountain views. Lot 1 Great Alpine Road, Mount Hotham; (03) 5759 3523; thegeneral.com.au.
- **Harrietville Snowline Hotel:** This motel-style establishment is family friendly and good value for money, with double and family rooms available. Having a legendary pub onsite serving hearty food is a bonus. 237 Great Alpine Road, Harrietville; (03) 5759 2524; snowlinehotel.com.au.
- **Tree tent glamping:** For a full alpine immersion, sleep in cosy tents suspended in the snowgums at this eco camp situated between Mount Hotham and Dinner Plain. A communal Nordic tipi is where meals are served, and those staying in the premium vista camp even get a private outdoor wood-heated bath. Alpine Nature Experience; 0466 280 603; alpinenatureexperience.com.au.

WHILE YOU'RE HERE

- **Ride a bike:** The Mountains to Murray Rail Trail stretches over 100km from Bright through Myrtleford and Beechworth to Wangaratta, combining scenic alpine countryside and the occasional winery or brewery. Mountain bikers can explore 24km of cruisy trails at Dinner Plain Mountain Bike Park or get serious at Mystic Mountain where there are 30+ graded trails (flow and downhill) and over 500m of vertical; ridehighcountry.com.au.
- **Bright Adventure Company:** Whether you want to kayak on the beautiful Ovens River, try your hand at rock climbing, abseiling or even underground river caving, BAC has plenty of ideas for all ability levels; (03) 5756 2486; brightadventurecompany.com.au.

Climb from the base of Mount Buffalo to the high plateau to witness epic views and striking granite formations.

The Big Walk, Mount Buffalo

This walk is on <u>Taungurung Country</u>.

WHY IT'S SPECIAL

Explorers Hume and Hovell named this granite mountain in 1824 for its resemblance to a lying buffalo, on account of the long plateau that caps it. Walking from its base to The Gorge on the edge of the plateau is a journey through changing habitats, from tall forest lined with bracken ferns to stunted snow gums littered with granite boulders and tors. The views increase in drama with altitude, from early outlooks over the surrounding valleys, to the jaw-dropping lookouts scattered around the rim of The Gorge, where sheer rock walls drop up to 300m. A wander around the manicured gardens of the grand old Mount Buffalo Chalet is a cool way to finish.

The alpine holiday town of Bright is a 15min drive from the trailhead so you can have a hearty pub or restaurant dinner after your walk and enjoy this picturesque adventure playground town. Alternatively, you can camp at Lake Catani on the Mount Buffalo plateau (*see* p. 109).

WALK IT

This is a one-way walk from Eurobin Creek picnic area at the park entrance to the Gorge Day Visitor Area on the plateau. While it's nice to finish with the spectacular views from the top, it means you'll be climbing steadily most of the time when walking in this direction.

If you're travelling with friends you can do a car shuffle, or alternatively park your car on the plateau and arrange for a taxi to drop you off at Eurobin Creek to begin the walk back up. If you're fit, it's perfectly doable to make this a full day return hike with no car shuffles required.

Most of the juicy stuff is in the top half of the track so if you prefer a 'Not Quite So Big Walk', start the climb from Mackeys Lookout instead (note that car parking is limited here).

→ Trail talk

- Distance: 11.3km
- Time: 4-5 hours one way
- Rating: Moderate-hard
- Technicality: A mix of well-defined trail, rough track and a little rock hopping.
- Puff factor: Have a good breakfast because it's uphill all the way with 1000m to climb!
- Watch out for: Rocks get slippery in wet conditions. It's alpine country and weather can change suddenly so pack a jacket and supplies.

ⓘ When to go

Spring to autumn is best. Snow blankets the mountain in winter, making parts of the trail potentially risky. Autumn colours in the region are worth the trip alone.

Ⓘ Resources

Download the Mount Buffalo National Park Visitor Guide from parks.vic.gov.au for maps and trail notes for all walks across the mountain.

Opposite Wilkinson Lookout overlooks the gorge and the Mount Buffalo Chalet, perched on top of the cliffs

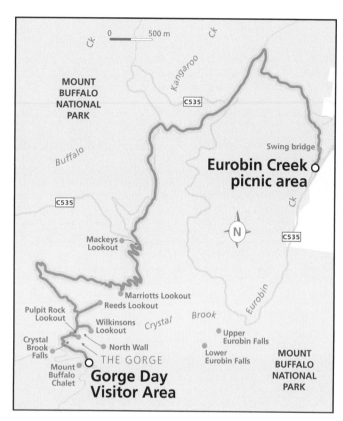

MOUNT BUFFALO NATIONAL PARK

0 — 500 m

Kangaroo Ck

Ck

C535

Buffalo

C535

Swing bridge

Eurobin Creek picnic area ○

Ck

N

C535

Mackeys Lookout ●

Marriotts Lookout ●
Reeds Lookout ●

Pulpit Rock Lookout

Wilkinsons Lookout

Crystal Brook

Crystal Brook Falls ●

● North Wall

● Upper Eurobin Falls

● Lower Eurobin Falls

MOUNT BUFFALO NATIONAL PARK

Mount Buffalo Chalet

THE GORGE
Gorge Day Visitor Area ○

◉ LOCAL SNAPSHOT

Mount Buffalo has been drawing tourists since the 1850s, a road was constructed to the plateau in 1908, and the Mount Buffalo Chalet opened in 1910. Dramatically positioned on the edge of the gorge, it's a grand timber building constructed in European chalet style. In its heyday it was considered the epitome of luxury, with large sitting rooms, cosy fireplaces, a ballroom, billiard room and accommodation for up to 200 guests. The 1920s saw Mount Buffalo bloom as the state's premier ski resort (Australia's first ski tow was here in 1937 on the Cresta Run), but tourists also flocked to ride horses, bushwalk and simply enjoy the spectacular setting. The Chalet closed in 2007 and is now only open for occasional guided tours, however it's still an impressive vision from the outside, and the surrounding manicured gardens are a reminder of a bygone time.

The glass-bottomed lookout at the Gorge day-visitor area

Top The North Wall *Opposite* Crystal Brook at the base of the gorge

ITINERARY

I'd be lying if I said the prospect of a 1000m climb isn't just a little bit daunting. When I set out from the Eurobin Creek picnic area, across the swing bridge over Eurobin Creek, I'm conscious that the only thing that'll give my lungs a reprieve over the next 4hr walk is perhaps admiring wildflowers (Hop Bitter Peas sprinkle orange and yellow through the forest in spring), studying trees and rocks (I do this anyway), or pausing for a view.

The trail is well graded in the lower half, roughly following an old horse route cut in the 1890s. Somewhere in the forest of peppermints and grey mountain gums, I hear a lyrebird running through his playlist, while cockatoos screech in the treetops. The track crosses Mount Buffalo Road a few times as it weaves and winds to the plateau, and I feel a kindred spirit with a few cyclists breathlessly inching their way uphill.

It takes almost 2hr to reach Mackeys Lookout, where the trail takes long zig-zags back and forth across a vast smooth flank of granite with expansive views over the surrounding valleys. Marriotts Lookout is next and it's here you get your first glimpse of just how impressive the sheer granite walls of this mountain can be. You can also visualise Buffalo's origin, as bubbling molten rock, once well below the surface (hundreds of millions of years ago), only later emerged when surrounding softer rock wore away.

The geological reminders continue in dry forest where the track is dotted with huge square boulders, like oversized wombat poo smeared in moss. As the trail shifts into snow gum territory the granite grows into huge tors, some seeming to balance precariously on their ends.

In blissful relief, the trail starts to flatten as the plateau draws near and the singletrack is lined with tufty grass and shrubs. A short detour to Reeds Lookout offers another huge sloping slab of granite with valley views. Wilkinsons Lookout is where the views get truly staggering, showcasing the gorge and the river that created it. Opposite, a 200m wall of rock is topped by the Mount Buffalo Chalet, looking tiny in comparison in its cliff-top nest of greenery. It's hard to fathom the size of this gorge. The North Wall plunges 300m – an objective that takes rock climbers up to three days to ascend – and at its base, Crystal Brook looks like a thin drizzle of milk, flanked by tiny trees and the odd tree fern.

In a string of 'wow' moments, the trail moves around the lip of the gorge from lookout to lookout. Pulpit Rock is as it sounds, raised and commanding as it leans out over the void. I cross

Crystal Brook where it spills over the precipice and it seems modest for all the impact it has had, eroding joint lines in the granite over millions of years to carve this place.

The grand finale is a suspended platform reaching out beyond the gorge rim, and through a glass square in its base I can peer beyond my shoes to the trees and rocks hundreds of metres below. It's tough deciding where to plonk myself for lunch: on the sweeping granite next to the paragliders' launch pad, in the flower gardens of the Chalet, or to stay put with eyes glued on the gorge. The gorge wins.

I had wondered about the possibility of chatting up one of the many picnickers for a lift back down the mountain to my car at Eurobin Creek picnic area but in the end I decide to walk it, an almost entirely downhill journey that's easy on the lungs and allows me opportunity to savour the scenery.

BEST EATS

- **Bright Brewery:** With huge capacity indoors and outdoors by the Ovens River, this place has a social vibe, great food and live music on Sun. 121 Great Alpine Rd, Bright; (03) 5755 1301; brightbrewery.com.au.
- **Ginger Baker Cafe:** This cafe has a mouthwatering menu (think ricotta hotcakes through to pork and fennel meatballs) and a riverside setting beneath the trees, and is a locals' favourite. 127 Gavan St, Bright; (03) 5755 2300; gingerbakercafe.com.au.

———

BEST SLEEPS

- **Lake Catani Campground:** There's space for tents, camper trailers and small caravans at this national park-managed camp on the Mount Buffalo plateau, right next to Lake Catani and walking trails. Lakeside Road, Mount Buffalo; 13 1963; parks.vic.gov.au/stay.
- **Bright Colonial Motel:** You'll find excellent accommodation at this recently renovated motel, along with a relaxing pool pavilion featuring a barbecue, pizza oven and communal tables. Cyclists are welcomed with a secure bike lock up, dedicated wash bay and maintenance bench. 56 Gavan St, Bright; (03) 5755 1633; brightcolonialmotel.com.au.

———

WHILE YOU'RE HERE

- **Keep walking:** There are nearly two dozen spectacular hiking trails across Mount Buffalo, and plenty are short enough that you can knock off a handful in a day. The 45min Horn Track leads to a striking lookout from Mount Buffalo's highest point at 1723m, with views across the plateau to the impressive Back Wall and surrounding valleys. For fantastic views of the Cathedral, Cresta Valley and the Horn, walk the 1hr Hump Track. Amble 1.5hr around Lake Catani, tackle a challenging 1hr scramble through the rock squeezes at Chalwell Galleries, or see water washing over vast smooth flanks of granite at Eurobin Falls on a moderate 45min hike.
- **Bright Adventure Company:** Epic views are guaranteed when you abseil down to a private ledge suspended 300m above the valley at Mount Buffalo Gorge to tuck into a hamper made for 2-4 people. Go for sunrise, lunch or dinner; (03) 5756 2486; brightadventurecompany.com.au.

Descend into Mitchell River Gorge for lush rainforest, waterfalls, sacred Gunaikurnai sites and dramatic views of a wild river.

Den of Nargun & Mitchell River Track

This walk is on Gunaikurnai Country.

WHY IT'S SPECIAL

The Mitchell River flows 260km from the Victorian Alps out into the sprawling coastal Gippsland Lakes. It's Victoria's largest remaining wild river, having managed to escape the taming of dams, and has cut an impressive gorge through ancient sandstone and mudstone, revealing blocky rock walls over 100m high.

It's some 300km east of Melbourne in Gippsland, and the fact that it's not a heavily trafficked trail only enhances the wild vibe. There's loads of variety on this walk, from lush mossy rainforest and waterfalls on the Den of Nargun loop, to the bubbling rapids and spectacular gorge views that accompany the undulating river route along with its truly gobsmacking ridge-top lookout at The Amphitheatre. Perhaps most special though is the sense of spirit you feel at Den of Nargun and Deadcock Den, two hugely sacred caves home to Gunaikurnai spirit creatures (*see* p. 112).

WALK IT

The Den of Nargun is a loop walk on to which you can add an out-and-back walk following a section of the Mitchell River Walk as far as Billy Goat Bend (BGB) and the spectacular Amphitheatre lookout. If you're pushed for time, just do the Den of Nargun loop, a stunning and moderate-graded hike, whose atmospheric forest is reminiscent of Wonderland. Rock-hopping on it could be super fun for active older kids. Branching out along the river trail will let you dip your toes in this wild river region and give stunning views over the gorge. Wander out and back for as long as you fancy or push on all the way to Billy Goat Bend (BGB). There's a carpark at BGB so you can do a car shuffle if you only want to walk the river one way.

If you don't want to miss a thing, consider tackling the full Mitchell River Walk, which continues past BGB all the way to Angusvale. The 18km distance (one way) is often tackled over two days with camping at BGB.

An unsealed but well-graded road leads to the trail's start at Den of Nargun carpark where there are picnic shelters and a gas barbecue. The road to BGB is a bit rougher.

 Trail talk
- Distance: 3.4km for Den loop + 7km one-way for Mitchell River track.
- Time: 1.5hr for Den loop + 3.5hr one-way for Mitchell River track.
- Rating: Moderate-hard
- Technicality: Lots of rock hopping on the Den of Nargun loop. Continue on the river track and you'll face a potentially muddy, narrow and off-camber path, at times sprinkled with rocks.
- Puff factor: The Den just has one big flight of steps to contend with, while the river section is a fairly steady puff-fest with lots of undulations and occasional sections of challenging terrain.
- Watch out for: Rocks and mud are slippery. This is a good walk to take your hiking poles on for added stability.

 When to go
It's doable year-round but avoid super-wet conditions when the mud factor will be dialled to eleven (unless you like mud).

 Resources
Download the Mitchell River National Park Visitor Guide from parks.vic.gov.au.

Opposite The Den of Nargun

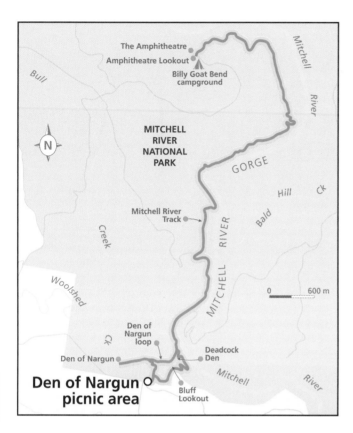

MITCHELL RIVER NATIONAL PARK

GORGE

Bull

Mitchell

River

The Amphitheatre
Amphitheatre Lookout
Billy Goat Bend campground

Hill Ck

Bald

MITCHELL RIVER

Mitchell River Track

Creek

Woolshed

Ck

0   600 m

Den of Nargun loop

Den of Nargun

Deadcock Den

Den of Nargun picnic area

Bluff Lookout

Mitchell

River

LOCAL SNAPSHOT

According to the Gunaikurnai People, the Nargun is a fierce being not to be trifled with. Half human, half stone, it lives in its cave, taking any children who dare visit the rockpool before it. Spears don't work against the Nargun - they'd only be reflected back at the thrower. Den of Nargun is a site of great significance to Gunaikurnai women.

This story is one of many in a region rich with First Nations culture (one of the reasons the Mitchell River is heritage-listed). The mighty waterway once divided two clans, and stories of conflict, ceremonies and spirits are many. Visitors are asked to treat the area with respect and leave it as they found it.

Bottom Moss and fungi *Opposite* The rock overhang at Deadcock Den

ITINERARY

From the carpark, set in dry stringybark forest, you wouldn't imagine there was a moss-filled rainforest hiding just moments away. I start the steep zig-zag descent through the forest from the Den of Nargun picnic area, catching glimpses of grey and orange rock-walls, appearing as though made with building blocks. Moss starts to coat trackside tree branches and by the time I reach the gorge floor 15min later, I'm deep in a furry green Wonderland. Rocks, sheared off the gorge walls, lie in jumbles about my feet. Kanookas, lilly pillies, blue oliveberrys and muttonwood compete with thick and twisting liane vines. Ferns cluster and tiny parasols of blue fungi sprout from fallen logs.

It's a short side trip to the sacred Den of Nargun (*see* p. 112). The dark cave hides under a long rock-shelf, over which water cascades into a milky teal pool, and though its entrance was once fringed in stalactites, sadly visitors have broken most of them off. Please show appropriate respect to the Gunaikurnai People and do not enter the cave.

A stunning rocky route follows Woolshed Creek through the rainforest to another small pool and waterfall, beyond which you press pause on the Den loop and branch out on the Mitchell River Track as it heads upstream through the gorge.

The track is a gentle rollercoaster, dipping close to the river at times and then climbing high as it squeezes past moss-covered boulders and through gullies of lilly pillies heavy with lilac berries. I hear a lyrebird going through its repertoire of calls and spot king parrots diving across the pocked gorge walls. At times the river roars – its grade III and IV rapids are popular with kayakers – while other times it glides silently between forested banks.

By the time I reach Billy Goat Bend and The Amphitheatre, I'm high and dry, and slack-jawed at the epic view. Perched on the gorge's rim, a balcony looks out over a mighty horseshoe bend – The Amphitheatre. Giant boulders, sheared off the cliff, litter the base and a small green island in the river's midst has collected a tangle of logs that look like matchsticks. As far as the eye can see, thickly forested folds cradle the river. It's a stunning view to accompany lunch.

From here, the Mitchell River track continues all the way to Angusvale but I turn to retrace my steps along the river and rejoin the Den of Nargun loop track. I soon pass beautiful Deadcock Den, another hugely sacred cultural site with a small waterfall, cubed rouge red and ochre block walls smeared with lime moss, and an enormous overhang rock shelter. You can just imagine Gunaikurnai People sitting here over thousands of years – one part of a broad rock platform even has what looks like eight small grinding holes worn into it.

It's a mostly sealed track that climbs back out of the gorge via Bluff Lookout to the Den of Nargun carpark.

BEST EATS

- **Bark Hut:** Set in bushland, this tearoom and kiosk is your quickest option for pies, scones and ice-creams. It's only a few minutes' drive from the Den of Nargun carpark, or you can walk there off the Den trail. Echo Bend Camping Park 345 Dunbars Rd, Iguana Creek; (03) 5157 6317.
- **The Criterion Hotel:** There's seriously good food to be had in this stylish dark-timbered pub in Sale, plus accommodation too (*see* below). 90 MacAlister St, Sale; (03) 5143 3320; criterionhotelsale.com.au.

BEST SLEEPS

- **Echo Bend Camping Park:** Put up a tent or stay in onsite vans spread out across this pretty bush camp with ponds. There's a walking trail leading directly from camp onto the Den of Nargun loop. 345 Dunbars Rd, Iguana Creek; (03) 5157 6317; petfriendly.com.au.
- **The Criterion Hotel:** It's got all the exterior character you'd expect from a pub established in 1865, but with modern and stylish rooms. It's located in Sale, a 50min drive from the trailhead and the first major town en route to Melbourne. 90 MacAlister St, Sale; (03) 5143 3320; criterionhotelsale.com.au.

WHILE YOU'RE HERE

- **Raymond Island:** Catch the ferry over from Paynesville and walk the 20min Koala Trail for one of the best koala spotting opportunities around.
- **Mitchell River silt jetties:** Formed from the accumulation of river silt, these 8km long silt banks are the second longest in the world. A gravel road slides right up the centre. It's a good spot for fishing and birdwatching too.
- **East Gippsland Rail Trail:** Cycle part or all of this 96km trail running through scenic countryside between Bairnsdale and Orbost; eastgippslandrailtrail.com.au.

Lookout over Billy Goat Bend from the trail

South Australia

From the red earth of the outback to island trails nuzzled by aqua bays, SA is full of surprises.

Discover a rocky gorge, waterfalls and koalas on the fringe of Adelaide.

Third Falls Hike

This walk is on <u>Kaurna Country</u>.

WHY IT'S SPECIAL

It's hard to fathom that such an awesome bushwalk is only 10km from Adelaide/Tarndanya's CBD. Stand before First Falls as it spills 30m over sheer walls of orange quartzite and you could pretend you're in the outback. This trail passes through woodland and heath as it skirts around the inside of Morialta Gorge passing (you guessed it) three waterfalls along Fourth Creek. There are spectacular views across the escarpment and to the distant metropolis of Adelaide, plus the area is a hotspot for koalas. If you fancy a cooling swim, add on a side trip to the enticing pool at the base of First Falls.

WALK IT

There's a whole network of trails at Morialta Conservation Park, catering to all ages and ability levels, so if the Third Falls Hike is a little too long or energetic for your needs, consider one of the shorter options. A scenic amble to the base of First Falls is an easy 1hr return. If you're happy with some climbing, you'll get two waterfalls, plus panoramic views across the gorge and Adelaide, on the 2.5hr Second Falls Hike. With so many trails on offer, and to avoid any confusion, it's a good idea to carry a map with you for this one to complement the plethora of colour-coded directional markers en route.

→ Trail talk
- Distance: 7.3km loop
- Time: 3.5hr
- Rating: Easy-moderate
- Technicality: Generally well-graded track, a little rocky at times.
- Puff factor: A fairly steady climb to the upper regions of the gorge and then the undulations are gentle.
- Watch out for: Take care not to stray off the trail as there's often a steep drop to one side.

ⓘ When to go
Go after a decent rainfall for some pumping falls. Winter and spring amp up the green, plus you'll get wildflowers too. Midweek is less busy.

ⓘ Resources
Download the Morialta Conservation Park walking trails map from parks.sa.gov.au.

Opposite Fourth Creek *Previous* Tanderra Saddle

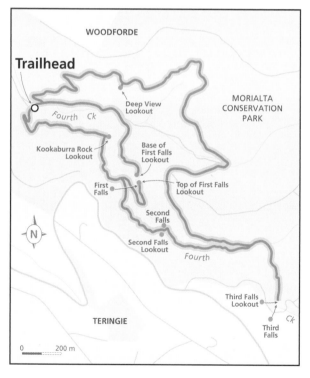

WOODFORDE

Trailhead

Fourth Ck

Deep View
Lookout

MORIALTA
CONSERVATION
PARK

Kookaburra Rock
Lookout

Base of
First Falls
Lookout

First
Falls

Top of First Falls
Lookout

Second
Falls

Second Falls
Lookout

Fourth

Third Falls
Lookout

Ck

Third
Falls

N

TERINGIE

0   200 m

LOCAL SNAPSHOT

The Kaurna People are the Traditional Owners of this area. Around 650 Kaurna People inhabited a 7200sqkm patch of country, incorporating what are now known as Morialta and Black Hill Conservation Parks. They lived off the land, hunting possums, bandicoots, kangaroos, fish and lizards - amongst other things. In summer they moved towards the sea, and in winter headed inland in search of better shelter and firewood. When Europeans settled in the 1840-50s the Kaurna peoples were so devastated by disease and dispersal that within 50 years they no longer lived the traditional lives here that they had for thousands of years previous.

Top Bushland right on the fringe of Adelaide *Opposite* The pool at the base of First Falls is great for a swim

ITINERARY

It's a big surprise when an Adelaide friend introduces me to Morialta Gorge. That such a dramatic chunk of bush could exist within 'cooee' of suburbia seems surreal, but at one point it was part of a private estate belonging to a Mr J.S. Reid. In 1913 he handed it to the government under the condition that it be preserved as a place of public recreation and it remains today a conservation park.

There are many ways to explore Morialta and though the Third Falls Hike officially peels off about 100m from the trailhead, we are lured by the park's glittering prize, First Falls, and fast track our way to its base via a wide path alongside Fourth Creek. The creek is rock and boulder-strewn and overhung with gum trees; this is the best place for koala spotting, though they remain elusive on my visit.

First Falls is an impressive sight. Water free falls from a 30m step in the gorge, past a wall of orange quartzite textured like ill-fitting building blocks, and a few swimmers revel in the sizeable pool at its base.

The Third Falls Hike itself traverses up the inside of the gorge, climbing gradually through woodland with increasing views across the treed valley falling away steeply to one side. Appropriately-named, Deep View Lookout puts us on the escarpment edge with views down the valley and west towards Adelaide. From this height, it's easy to appreciate the gorge's size and the bands of rock protruding on the opposite side.

Once initial height is gained, the gradient eases off and the dirt track is studded with rocks and lined with a smattering of grass trees. Things get increasingly bushy near the top of the gorge and Third Falls, which is way smaller than its lower sibling but still a pretty cascade over sloping rock.

Steps are retraced to a turn-off descending to Second Falls. Here, a bridge passes over Fourth Creek, which looks all modest and mild-mannered on one side, but disappears down a rock face on the other. Sidling around the southern side of the gorge offers a whole different vantage point over it.

It's a short side trip to look down over the top of First Falls, from where you can really appreciate the sheer drop to the round pool at its base, and get a closer look at its orange walls sprouting random tufts of green. Kookaburra Rock Lookout is the last chance for a look at the northern side's gentle folds and vertical seams of rock before the final descent to complete the loop.

Top Fourth Creek *Opposite* Tawny dragons are common

South Australia

122

BEST EATS

- **The Rolling Pin Bakery & Patisserie:** The French influence is evident in the selection of tarts, cakes, pastries and quiches offered at this bakery. You can also get a great pie, sausage roll or that all-important coffee. 92 St Bernards Rd, Magill; (08) 8331 7435.
- **Penfolds Magill Estate Cellar Door:** One of Australia's most famous winemakers has a casual diner and fine dining restaurant just 10min from the trail, and their views of the vineyard and beyond to Adelaide city are lovely. Try a tasting at the cellar door while you're there. 78 Penfold Road, Magill; (08) 8301 5569; penfolds.com.

BEST SLEEPS

- **The Osmond Motel & Apartments:** There is no shortage of options for places to stay in Adelaide city itself but if you want to base yourself just outside of the CBD, and on the right side for Morialta Gorge, then these newly opened rooms and apartments offer a stylish solution. 232 Glen Osmond Rd, Fullarton; (08) 8267 1556; adelaidedresscircle.com.au/fullarton.

WHILE YOU'RE HERE

- **Mukanthi Nature Play Space:** Kids of all ages will love this area, located at the Stradbroke Road picnic area end of Morialta. Five play areas include cool features built with natural materials and with designs inspired by nature, such as climbing boulders, huge 'bird's nests' and a giant snake tunnel.
- **Rock climbing:** The area between First and Third Falls, off Norton Summit Road, is one of Adelaide's most popular climbing areas, combining impressive scenery with quality routes. Earth Adventure operate guided climbs to suit all ability levels. 2 Pirie Street, Adelaide; (08) 8165 2024; earthadventure.securedirectbookings.com.

Breathe in fresh air blown up from Antarctica, while surrounded by wildlife on Australia's third largest island.

Kangaroo Island Wilderness Trail

CONTRIBUTION BY ALEXIS BUXTON-COLLINS

This walk is on Kaurna Miyurna, Ngarrindjeri, Ramindjeri and Barngarla Country.

WHY IT'S SPECIAL

When this trail opened in 2016, it was a revelation. Though South Australia already boasted one of the country's premier long-distance walks in the 1200km Heysen Trail, it was in need of a more attainable multi-day hike and the Kangaroo Island Wilderness Trail (KIWT) delivered. Situated at Kangaroo Island's rugged western end, it's an eminently approachable walk that rewards hikers by immersing them in the wild beauty of this iconic destination.

Over five days, the largely flat path follows tannin-stained creeks and sheer limestone cliffs, traversing open grassland and dense forest, with plenty of time to view Kangaroo Island's famous geological marvels, look out for koalas and echidnas and swim at secluded beaches.

In the summer of 2019–20, bushfires ripped through the island and burned 96 per cent of Flinders Chase National Park, destroying all trail infrastructure and altering the landscape irrevocably. Since then, regrowth has been remarkably swift and in some places it's so thick that visibility off the trail is just a few metres. Accessible as a series of day walks until autumn 2023 (when the campsites will reopen), the KIWT currently presents a unique snapshot of the Australian bush in recovery.

WALK IT

Much of the infrastructure for the trail and campsites was purpose-built when it opened in 2016 and this is built into the price tag that includes park entry fees, as well as an excellent booklet with details about the walk. For a small additional fee, hikers can add a transfer from the hike's endpoint back to the trailhead at Flinders Chase National Park Visitor Centre.

 Trail talk
- Distance: 64km
- Time: 5 days
- Rating: Easy-Moderate
- Technicality: Dirt and limestone tracks with some beach walking - take care with footing on the rocky sections.
- Puff factor: Elevation changes are few and far between, with only the beach walk presenting any real challenge.
- Watch out for: Days 2 and 3 are very exposed to any rough weather so check the forecast before leaving. Be careful around cliff-edges and on uneven surfaces, and watch out for snakes in the warmer months when the walk may be closed due to fire danger.

 When to go
Spring and autumn allow you to avoid the heat of summer and brutal storms of winter, which is especially important on Days 2 and 3. Spring has the added benefit of bringing a profusion of colourful wildflowers.

 Resources
Visit parks.sa.gov.au/experiences/kiwt for more information and bookings. A comprehensive guidebook, including maps, trail notes and plenty of information on the island's natural and human history is given to walkers on arrival.

Opposite Remarkable Rocks

The walk follows a broad semi-circle and is tackled in a counter-clockwise direction. With only 24 camping permits issued per day you may only encounter other walkers at the start and end of each day and the itinerary allows for plenty of time to take in the scenery. Despite the feeling of isolation, every campsite can be reached by road if necessary and the track intersects with two of Kangaroo Island's most popular sights; you can expect to find plenty of tourists at Admiral's Arch and Remarkable Rocks.

The walk itself is flat and well-marked; the most challenging section is probably the 2km section of soft white sand at Maupertuis Bay, but the chance to place the first set of footprints in a wild and remote beach more than makes up for it. In the cooler months, there's a chance you'll see southern right whales cavorting offshore (Rangers advise hikers not to join them as there can be strong rips and currents, but there are other chances to swim throughout the hike).

Note that with a population of just under 2000, Kingscote is the island's largest town.

 LOCAL SNAPSHOT

Many first-time visitors are surprised by Kangaroo Island's size - it's 145km long from end to end - and almost one-third of the island is given over to national and conservation parks. The majority of those protected areas are clustered at the island's western end, which is ripe for exploration.

Just 13km from the mainland at its closest point, Kangaroo Island, known as Karta Pintingga by its Traditional Owners, only became an island some 10,000 years ago, at which point it was home to a thriving First Nations community. Some First Nations in southern Australia still call it the 'Island of the dead'. A Creation story tells of an ancestor, Ngurunderi, who crossed to the island and then ascended to become the Milky Way, allowing the spirits of the dead to follow his tracks to the afterlife.

When Europeans arrived in the early 19th century, they found the island uninhabited. French explorer Nicolas Baudin was the first to circumnavigate it, and his legacy lives on in the many French place names that locals pronounce with a distinct Aussie twang. Matthew Flinders gave the island its current name when he landed there in 1802.

Whalers and sealers soon descended on the island, decimating local populations, while the farmers that came in their wake cleared much of the island's eastern half. The whalers and sealers kidnapped many Aboriginal women and took them to Kangaroo Island as slaves.

The island was colonised by the British in 1836. The government declared Flinders Chase a protected area in 1919, and the ensuing decades saw it turned into a 'Noah's ark' with the introduction of koalas, ringtail possums and platypus. Those species are still thriving today, along with plenty of other mammals that exist in such numbers it's best to avoid driving after sundown. First Nations communities are also working to share their long history on the island.

Top Goannas are plentiful *Opposite* Remarkable Rocks

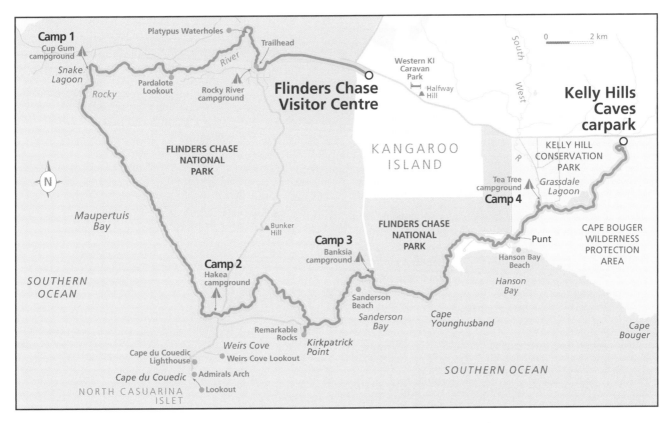

ITINERARY

DAY 1

Flinders Chase Visitor Centre to Cup Gum campground, 15.5km, 4.5hr

From the newly rebuilt Flinders Chase Visitor Centre, the walk begins with a gentle 5km stretch of new trail, through regenerating cup gum forest to the park's old HQ, where you'll find picnic areas, toilets and a campground. Regardless of whether you arrive on the island via plane or ferry, it's a long drive to the trailhead, but if you're determined to get straight into it, starting here can shave some time off the first day.

A series of day walks emanates from the campground and I see a few other visitors as I cross clearings full of morning flag tussocks being used as nests by Cape Barren geese. Sadly, not all of the local fauna is quite as easy to spot; after sitting at the nearby Platypus Waterholes for half an hour in the hope I might catch a glimpse of the eponymous residents, I continue along a path scarred by diggings that cheer me up with the suggestion of a healthy echidna population.

Entering a stretch of dense eucalypt forest, I'm soon hemmed in by thick vegetation on either side and the winding trail is rarely visible for more than a few metres ahead. Attention-seeking bottlebrush with lurid pink bristles, fragrant bush tobacco and yacca with extravagant headdresses of spiked fronds all fight for space beneath trees, whose fire-blackened trunks are completely hidden by thick blankets of new leaves.

Ascending a small hill to Pardalote Lookout reveals a view of the trail stretching out ahead alongside the tannin-stained waters of Rocky River, where brightly covered dragonflies hover above the surface and orange throated tawny dragons wait patiently for them to stray within striking distance. From there it's a pleasant walk to the ominously named Snake Lagoon beside Cup Gum campground, but fortunately the only creatures I encounter are the mobs of roos and wallabies gathering at the edges of a large clearing to enjoy their dinner as I prepare my own.

DAY 2

Cup Gum campground to Hakea campground, 14km, 5–6hr

Day 2 begins by continuing along the Rocky River, which cuts into the limestone to create a small but scenic gorge, before reaching a small cove, where it empties into the Southern Ocean and tints the frothing waves the colour of chai.

From here, the trail follows the coast south along a series of limestone cliffs buffeted by roaring winds. The next landfall looking west is Argentina, and it feels like I'm walking along the edge of the world but I'm far from alone – seabirds wheel overhead and I soon spot a pod of dolphins tracking my progress along the coast. In winter, whales also frequent these treacherous waters, which have claimed several ships over the years.

For most of the day the walk is rocky underfoot, but when it descends onto the sugar-white sands of Maupertuis Bay the going gets significantly harder. Finding a compacted section of sand is impossible and I sink into the beach with every step, so that it takes the better part of an hour to walk several kilometres. Tiny hooded plovers tease me by skittering over the sand in a blur of spindly red legs. Their nesting places among the dunes mean that at high tide the walk makes a detour inland, but the two paths rejoin at the other end of the bay where the cliff-top views recommence.

Shortly before reaching Hakea Campsite, the trail veers inland where there's more shelter from the wind, but I can still hear the waves (and traffic from a nearby road) when I drop my pack. That traffic is heading to Admiral's Arch at the island's south-west tip, where a side trip reveals fur seals and sea lions cavorting in the water below a large natural arch. Waiting until late afternoon means I avoid most of the tourists on the walk past Cape du Couedic lighthouse (1906–09), which is visible for much of the day's walk and is surrounded by a rare section of unburned vegetation that provides a refuge for a vocal community of small birds – and makes a great spot to watch the sunset.

DAY 3

Hakea campground to Banksia campground, 13km, 5hr

If you don't make it to Admiral's Arch on Day 2, there's an option to walk there in the morning before heading east through a windswept stretch of rocky ground that only supported knee-high growth even before the 2019–20 fires. The almost lunar landscape makes it one of the best areas to spot gorgeously decorated Rosenberg's goannas which, like many scavengers, thrived after the fires. It also means sweeping views of the trail ahead, including Remarkable Rocks.

Perched atop a large granite outcrop is a jumble of giant boulders that have been battered by the elements to create fanciful crenellations and overhangs so that from some angles they appear to be melting. A dusting of bright orange lichen makes them even more photogenic, and when the sun comes out the colours pop against the deep blue sea behind. It's a popular site, and from a distance I can see tourists crawling among the rocks like ants; when I arrive I drop my pack so I too can spend an hour wandering around the formations.

As I continue past them, the trail hugs a wild section of coast where azure bays are ringed by precipitous cliffs, but I can't help turning around frequently to see the rocks receding in the distance, looking slightly different from each new vantage point. The uneven ground and sometimes sharp limestone means it's important to pay attention to where I put my feet, but thoughtfully spaced out benches provide an excuse to stop regularly and take in the views.

At the end of the day, the trail once again tracks a short distant inland to the enchanting Banksia Campsite tucked into the bush. Even better, an easy 700m side trip leads to Sanderson Bay, a secluded cove where I see roo prints coming down to the high tide line as I cool my heels in the water.

DAY 4
Banksia campground to Tea Tree campground, 13.5km, 5hr

Despite having no headline attractions, this is one of the most pleasant days of the walk, with plenty of time to pay attention to the landscape I'm passing through. For hours I follow towering cliffs covered in low coastal heath, setting a modest pace with the sharp wind to cool me.

Headlands that jut defiantly southward bear the full brunt of the Southern Ocean's fury, as breakers crash into their bases with a roar and throw spray high into the air. With a thick cover of cloud overhead, the atmosphere is brooding and vaguely threatening, but whenever the sun flashes through the showers of foam are struck through with rainbows, and the sandy-bottomed coves are transformed into an alluring peacock blue.

When the track wanders inland through tall dunes carpeted in thick mallee and tea tree forest, the ceaseless roar of the ocean is replaced by birdsong and the extra cover hides plenty of roos that bound off at my approach. At the South West River, a punt that allows me to pull myself across on a rope provides a memorable interlude and on the far bank of the river a short side trail leads to Hanson Bay. This idyllic beach is justifiably popular with locals (including a pod of dolphins and several sea lions that frolic in the water as I watch) and is the perfect spot for a quick dip, before continuing on to Tea Tree Campsite located next to a historic cottage. As the golden hour illuminates the large gums that surround a massive cleared area, hundreds of roos hop out to graze and a dedicated fireplace with supplied wood is a great way to ensure a memorable final night on the trail (outside of fire ban season).

Cape du Couedic Lighthouse

DAY 5
Tea Tree campground to Kelly Hill Caves, 7.5km, 2hr

More a triumphal procession than a full day of walking, the final section passes through sugar gum forest that supports so many koalas I soon lose count of the furry grey balls wedged into the branches above me. The dappled light filtering onto the trail also creates excellent growing conditions for wildflowers, like the delicate lilac sun orchid, and goannas take advantage of the open ground to sun themselves on the path, barely rousing themselves to scurry off before I'm upon them.

Even after five days of walking there are new ecosystems to explore, most notably the broad freshwater lakes filled with waterbirds that appear regularly. Sinkholes beside the trail hint at the vast system of underground caverns beneath the karst landscape, and after a few small climbs on the final stretch I emerge at the Kelly Hills Caves carpark.

South Australia

BEST EATS

- **Vivonne Bay General Store:** There are precious few places to get food or fuel on the island's western half, but this cute roadside stop is justifiably famous for its local whiting burger (actually more of a roll). 4417 S Coast Rd, Vivonne Bay; (08) 8559 4285.
- **Cactus:** The best spot in Kingscote for a big brekkie or lunch is this easy-going cafe serving fresh fusion dishes and pastries baked daily. 54 Dauncey St, Kingscote; 0473 311 049.

———

BEST SLEEPS

- **Western KI Caravan Park:** The closest accommodation to the trail is just minutes from Flinders Chase National Park's entrance on a property with plenty of resident koalas and roos. The friendly owners run shuttles for day walkers who want to see the trail without camping, and a small general store in case you've forgotten anything (the closest supermarket is 60km away in Parndana). 7928 S Coast Rd, Karatta SA 5223; (08) 8559 7201; westernki.com.au.
- **Ecopia Retreat:** If you want to spoil yourself after the trail but you're not ready to head back to civilisation yet, these two off-grid cabins hidden in the centre of the island let you enjoy a warm shower and comfortable bed with only the wildlife for company. A firebreak through the centre of the property also lets you see before and after versions of the vegetation. 563b Gregors Rd, Seddon; 0414 751 733; ecopiaretreat.com.au.

WHILE YOU'RE HERE

- **Seal Bay Conservation Park:** Head some 60km from Flinders Chase back along the southern coast and you'll reach this small bay, which was inaccessible to 19th-century sealers and thus still protects about 800 endangered Australian sea lions. Join a tour and you can walk onto the beach with these gorgeous beasts. Seal Bay Rd, Seal Bay; (08) 8553 4463; parks.sa.gov.au/experiences/seal-bay.
- **Kangaroo Island Spirits**: A remote island might seem like an unusual spot for the nation's first craft gin distillery, but this is ground zero for the local industry. You can stroll round the fragrant botanic garden, taste some of the award-wining concoctions or even blend your own gin. 856 Playford Hwy, Cygnet River; (08) 8553 9211; kispirits.com.au.
- **Visit a hidden beach:** The 'where is the beach???' sign at Stokes Bay is the first hint there's something unusual going on. Follow the markers along a hidden path through the jumble of boulders lining a nearby hillside and you'll emerge at a gorgeous bay on the island's protected north coast, where a built rockpool ensures you can have a peaceful float on even the roughest days.

Opposite Cliff-top trails provide epic ocean views

Follow the route of Alligator Creek as it squeezes between ochre rock walls in the Southern Flinders Ranges.

Alligator Gorge Ring Route

This walk is on <u>Nukunu Country</u>.

WHY IT'S SPECIAL

The universe gave the Alligator Creek a few million years, and the Alligator Creek gave us a gorge. These days the creek is often a modest trickle, but the rough route of loose rocks trailing between orange quartzite walls makes for an exciting walk. At The Narrows, the gorge's cool passageways are only a few metres wide, while the cascading rock platforms of The Terraces occasionally reveal the ripples of an ancient sea. It changes with conditions: rock glows red when the sun hits it, festooning foliage ripens into brilliant green after rain, and in spring, wildflowers carpet the place in colour.

WALK IT

If you're not in the mood for a 4hr adventure, the Gorge Circuit Hike takes half that time and incorporates the spectacular Narrows. Add a little side trip and you can tick off The Terraces too. Conversely, if you want the full Mount Remarkable National Park experience, you can make a two-day/34km hike by walking from Mambray Creek right through to Alligator Gorge and back, taking in the spectacular Hidden Gorge.

The 12km drive off the main highway to the Alligator Gorge carpark is steep and winding in places (not ideal for caravans or trailers) but once you arrive there's a decent-sized parking area and good toilet facilities. For amazing views over the top of the gorge, don't miss the 5min ambles from the carpark to Ali Lookout and Gorge Lookout.

→ Trail talk
- Distance: 9km loop
- Time: 4hr
- Rating: Moderate-hard
- Technicality: Lots of rock hopping on uneven and loose rocks along the gorge floor.
- Puff factor: There's a steep flight of steps in and out of the gorge but otherwise the undulations are gentle.
- Watch out for: After heavy rain, you might have to dodge around the creek. Take care on the rocks - they're extra slippery when wet.

When to go
Spring is ideal for abundant wildflowers, mild temperatures and water in the gorge.

Resources
Download the Mount Remarkable National Park - Alligator Gorge map and buy national park passes from parks.sa.gov.au.

Opposite Wandering through The Narrows

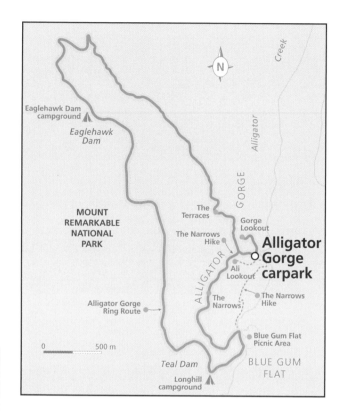

LOCAL SNAPSHOT

There are no alligators in Alligator Gorge but legend has it the gorge was named after a shepherd called Ally who once lived in the area. It's part of Mount Remarkable National Park, overlooked by Mount Remarkable - or 'Wangyarra', according to the Nukunu People. Alligator Creek is one of three significant watercourses in the park, along with Mambray and Spring Creek, and they're magnets for wildlife. The area is home to lace monitors, echidnas, emus, western grey kangaroos, euros, scorpions, wedge-tailed eagles and even the endangered yellow-footed rock wallaby, for whom the park's rocky outcrops make the ideal home.

Right The Narrows lives up to its name *Opposite* Alligator Gorge's orange walls change with the light

ITINERARY

It's easy to be oblivious to the spectacular secrets hidden in a gorge until you go down and have a good poke around. From Alligator Gorge carpark, I descend the few hundred steps and my world transforms. Soon I'm on the bottom of a dry creek bed squeezed by magnificent walls of orange rock, layered and blocky. The ground is littered with rock and a smattering of white-trunked river red gums, and the giggles of a passing flock of corellas floats on the breeze.

I'm immediately drawn towards The Narrows, setting me off on a clockwise loop, and within 15min the walls are not much wider than my outstretched arms, the rock's angular edges smoothed off by raging torrents past. Today the Alligator Creek is bone dry but after high rainfall this section can be a shallow wade, so check ahead, though rarely is the water too high to pass.

It's a dazzing stretch. The walls occasionally lean inwards in a gentle overhang but eventually they widen, spitting me out near Blue Gum Flat Picnic Area. A junction bears left to complete the Gorge Circuit, however I head right to continue on the longer Alligator Gorge Ring Route. It's fast progress on 4km of fire trail over hardpack orange earth and I pass two campsites before I return to the gorge via its tree-filled wide mouth. What starts as a narrow track slowly gives way to a rough and rocky route between the gorge walls. It's grand and dramatic. Large boulders that have sheared off the cliffs and logs litter the floor and at times it's a scramble to negotiate around them. Undercuts eat into the walls and the sun's rays turn the rock bright rust.

Entry to The Terraces is heralded by shallow cascading quartzite platforms dotted with still pools of water. It's hard to grasp the scale of Alligator Gorge's ancient backstory but you can literally see it here in the ripple marks, a link to 600 million years ago when an inland sea had its sandy undulations forever immortalised. By the time I climb back out of the gorge to Alligator Gorge carpark and wander to the Gorge Lookout (600m return), with its view over the great rusted incisions in the land, I have a whole new appreciation of this outback 'gator.

Wandering The Terraces

BEST EATS

- **Store 54:** This cool cafe is the go-to for hearty breakfasts, burgers, focaccias and wraps. 24 Stuart St, Melrose; (08) 8666 2057.
- **North Star Inn:** It's one of the best-looking buildings in town, built in 1881 and oozing with character, and the food and beers are good too. 43 Nott St, Melrose; (08) 8666 2110; northstarhotel.com.au.

BEST SLEEPS

- **Alligator Lodge:** Just minutes from Alligator Gorge, this former ranger's residence makes a tranquil option, immersed in the bush. With three bedrooms sleeping up to 10 people, it's good value for families or groups. Off Alligator Gorge Rd, Wilmington; (08) 8207 7700; parks.sa.gov.au/booking and search for the property.
- **Under the Mount:** It's a favourite of mountain bikers, but even if you're sans wheels this sprawling property with fire-pits and communal hangouts is a popular choice. Choose from ensuite cabins or bunk rooms. 9-11 Jacka Street, Melrose; 0409 093 649; underthemount.com.au.

WHILE YOU'RE HERE

- **Melrose:** Officially the oldest town in the Flinders Ranges (established in 1853), this cute town is full of picturesque historic buildings set against the backdrop of Mount Remarkable. It's also a magnet for mountain bikers who are spoiled for choice here with over 100km of singletrack and the new 37.5km IMBA-certified (International Mountain Bike Association) EPIC mountain bike trail slated for opening late 2022/2023; melrose-mtremarkable.org.au.
- **Wirrabara Silo Art:** Who doesn't love a painted silo? Drop in at the 28m-tall Wirrabara Silos on your way to the gorge; wirrabara.com.au/silo-art.
- **Hidden Gorge:** Another spectacular walk in Mount Remarkable National Park is Hidden Gorge, accessible from Mambray Creek on the western side of the park. Allow 6-8hr for the 18km circuit; parks.sa.gov.au.

Climb to the rim of Wilpena Pound/Ikara for epic views of the Northern Flinders Ranges.

Tanderra Saddle (St Mary Peak track)

This walk is on <u>Adnyamathanha Country</u>.

WHY IT'S SPECIAL

The state's longest mountain range starts 200km north of Adelaide and stretches for 430km, rising and submerging in a discontinuous line as it pushes deep into the outback. At Wilpena Pound/Ikara, millions of years of folding and erosion have seen the sedimentary mountain range uplifted and wrapped back on itself, leaving a 17km-long oval-shaped amphitheatre enclosed by serrated peaks. Wilpena Pound/Ikara is sacred to the Adnyamathanha People, the Traditional Owners of the Flinders Ranges and co-managers of Ikara-Flinders Ranges National Park. St Mary Peak/ Ngarri Mudlahnha is the highest point and central to the Adnyamathanha creation story. Although visitors are asked not to walk to its rocky summit, Tanderra Saddle, 1.6km shy of the peak and 220m lower, affords spectacular views both inside the Pound and across the surrounding outback. One thousand million years in the making, this is one of those places where the land's ancient energy is palpable.

WALK IT

This circuit walk climbs the steep and rocky outer flanks of the Pound and over its rim, before returning via the far more gentle inside route – across the Pound floor. A shorter option is to take the outside route there and back, although you won't get the full gamut of scenery available on the circuit. Tackling the circuit anticlockwise means you can climb the steeper and gnarlier section first and enjoy a relatively straightforward and gentle descent to finish.

If you're staying at Wilpena Pound Resort (*see* p. 143), trail access is easy, starting at the Visitor Centre.

Trail talk
- Distance: 18.5km loop (or 11.5km return via outside route only)
- Time: 6-8hr (or 4-5hr via outside route only)
- Rating: Moderate-hard
- Technicality: The outside route has some rock hopping and one short section of challenging scrambling near the saddle, but otherwise the route is well graded.
- Puff factor: There's an hour or two of steady climbing to reach the saddle but beyond that it's a pretty mellow walk.
- Watch out for: Take care on loose rocks and on the final steep and exposed scramble to the saddle.

When to go
April to Oct is best. The trail closes Dec to Feb when conditions are dangerously hot. Spring sees a feverish burst of flowering and seeding after winter rains, bringing a riot of colour.

Resources
Download the Bushwalking in Ikara-Flinders Ranges National Park guide from environment.sa.gov.au. Visit parks.sa.gov.au for more info on Ikara-Flinders Ranges National Park.

Opposite top Ring-neck parrots are common
Opposite bottom Photo-worthy stop

Tanderra Saddle (St Mary Peak track)   139

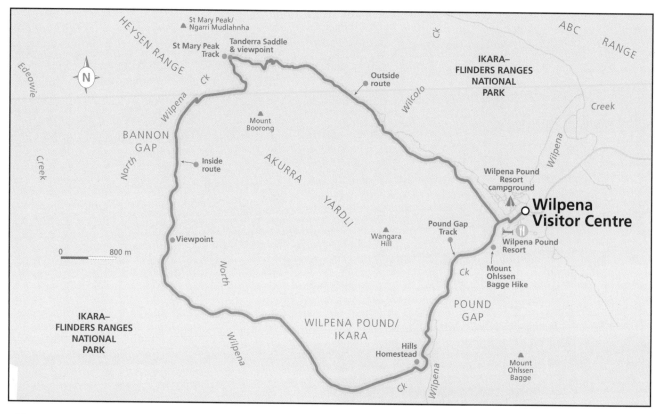

⊙ LOCAL SNAPSHOT

Adnyamathanha habitation in the Northern Flinders Ranges can be traced back around 15,000 years. Their name translates to 'hills or rock people', and evidence of their culture and creation stories are embedded in their Country, from engravings of circles in the rock at Sacred Canyon to the ochre paintings at Arkaroo Rock. For the pastoralists who farmed here in the latter half of the 1800s, the curved rippling mountains were a perfect natural stock pen (a 'pound') but for the Adnyamathanha People, the mountains were created by serpents and held great spiritual meaning. They call it Ikara - meaning 'meeting place' - and for thousands of years it had been just that, a place for local groups and neighbours to hold ceremonies and have discussions. Today, Wilpena Pound/Ikara is jointly managed by Traditional Owners and Indigenous Business Australia, and around half the workforce here consists of First Nations People.

Right Enjoying snow gum scenery and level ground
Opposite Climbing the rocky route up Ikara's outside edge

ITINERARY

It's difficult to fully grasp what Wilpena Pound/Ikara is until you're looking down over it, but to get that view I need to climb. From Wilpena Visitor Centre, it's 6km to the saddle via the outside route, a trail that starts as a gentle amble through sparse native pine, before transitioning midway to a steep and uneven track that looks as though someone has tipped a tray-load of orange rocks down it. As height is gained, the trees lessen and hardy bushes in fiery shades of red, orange and yellow take over. The views are increasingly impressive too, across the Heysen and ABC ranges rippling outwards in a gnarly contrast against the flat and barren land crossed during the drive to get here.

The last push to Tanderra Saddle is the hardest, a short scramble up a reasonably sheer and exposed section of rock that could be a tad unnerving for those with a fear of heights,

but once on top the views are ample reward. From my viewpoint at the northern end of Wilpena Pound/Ikara, I'm able to peer inside what looks like a vast sloping soap dish fringed with serrations from the tilted and eroded mountain ranges. Sedimentary layers are easily visible, streaking great bands of orange across the land. It's a view you can happily soak up for some time. A trail continues a further 1.6km to the summit of St Mary Peak/Ngarri Mudlahnha – it's far steeper and more scrambly than other parts of the trail – but the Adnyamathanha People prefer walkers end their ascent here rather than stand on the head of the serpent that created this striking formation (*see* p. 140).

From here the trail begins its descent, curving around the inside of the Pound and showing off expansive views of the interior. After about 3.5km it meets the floor of the Pound, diving into forest and an easy trail. Wildlife love this place

and if you don't manage to spot emus, kangaroos or koalas, you'll definitely see birds. Most plentiful are the ring-neck parrots with blue-green plumage and yellow necks.

In the trail's final quarter, where it turns north-west back towards Wilpena, the historic Hills Homestead appears. From 1899 the Hill family grew wheat inside the Pound, until severe floods in 1914 destroyed their access road and they gave up trying to work the harsh land, but their stone cottage remains.

If you're feeling weary, you can flag a shuttle bus from here back to Wilpena Pound Resort, however the easy walk along Wilpena Creek, with its streaked and gnarled river red gums, is a lovely way to finish.

BEST EATS

- **Wilpena Pound Resort:** Head to the Ikara Lounge Bar & Bistro for quick bites or to the Dining Room for quality pub fare made from local and indigenous seasonal produce. Wilpena Road; (08) 8648 0004; wilpenapound.com.au.

BEST SLEEPS

- **Wilpena Pound Resort:** This expansive resort incorporates everything from campgrounds to glamping tents and hotel rooms, and walking trails are right on your doorstep. Wilpena Road; (08) 8648 0004; wilpenapound.com.au.

WHILE YOU'RE HERE

- **Brachina and Bunyeroo gorges:** An 8km route through layers of rock is littered with fossils that trace the evolution of life over a 100-million-year period, from stromatolites to soft-bodied animals with shells. Though you can self-drive this 'corridor through time', you'll see and learn a lot more on a half-day guided Time Travel and Gorgeous Gorges tour from Wilpena Pound Resort. (08) 8648 0004; wilpenapound.com.au.
- **Scenic flight:** The only way to fully appreciate Wilpena Pound/Ikara's extraordinary size, shape, and the snaking ochre mountains that surround it, is from up above. Book a flight through Wilpena Pound Resort; (08) 8648 0004; wilpenapound.com.au/do/flights.
- **Keep walking:** There are over a dozen trails across this part of the Flinders Ranges, revealing different aspects of a unique and striking region. To see Adnyamathanha rock carvings and paintings, walk to Sacred Canyon and Arkaroo Rock or book a Sacred Canyon Yura Mulka Cultural Walk with an Adnyamathanha guide; wilpenapound.com.au/do/cultural-tours. Mount Ohlssen Bagge is another popular hike with excellent views of the Pound. Download the Bushwalking in Ikara-Flinders Ranges National Park guide from environment.sa.gov.au.

The impressive Wilpena Pound/Ikara

Western Australia

From half-day ambles to a 1000km epic,
WA has a trail to wow everyone.

Discover salt lakes, quokkas, white beaches and turquoise bays on Rottnest Island/Wadjemup.

Gabbi Karniny Bidi

This walk is on <u>Whadjuk Country</u>.

WHY IT'S SPECIAL

As a car-free island, 19km off the coast from Perth/Boorloo, Rottnest Island/Wadjemup lends itself to exploration on foot. This walk is just one loop within the Wadjemup Bidi (Rottnest Island Walk, in Noongar language), a network of 45km of trails that circumnavigate the island and reach into its interior.

The focus of the Gabbi Karniny Bidi loop is the salt lakes at the island's eastern end – recognised as a 'Wetland of National Importance', as well as being bird magnets – but you also get to take in the island's famously blinding white sand beaches, turquoise bays and cute quokkas. Pack your swimming gear and a very good pair of sunglasses.

WALK IT

From Fremantle, it's half an hour by ferry to the island (90min from Perth) and once you're there, it's really worth exploring more of Wadjemup Bidi. Five bite-size segments ranging from 6 to 10km in length reveal more of the island's epic coastline, World War II defence systems, the world-class surf break and a colony of New Zealand fur seals.

If you're in any way into swimming or snorkelling, explorations will require plenty of time. Little Salmon Bay and Parker Point have underwater snorkelling trails that follow plaques highlighting points of interest; expect to see coral, limestone outcrops, tropical fish, sponges, molluscs and rays. Wadjemup Bidi trailheads can be reached by bicycle or on the Island Explorer hop-on-hop-off bus.

→ Trail talk
- Distance: 9.7km
- Time: 3-4hr
- Rating: Easy
- Technicality: Easy wide limestone track, boardwalk and sandy beaches.
- Puff factor: Undulations are gentle.
- Watch out for: It's largely an exposed trail so sun protection is a must.

When to go
Sunny days bring out the spectacular colours. It's good year-round but Oct-Mar is ideal for swimming and Apr-May is much quieter than in summer.

Resources
Download the map and fact sheet from rottnestisland.com.

Opposite Bathurst Lighthouse *Previous* Cape to Cape Track

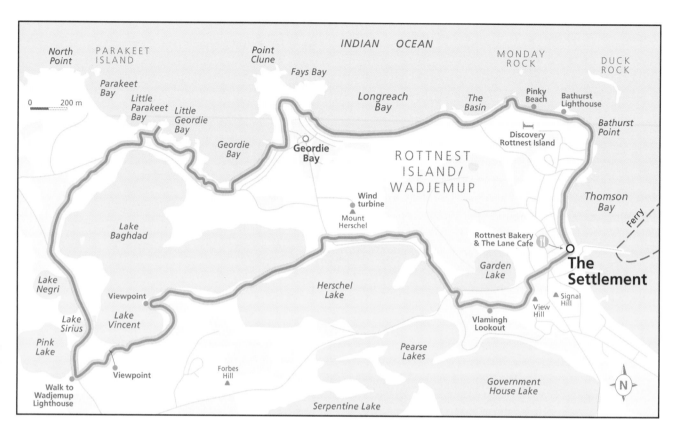

Western Australia

◉ LOCAL SNAPSHOT

The Whadjuk People occupied Rottnest/Wadjemup for up to 30,000 years when it was still part of the mainland - during the last ice age - and artefacts found here predate 6500 years ago. Even when sea levels rose and the island formed, it remained extremely culturally significant and was named Wadjemup, meaning 'place across the water where the spirits are'. It's considered to be a place of transition, a place where a whale meets spirits at the island's western end to escort them to their final resting place in the ocean far on the horizon. For the Whadjuk People it holds a spiritual significance. But from 1838, for almost a century, the island was used as a prison and forced labour camp for Whadjuk men and boys who came into conflict with colonial settlers over the loss of their land. When the prison closed in 1907, plans were made to transform Rottnest/Wadjemup into a holiday island. In 2020 the Wadjemup Project, led by Noongar Elders, was initiated to determine how to conserve and reconcile the history and how to commemorate the prison and burial grounds.

Top The island's famously cute quokkas *Opposite* Vlamingh Lookout

ITINERARY

Arrive on Rottnest/Wadjemup on a sunny day and the first thing that hits you is the light; it shines from above and bounces off that brilliant white sand to sneak under hats and sunglasses. The ferry lands at Thomson Bay, ideally situated to hit the trail immediately, but it's hard to resist lingering to meet the island's most famous residents that loiter around the Settlement – hello quokkas!

Quokkas have the kind of animated smile that deserves to feature in a Hollywood cartoon. They're incredibly cute and have been snapped alongside many of the world's famous but if you're planning on capturing your own quokka selfie, be sure not to touch or feed them (there's a $150 fine if you do). Actually wallabies (not rats, as Dutch explorer Willem de Vlamingh thought in 1696, leading him to name the island 'Rotte nest', or 'rats nest'), they were once abundant on the mainland until dingoes arrived 3500 years ago.

The fact that quokkas can tolerate environments virtually devoid of freshwater has worked well for them on Rottnest/Wadjemup. Around 10 per cent of the island is salt lakes (there's a smattering of freshwater seeps too) and you get an introduction to them from Vlamingh Lookout, the first point of interest flagged on the trail map. It's not very high but you don't need much altitude to get a view here – the island's highest point is only 46m – and the outlook extends down the island.

After passing a wind turbine – part of the mix of wind, solar and diesel used to power the island – the trail embraces the salt lakes. They're a hive of life, recognised as an Important Bird Area for seabirds (i.e. a priority conservation area) and rich in invertebrates that in turn feed the island's reptiles, amphibians, mammals and birds. Lake Baghdad is an ideal location to linger and spot a few banded stilts. The track slides between Baghdad and Herschel Lake and on to Lake Vincent where a feature boardwalk hovers over the water's edge and

protects fragile communities of samphire (succulent salt-tolerant plants). In the right conditions, the lake's mirror-like reflections of clouds and sky are extremely photogenic, the boardwalk giving the illusion of walking across the sky.

Off to the west, Wadjemup Lighthouse (1896) peeks out from its inland perch, and if you take the 1km side trip to visit it you'll pass Pink Lake. It doesn't always live up to its name, and in summer it can dry out completely, but if you catch it on a day when the algae is blooming it is delightfully pink.

A short section of thick bushland offers a nice change of pace and a rare bit of shelter from the sun, and when the trail hits the island's north coast it exchanges salt lakes for a string of beaches of dazzling beauty. First is Little Parakeet Bay, a cove of turquoise perfection sheltered by craggy limestone headlands and great for snorkelling. The long sweep of sand hugging Geordie Bay is lined with holiday accommodation, plus there is a general store, cafe and art gallery. Longreach Bay is home to The Basin, a natural 'swimming pool' sheltered by reefs, making it one of the island's most popular places for a swim. Pinky Beach, overlooked by Bathurst Lighthouse (1900), is the last place for a dip before completing this beautiful loop.

Bottom Approximately 10 per cent of the island is covered in salt lakes *Opposite* Bathurst Lighthouse

BEST EATS

- **Rottnest Bakery:** There are bakeries and then there's Rottnest Bakery. This place is well known for its tasty pies, sausage rolls, fresh pastries, sandwiches and sourdough baked daily. The adjoining Chook Shack is the go-to for chicken and chips. Maley St, The Settlement; (08) 9292 5023.
- **The Lane Cafe:** Some say this place serves the best coffee on the island, along with fresh juices, fancy burgers, crayfish rolls and lunch bowls. Somerville Dr, Thomson Bay, Rottnest; 0407 366 447.

BEST SLEEPS

- **Rottnest Island Authority accommodation:** There's a huge range of accommodation to suit all needs and budgets, from camping and hostel beds to seaside units and cottages, and everything is a stone's throw from the waterfront; rottnestisland.com/accommodation.

- **Discovery Rottnest Island:** These glamping eco tents set in the dunes at Pinky Beach are the best place to immerse yourself in Rottnest's coastal vibe. Choose from standard double tents, family size or deluxe oceanside tents with unhindered sea views. (08) 6350 6170; discoveryholidayparks.com.au/discovery-rottnest-island.

WHILE YOU'RE HERE

- **Pedal & Flipper bike hire:** Bicycle is the best way to get around Rotto. Pack snorkelling gear and hiking shoes and go explore the 20 bays, 63 beaches and kilometres more of walking trails. Equipment can be rented from Pedal & Flipper, Bedford Ave, Rottnest; (08) 9292 5105; rottnestisland.com/pedalandflipper.
- **Sea Kayak Rottnest:** The island's famously clear water comes in handy when you're peering through the bottom of a kayak while cruising over coral reefs. On a guided tour with Sea Kayak Rottnest you also get to learn all about the island's wildlife and history. Pinky Beach, Rottnest; (08) 6219 5164; rottnestkayak.com.au.

Australia's best long-distance hike offers a moving feast of unique landscapes and a chance to get off the grid, connect with nature, and reset the body and mind.

Bibbulmun Track

This walk is on <u>Whadjuk</u>, <u>Pinjarup</u>, <u>Wiilman</u>, <u>Kaniyang</u>, <u>Bibulmun</u> and <u>Minang Country</u>.

Western Australia

WHY IT'S SPECIAL

Magic happens on a long walk, such as serious stress-busting forest bathing, boosted self-confidence and occasionally life-changing epiphanies. With well-graded tracks and great campsites, there can be few more hiker-friendly long-distance trails to cut your teeth on than the Bibb.

Stretching between Perth/Boorloo and Albany on the south coast, the Bibbulmun Track passes through a remarkable variety of terrain, from dry woodland to granite-domed peaks and lush mossy forests, as well as along dazzling white beaches.

Western Australia's south-west corner is a biodiversity hotspot with almost 80 per cent of the plant species here not found elsewhere – the giant tingle trees are a highlight. Go in spring and you'll be drowning in wildflowers, including tons of weird and wonderful orchids.

WALK IT

Yes it's long and you'll need energy, but the terrain is relatively easy and the logistics are also easy with welcoming three-sided shelters, toilets and water tanks provided at every camp. Adopt the mantra 'one step at a time', and it's completely doable for anyone with the will. The trail passes through a town every three to seven days, allowing you to take a rest day, get a comfortable bed and a good feed, do some washing and resupply food for the next section.

For those without the time or inclination to through-hike it in one go, the Bibb can easily be tackled section by section, plus there are additional vehicle entry/exit points. Alternatively, just pick one section that appeals or do a day hike. Check out bibbulmuntrack.org.au for dozens of suggestions for day walks and short multi-day sections along the route.

If you're someone who divides their loyalties between boots and trail runners, you might prefer runners for this one. The terrain is rarely difficult and frequent long flat stretches can be tough in boots.

 Trail talk

- Distance: 1000km
- Time: 6-8 weeks
- Rating: Moderate
- Technicality: Aside from a handful of rocky sections, this is overwhelmingly a well-graded route with pretty solid signage.
- Puff factor: There are a few climbs along the way but none are very long. Beach walking and the vegetated dunes down south can be tiring, and the trail's sheer length alone requires some energy.
- Watch out for: It's a relatively 'snakey' corner of the country, so keep your ears and eyes open for creatures slithering across the track. Rats can be a problem in just a few of the shelters so always keep your food secure. Be careful on slippery rock in the wet or after rain.

 When to go

Apr-May or Sep-Nov are ideal times, when it's not too hot and not too cold or wet. Spring is an absolute feast of wildflowers. Avoid in summer when bushfire risk is high.

 Resources

Get planning information at bibbulmuntrack.org.au. Maps and trail guide booklets (produced section by section) are available for purchase.

Opposite top Wandering in the White Horse Hills *Opposite bottom* Three-sided shelters at every camp make life easy

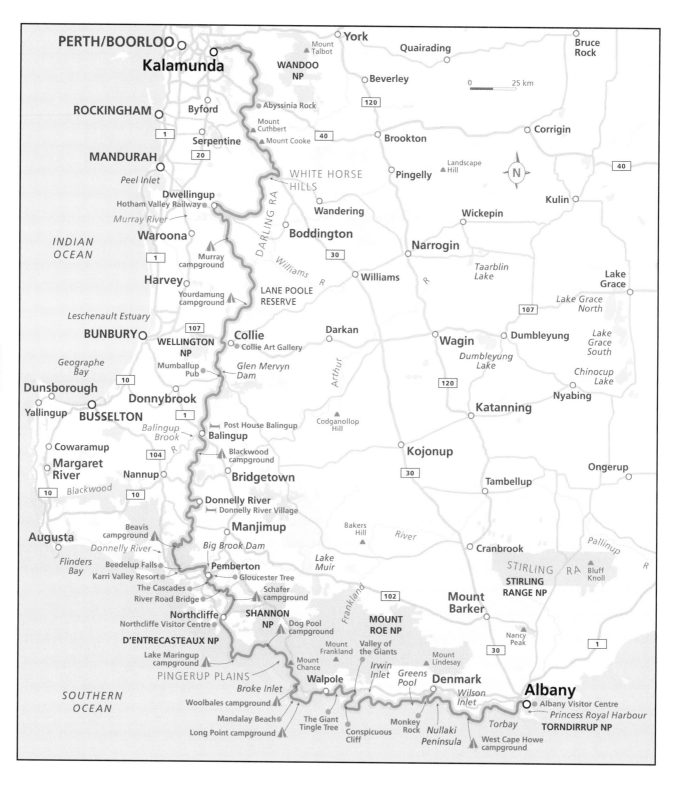

PERTH/BOORLOO

Kalamunda

ROCKINGHAM   Byford

Serpentine

MANDURAH

Peel Inlet

Dwellingup
Hotham Valley Railway
Murray River

INDIAN
OCEAN   Waroona

Murray
campground

Harvey

Yourdamung
campground

Leschenault Estuary

BUNBURY   WELLINGTON
NP   Collie
Collie Art Gallery

Geographe   Mumballup
Bay   Pub

DUNSBOROUGH

Yallingup   BUSSELTON   Donnybrook

Cowaramup   Balingup
Brook   Post House Balingup
Balingup

Margaret
River   Nannup   Blackwood
campground

Blackwood   Bridgetown

Donnelly River
Donnelly River Village

Augusta   Beavis
campground   Manjimup

Donnelly River   Big Brook Dam

Flinders   Beedelup Falls
Bay   Karri Valley Resort   Gloucester Tree
The Cascades   Schafer
River Road Bridge   campground

Northcliffe   SHANNON
Northcliffe Visitor Centre   NP   Dog Pool
campground

D'ENTRECASTEAUX NP   MOUNT
ROE NP

Lake Maringup   Mount
campground   Chance

PINGERUP PLAINS   Walpole

SOUTHERN   Broke Inlet
OCEAN

Woolbales campground

Mandalay Beach   The Giant
Long Point campground   Tingle Tree   Conspicuous
Cliff

York   Mount
Talbot   Quairading   Bruce
Rock

Beverley

Abyssinia Rock   120

Mount
Cuthbert   Brookton   Corrigin

Mount Cooke   40

WHITE HORSE   Pingelly   Landscape   N   40
HILLS   Hill

Wandering   Kulin

Boddington   Wickepin

30   Narrogin

Williams   Taarblin
Lake   Lake
Grace

Darkan   Lake Grace   107
North

Wagin   Dumbleyung   Lake
Grace
South

Dumbleyung   Chinocup
Lake   Lake

Arthur   120   Nyabing

Codganollop   Katanning
Hill

Kojonup   Ongerup

30   Tambellup

Bakers
Hill   River

Lake
Muir

Cranbrook   Pallinup

STIRLING   RA   Bluff
Knoll

STIRLING
RANGE NP

102   MOUNT
ROE NP   Mount
Barker   Nancy
Peak   1

Mount   Valley of   30
Frankland   the Giants
Irwin   Greens   Mount
Inlet   Pool   Lindesay   Denmark   Albany

Wilson   Albany Visitor Centre
Monkey   Inlet   Princess Royal Harbour
Rock   Nullaki   Torbay   TORNDIRRUP NP
Peninsula   West Cape Howe
campground

Western Australia

0   25 km

INDIAN
OCEAN

SOUTHERN
OCEAN

◉ LOCAL SNAPSHOT

In Noongar Dreaming, the Waugal, a great serpent spirit, created all the contours of the land. Its body carved the hills, rivers and trees and, when it paused to rest, bays and lakes were formed. The Bibulmun People once walked long distances across this south-west corner of the state for ceremonial gatherings, providing the inspiration for the creation of this epic modern-day route. Walkers on the Bibbulmun Track are now guided by the Waugal, which is imprinted on every yellow trail marker along the route.

Section number	Section start	Section finish	Distance	Days
1	Kalamunda (Perth)	Dwellingup	211km	9-12
2	Dwellingup	Collie	128km	7
3	Collie	Balingup	86km	4
4	Balingup	Donnelly River Village	58km	3
5	Donnelly River Village	Pemberton	109km	4-5
6	Pemberton	Northcliffe	59km	3
7	Northcliffe	Walpole	142km	7-8
8	Walpole	Denmark	126km	6-8
9	Denmark	Albany	85km	4-6

Waugul trail markers lead the way

ITINERARY

SECTION 1

Kalamunda to Dwellingup, 211km, 9–12 days

It's a funny thing to start a long distance bushwalk within 'cooee' of a state capital. A friend drops me off at the northern trail terminus on the corner of Mundaring Weir Road and Railway Road in Kalamunda, an outer suburb of the Perth Hills, early on a spring morning, and I'm conscious that I'm about to leave the modern world behind for a few months.

The first section is the longest, though there are a number of entry points where friends can drop in with extra food if desired. It's also the hilliest but heavy packs are more easily forgotten when you're surrounded by beautiful scenery and the Darling Ranges have plenty of it. Most notable is the regular eruptions of granite that reveal themselves in vast sloping slabs streaked in emerald moss, such as at Abyssinia Rock, or enormous domed peaks like Mount Cuthbert, Mount Cooke and the White Horse Hills. They're not exactly Everest – Cooke

is the trail's highest point at 582m – yet all offer epic 360-degree views over distant treed plains. I love kicking my shoes off for a break on these high points, feeling the heat of the rock beneath me while clouds swirl overhead.

Sandy trails undulate quite a bit through dry woodland – jarrah, marri and white gums – dotted with grass trees, and within days on the trail the flowers are staggering. Blooms of every colour under the rainbow fill the air with fragrance – hay fever sufferers, beware.

Though I walk solo, I'm not alone, accompanied by the mournful shriek of red-tailed black cockatoos and the chatter of ringneck parrots, and shadowed (literally) by huge wedge-tailed eagles. Wallabies, kangaroos and emus occasionally drop in too.

Trail town: The section ends in Dwellingup, a peaceful one-pub town surrounded by forest with a caravan park and numerous lodges and holiday cottages. Awarded as WA's Top Small Tourism Town 2021, it's a popular weekend destination for Perth residents looking to explore the outdoors and to ride the historic steam Hotham Valley Railway that departs from here. There's a small IGA general store but you won't get a massive choice on lightweight hiker food, so many walkers opt to post a food resupply box to themselves ahead of time via the post office.

SECTION 2
Dwellingup to Collie, 128km, 7 days

After two nights and a day of rest in Dwellingup, involving numerous chicken parmis at the pub, I'm ready to hit the trail again and it's suddenly a busy place. Two new through-hikers and seven section-hikers join me and it's a full house on the sleeping platforms in the three-sided shelter at camp, though there's always plenty of tent space.

The Murray River leads the way on this section, carving through forest scattered with banksia, grass trees, and zamia with huge seed pods sprouting from their centre like pineapples. Everything is decorated with the ever-present wildflowers. Some days are dominated by pink and orange coral vine that drapes over everything like a camo net, while other days it's white clematis, red grevillia or orange bookleaf pea. One valley is so thick with yellow wattle it looks on fire. Murray camp, on night two, is a treat, overlooking the river and with easy access for a swim.

The forest is interspersed with pockets of banksia and sandy tracks. I find myself lured into the thrill of a treasure hunt, one eye always peeled for the orchids that come in wild designs and colours. There's the silky blue, white spider, cowslip, rabbit orchid (looks like a chubby bunny face with two ears poking up), snail orchid (looks like a snail) and donkey orchid (... have a guess).

Such landscapes provide great habitat for birds and I regularly spy scarlet robins and a few threatened red-tailed black cockatoos. At Yourdamung camp (Day 5 of this section) six emus wander in for a look around while everyone is having an afternoon siesta, though sadly I sleep through the whole thing.

There are a few hills to tackle on this section and though it feels more remote than the first stretch out of Perth, there is still a reminder of humanity when you pass beneath the huge overhead conveyor belt of a bauxite mine.

Trail town: Collie is by far the largest town on the Bibbulmun and has everything a hiker needs, including two major supermarkets, a camping store, loads of restaurants and a handful of pubs. It's worth dropping in at the snazzy Collie Art Gallery (collieartgallery.org.au), which often hosts some quite significant exhibitions.

SECTION 3
Collie to Balingup, 86km, 4 days

I walk alone from Collie to Balingup and the solitude gives me a chance to slow down and tune in to my surroundings. Walking can be a meditation and without people to talk to, the internal monologue quietens as well. I become far more conscious of the soft earth beneath my feet, the scent of tree oils and the squawks of birds. Everything I do is mindful, yet it's without effort. Food is savoured and sights are appreciated, simply because there is nothing else for the mind to do.

Tunnels of forest lined with yellow flowers leads to Glen Mervyn Dam, pumping on weekends with waterskiers, fishing and swimming but resting peacefully on my visit. Following old rail formations keeps the track flat and easy for a while, allowing ample opportunity to admire the forest. I even spot an emu running in the distance.

A short road section passes Mumballup Pub, over a century old and with a beer garden out the back. Such rare moments of culinary excitement are hotly anticipated by hikers and I start dreaming of a hamburger and chips for lunch only to discover it's closed on the one day of the week that I walk by.

Beyond rolling farmland dotted in yellow daisies and cows, I slip into some of the best virgin jarrah forest in the south-west. Endemic to WA, this myrtle grows around 40m tall and its pale bark comes alight with the lowering sun. It's the perfect place for some forest bathing – the Japanese concept of 'shinrin yoku', where you immerse yourself in nature and slow down, look around and breathe in the scents and stillness of a forest.

It's then a steep descent into Balingup Brook valley from where the track follows a pretty route along the river, through pine forest carpeted in soft needles and beneath boughs of weeping willow to the quaint and picturesque town of Balingup.

Trail town: Balingup is tiny, yet vibrant and full of character with lots of boutique artsy shops and quality cafes. At the time I visited it was hard to find anything open for dinner, but if you stay in the hostel accommodation at the cute Post House Balingup (a working post office) you can cook your own in the communal kitchen. Alternatively, there are plenty of self-contained cottages and B&Bs for a bit of comfort. There is only a small general store – i.e. expensive and limited selection – so this is another place where you might want to consider posting a food box to yourself for food resupply.

SECTION 4
Balingup to Donnelly River Village, 58km, 3 days

A friend catches a bus to Balingup to join me for the week's walk (Section 4 and 5) through to Pemberton. Our energy levels wax and wane; mine descending from trail-strong to one of the inevitable troughs that comes with a long-distance walk, while his grow from trail newbie to trail fit.

Skirting farmland, we climb to Blackwood Camp for a night, overlooking the Blackwood River valley, and awaken to the thick mist that regularly cloaks the area.

Long stretches of flat walking are both a blessing and a curse, easy on the lungs but unforgiving on the feet. Old railway formations and 4WD tracks carve the forest, sections of which are recovering from one of the many bushfires that seem to hit this corner of the state. Blackened trunks are fluffy with regrowth and draped in vines of white clematis or purple wisteria. Another emu makes an appearance, this time trailing eight chicks.

On arrival at Donnelly River Village (DRV) I'm up to my armpits in emus. The heritage-listed timber mill town was a hive of activity in the 1950s, providing employment for enough people to warrant the construction of 35 workers' cottages and a schoolhouse. The steam mill fell into disrepair after closing in 1978 and now the town is purely a holiday village with cottages rented to holiday-makers and the schoolhouse utilised as a hiker's dorm. Quaint architecture aside, one of the most appealing aspects of DRV is the resident population of emus and kangaroos that loiter in front of the general store, waiting for handouts.

Trail town: There are no facilities at DRV other than the General Store but here you'll find a few basic groceries, a good supply of dehydrated hiker meals, and a cafe. They also sell frozen homemade dinners that you can take back to your cottage or the communal kitchen in the schoolhouse and enjoy with a bottle of wine. All accommodation bookings are handled by the General Store (donnellyriver.com.au).

SECTION 5
Donnelly River Village to Pemberton, 109km, 4–5 days

In the middle of thick forest, a day's hike south of DRV, a lone directional sign marks the halfway point of the Bibbulmun. Towering old-growth forests become scattered with karri, tall pale ghosts amid the moss and greenery; they're the second tallest flowering tree in the world.

Top The trail's mid section is marked by lush forests

The trail gets cosy with the Donnelly River for much of this section and it makes for some super pretty walking. Dark water cuts a passage through the greenery in still flows or cascading over slabs of rock. In contrast to the northern section, here the forests become dense and damp and though several riverside camps, such as Tom Road camp, are perfect for an afternoon swim, my friend and I don down jackets and crank up the fire-pits instead.

Undulations carry us from damp forests scattered with purple wisteria and moss-covered granite boulders, up to dry terrain dotted with grass trees. These damp forests get cold, even in early October, and I start hanging my silver foil emergency blanket over the tent inner at night to reflect my body heat back at me. I feel like a chicken at a deli counter but it works.

The third day of this section features a few decent ups and downs described in the trail notes as the 'Rollercoaster'. The effort is enough to keep me warm in a T-shirt until I arrive at Beavis camp and stop moving. A thermometer in the hut declares it nine degrees at 3pm and it's so cold overnight that I'm reluctant to breathe too deeply at the icy air which chills me from the inside.

There are a few decent climbs on this section, mixed in with flatter stretches of old timber railway and trestle bridges. Big Brook Dam has the feeling of a summer camp, a vast lake with a sandy beach popular with families canoeing, swimming and fishing, and we lose a few hours reclined in a deck chair with faces tilted to the sun. The Karri Valley Resort here has a restaurant and kiosk.

The section finishes with Beedelup Falls, which spreads itself over winding cascades viewed from an elevated walkway.

Trail town: Pemberton is a decent-sized town in a valley surrounded by karri forests. There's plenty of accommodation and dining options here, as well as art and craft galleries. This corner of the state is a fertile place and Pemberton is the perfect base from which to explore the region's gourmet food and wine, such as truffles, marron and wineries.

SECTION 6
Pemberton to Northcliffe, 59km, 3 days

The south-west has a long history with logging and the sawmill at Pemberton was in operation for over a century before closing in 2016. On the town's outskirts grows the Gloucester Tree, one of eight karris used as fire lookouts until the 1970s. You can still climb to the tiny platform in the tree's 61m canopy but it's not for the faint-hearted. Hammered in a giant swirl around

the trunk are 153 steel pegs with only a flimsy wire cage around them to give some semblance of protection. I'm fine while focusing on the rungs but when I let my gaze wander to the increasingly distant forest floor below, my legs turn to jelly.

The Lefroy Brook rushes over a series of rock slabs at The Cascades, a popular picnic area. The route continues along pretty trails through towering karri forest and a highlight is the long River Road Bridge, a historic wooden trestle bridge over the Warren River.

The last stop before Northcliffe is idyllic Schafer camp, sitting on the banks of a picturesque dam that has a designated swimming area.

Trail town: Northcliffe is essentially a tiny one street town but has a decent pub and a small general store where you can stock up on a few supplies. Visit the Northcliffe Visitor Centre and its adjacent art-in-nature experience, Understory, a 1.2km nature trail through the forest featuring sculptures, poetry, stories and music from 40 artists.

SECTION 7
Northcliffe to Walpole, 142km, 7–8 days

After weeks of chilly forests and rivers, the trail begins a transition as it draws closer to the ocean. The towering trees fall away, depositing me on open heath and swampland and suddenly I'm faced with long stretches of tannin-stained water, thigh-deep at times and wriggling with tadpoles.

Campsites in this section are awesome. Lake Maringup sits immersed in bracken ferns and karri forest with water views over one of the south-west's biggest freshwater lakes, and the birds and frogs here create a cacophony. More wading, through flowering heath, leads to Dog Pool camp, another gem set on rocky cascades on the Shannon River. The frogs here are a constant roar all night and the fact that snakes like to eat them is probably why I spot half a dozen of them on this stretch, though all avoid me without fuss.

The Pingerup Plains are marked on the map as being 'seasonally inundated' and all up I spend four days with wet feet as I wade in and out of sprawling puddles across flooded sandy trails, but blue skies and warm weather temper any real discomfort. Inundated sections are mixed with a smattering of karri and jarrah forest and then the enormous granite domes are back. Sunset from the top of Mount Chance (5min walk from Mount Chance camp) is dazzling with sunbeams threading holes through dark clouds. Lines of pink flowers and moss sprout from fracture lines on the mighty granite Woolbale

Hills and 360-degree views stretch to distant Broke Inlet. It's another great place to linger at sunset, being just a short walk from Woolbales camp.

There's a scent on the breeze, a faint roar. Anticipation builds and after 40 days of walking I finally arrive at the Southern Ocean. It's raining and blustery but even in the flat light Mandalay Beach seems to generate its own luminescence with a perfect white powder beach and clear aqua water.

I follow the trail across open dunes covered in low heath and flowers for hours and it's slow going at times in soft sand. A squall of horizontal rain lashes through and after 10min it passes and I watch it charge on across the green dunes, a sweep of fury and chaos, leaving sun and glistening green bushes behind. A massive thunderstorm breaks on the last night at Long Point camp and again I'm grateful for this trail's three-sided shelters that always ensure that no matter how challenging the elements are during the day, there's always somewhere dry to retreat to at night.

Trail town: Situated on the banks of the Walpole Inlet, Walpole has a lovely coastal holiday town vibe going on. There's plenty of accommodation to suit all budgets, some lovely cafes, a supermarket and a pub. Hugely popular is joining a WOW Wilderness Eco Cruise to explore the inlet and learn more about the area's history, culture and ecology.

SECTION 8
Walpole to Denmark, 126km, 6–8 days

Part of the trail's great appeal is its steady stream of the rare and wonderful, and the first few days out of Walpole are no exception. Red tingle trees grow up to 75m tall with huge buttressed trunks whose girths reach over 20m, and they only grow around Walpole and Nornalup. The trail winds through two pockets, first at The Giant Tingle Tree (you can walk around inside this fire-hollowed monster) and then the Valley of the Giants where an optional Tree Top Walk (for a fee) hovers 40m high amid the canopy.

After the forests and the dark pools and rapids of the Frankland River, the Bibb is lured back to the coast at Peaceful Bay where there's a caravan park, a tiny mini-mart and good fish and chips. From there I wander for days on white sandy paths undulating across vegetated dunes, hand-in-hand with the vast blue ocean. Kangaroos graze amid carpets of banksia and pink and yellow flowers and lift a head as I pass.

The sun's out at Conspicuous Cliff, sending colours soaring: green cliffs, a long sweep of white sand, and rolls of baby-blue surf. It's a vision of perfection. A lookout provides the ideal spot to watch whales passing by between winter and spring.

Boatsheds at either side of the Irwin Inlet store a stash of canoes to assist hikers in the 200m crossing, and the several days of steep dunes and beach walking south of it are exhausting. Every powdery arc of white sand and adjacent blue bay is a stunner though and perhaps no more so than at Greens Pool where large water-bound granite boulders shelter the turquoise water, creating a swimmer's paradise.

One final climb over the forest and granite playground of Monkey Rock wraps up a particularly stunning section.

Trail town: There's no problem finding good food in Denmark, a popular tourist town set on the Denmark River as it flows into Wilson Inlet and on to the Southern Ocean. Choose from cafes and restaurants, supermarkets stocking gourmet items, or the abundance of wineries and cellar doors that surround it. With so much water around, it's also a great place to hire a canoe, paddleboat or motorboat, or relax on nearby beaches.

Warming up by the fire at Tom Road camp

SECTION 9
Denmark to Albany, 85km, 4–6 days

The first challenge of this final leg is crossing the huge Wilson Inlet. I share a taxi with a few other hikers around to the Nullaki Peninsula and prepare for the final leg.

It takes a few days to reach West Cape Howe, on sandy paths through dunes and along ocean cliffs pounded by foaming waves. Belts of pelting rain sweep across the land and there's not a lot of shelter along this stretch – the best I can do is crouch into stunted peppermint thickets – so it's no surprise that a string of wind farm turbines exploit the natural power that is abundant here. West Cape Howe camp has epic views from its cliff-top position, stretching all the way down the rugged coast.

East of the cape feels just a smidge calmer and the route undulates gently between cliff-tops and beaches linked by rolling vegetated dunes. Up high I pass hang glider launching pads and peek into bays scattered with surfers and sheltered beaches. Down low I walk long stretches of sand and wade across Torbay Inlet. It's a beautiful stretch, though the wind is ever-present and there's sand in my ears at day's end.

In Torndirrup National Park I spot my last orchids, just hours before skirting Albany's Princess Royal Harbour and the trail's southern terminus. It's the done thing for thru-hikers to ring the Bibbulmun bell at the Visitor Centre to announce the arrival of a long-distance legend.

Be aware, it can be hard to rejoin society after a long-distance hike. Despite the physical challenge, many through-hikers become addicted to the simplicity, solitude and peace of life on the trail where all that needs to be done is put one foot in front of the other. I met one Bibb hiker who once he finished hiking south, turned around and walked back north again. You've been warned.

Trail town: After such an adventure it's worth lingering a few days in picturesque Albany (*see* p. 173).

The Darling Ranges are full of granite hills

Western Australia

See striped sandstone formations, black swans and the iconic Nature's Window on this outback loop around Murchison River Gorge.

Kalbarri Loop Trail

This walk is on <u>Nanda Country</u>.

WHY IT'S SPECIAL

At nearly 800km, the Murchison River is the second longest river in WA. Where the river nears the Indian Ocean, it has carved a gorge 85km long and up to 150m deep, revealing a cross-section of banded red and white Tumblagooda Sandstone that was laid down 400 million years ago. It makes for an impressive landscape and this loop walk follows a switchback in the river's course, at times skirting the rocky gorge rim and at others walking the soft sand alongside the river where river red gums sprout.

Hikers pass Nature's Window, one of WA's most famous sights, where a wind-eroded hole in the layered sandstone frames a view of the khaki river and surrounding orange sand plains, which are spectacularly carpeted in wildflowers from late winter to early summer. The route also reveals Kalbarri's water ripples and fossils immortalised in the rock; the park is one of the best locations in the world to view fossil traces of some of the earliest animals (arthropods) to walk on land.

WALK IT

The Loop Walk starts from the Nature's Window carpark, off Murchison Gorge's access road. Apart from the cover provided by a few river red gums on the gorge floor, most of this walk is unshaded, and temperatures can skyrocket to 50°C in summer, so it's best saved for winter months. If you are there between Nov and Mar, you'll be required to hit the trail before 7am. People have died here from dehydration and heat exhaustion, including the young and fit, so don't underestimate the dangers. Wear a broad-rimmed sunhat, pack double the water you'd normally carry on a hike (there's none in the park so bring your own), and bear in mind it can be considerably hotter in the depths of the gorge. If you can head out at sunrise you'll avoid the worst of the heat. Flies can be a pain here so you'll likely appreciate a face net, and when deciding on your outfit for the day, bear in mind that research shows flies love blue and are repelled by yellow.

If you're not up for the whole loop, just follow the mostly sealed path to Nature's Window, a 1km return walk that should take around 30min.

The snaking Murchison River

Trail talk
- Distance: 9km loop
- Time: 3-4hr
- Rating: Moderate
- Technicality: A mix of rugged rock walking and soft sand with a few brief challenging scrambles. It's well marked.
- Puff factor: Pretty gentle undulations, apart from the big descent in and out of the gorge. The soft sand sections can get you huffing too.
- Watch out for: The trail is exposed and can be very hot so be prepared (see Walk it section opposite), leave early and carry plenty of water. Be careful around unstable cliff edges.

When to go
May to Oct is best, when the weather is cooler. Wildflowers are spectacular from late winter, through spring and into early summer.

Resources
Go online to parks.dpaw.wa.gov.au and trailswa.com.au for more information. Entry fees apply for Kalbarri National Park ($15 per vehicle per day).

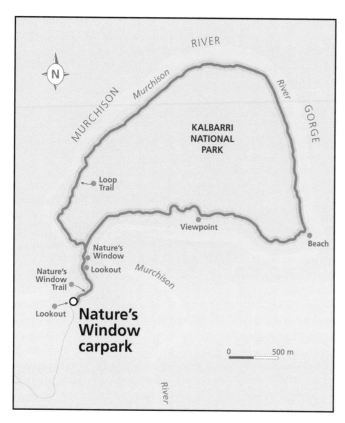

◉ LOCAL SNAPSHOT

For thousands of years the Nanda People have inhabited the region now known as Kalbarri National Park and beyond, from Woomerangee Hill in the north to Northampton in the south. For the Nanda People, there is spiritual power in the landscape and the Murchison River is of particular importance. The Dreaming tells of a serpent called Beemarra moving down the river, drawn by the sound of the ocean, however once she caught sight of its crashing waves she fled in fear back upstream again, tunnelling through the red sandstone and resting along the way to leave the permanent river pools of today. Of the 67 Aboriginal sites recorded as at 2015 - such as artefacts, middens, paintings and a quarry - most were found riverside. However surveys so far have been limited and it's likely there are many more sites yet to be discovered. The Nanda People are involved in the cultural management of the national park to ensure conservation and protection of cultural heritage.

ITINERARY

Kalbarri is big sky country, and from the top of the steps that mark the beginning of this walk, there is nothing to interrupt the line of sight across gently undulating and heath-covered sand plains, all the way to the horizon and the vast blue above. Snaking through this scene is the Murchison River Gorge, but only its upper heights are visible at this point.

To access the Loop Trail, you first need to set out on the Nature's Window Trail, a 500m walk which descends a few steps to follow a mostly sealed path, before a final little rock hop up to the icon itself. Formed from rugged layers of orange sandstone, Nature's Window sits on the gorge rim like the eye of a needle. It's not huge but it's highly effective as a picture frame for the winding river below, flanked by the striated and sloping gorge walls. It's a beautiful formation but fragile, so resist the temptation to stand or climb on it (and remember it's a steep drop into the gorge on the back side). The cascading red and orange rock slabs surrounding it clearly reveal ripple marks from the shallow sea that once ebbed and flowed here.

It's from Nature's Window that the Loop Trail begins in an anticlockwise direction, first staying high along the gorge rim, then descending to the river to rock hop the narrow ledges alongside it, and finishing with open sandy country along the river's edge, before a climb back to Nature's Window completes the loop.

While the trail to the window is a busy one, there are far fewer people on the loop track. It begins trailing across slabs of orange rock on a flat-topped ridge that falls steeply to the khaki river on the right. On the left, in the distance, can be seen Kalbarri Skywalk, two cantilevered viewing platforms jutting out 100m above the gorge.

It's quite likely you'll be doing the 'Aussie wave' on this walk, keeping up a fairly regular flap of the hand to deter flies from exploring your nostrils, eyes, mouth and ears. They get worse as the day heats up – another reason to start your walk early.

The track descends the ridge and though it dissolves into a path of chunky rocks flanked by low scrub, the way is clearly marked by white posts, finally reaching a decent-sized termite mound and the sandy beach of the Murchison River, backed by the gorge's striped and layered sandstone walls that rise steeply. The Murchison is ephemeral, sometimes wide and sometimes, during summer, shrinking to a string of large permanent pools. The sight of black swans – WA's emblem – here can feel like a surprise, but the water is brackish and makes an ideal habitat. It's also excellent for humans seeking a cool down.

The gorge squeezes the river in places and the most challenging, yet exciting, part of the walk involves rock hopping a series of narrow and shelved ledges that skirt the river's edge. Wind erosion has scooped out overhangs, revealing the sandstone's layers in swirls of cream and rust, and in places you may spot the fossilised burrows of ancient worms. For the most part this section is straightforward but there are a few pinches tight enough to have you groping the rock for security. Try not to stand on any particularly jutting-out bits as they occasionally break off.

At around halfway, the gorge broadens and opens up and for about a kilometre the route alternates between soft sand and rock hopping, alongside honeycomb formations and overhangs. River red gums, occasionally clogged with the flotsam of earlier floods, dot the gorge base and offer a little shade if you need respite from the sun. Keep an eye out for kangaroos, feral goats or possibly even wedge-tailed eagles soaring overhead.

The last few kilometres follow a wide sandy section through scattered shrubs and acacias and soft sand makes the going a little tiring, but there's opportunity for one more swim before the climb back out of the gorge. You'll spot Nature's Window, perched on the gorge rim ahead, well before reaching it on the zig-zag climb up loose rock. When you return to it, it's worth pausing again for another gaze through as the view changes with the light.

The trail shadows the Murchison River

Nature's Window

BEST EATS

- **The Gorges Cafe:** Offering wholesome fresh food, homemade cakes, excellent coffee and views overlooking the river, this place is super popular for breakfast through to lunch. 166 Grey St, Kalbarri; (08) 9937 1200.
- **Kalbarri Edge Resort Restaurant:** Eat indoors or outside at this a la carte restaurant serving up dishes such as slow-cooked pork belly, porterhouse steak with cabernet jus, or roast vegetable salad drizzled in hazelnut oil and sticky balsamic. 22 Porter St, Kalbarri; (08) 9937 0000; kalbarriedge.com.au.

BEST SLEEPS

- **Kalbarri Edge Resort:** This popular resort has studios, one-bedroom and two-bedroom apartments and is just a 100m walk from the township of Kalbarri and the Murchison River where it flows into the ocean. 22 Porter St, Kalbarri; (08) 9937 0000; kalbarriedge.com.au.
- **Kalbarri Gecko Lodge:** Aimed at couples and singles looking for a little peace and privacy, this luxury B&B is just moments away from Blue Holes Beach, renowned for its exceptional snorkelling. 9 Glass St, Kalbarri; (08) 9937 1900; geckolodgekalbarri.com.au.

WHILE YOU'RE HERE

- **Kalbarri Skywalk:** Reaching out 17m and 25m beyond the gorge rim, the two cantilevered lookouts at Kalbarri Skywalk hover 100m above Murchison River gorge in an impressive feat of engineering that delivers some epic and expansive views. Interpretive signage and artwork informs visitors about Nanda culture, as well as the park's fauna, geology and fossils. (08) 9937 1140; parks.dpaw.wa.gov.au/site/kalbarri-skywalk.
- **Hutt Lagoon (Pink Lake):** Coloured by algae, this salt lake is seriously pink and an Instagrammer's dream. If you've packed a drone, you'll be able to capture the surreal contrast between the lake (at times, hot pink or even red) and the cobalt Indian Ocean adjacent. Bright sunny days will show it at its best. Head to Pink Lake Lookout on Port Gregory Dr, a 35min drive south of Kalbarri.
- **Wagoe Beach Quad Bike Tours:** Riding down Wagoe Beach and across the rolling sand dunes that overlook the Indian Ocean makes for an exhilarating adventure. You might even spot some dolphins offshore. (08) 9936 6060; kalbarriquad.com.
- **Keep walking:** There are a dozen trails in Kalbarri National Park, from 20min to a few hours (or even a four-day river gorge hike, if your skills are aligned with Bear Grylls) and, with the park stretching to the Indian Ocean, the terrain is diverse. The 3hr Bigurda Coastal Trail is a popular option. Download the Kalbarri National Park Visitor Guide; parks.dpaw.wa.gov.au/park/kalbarri.

A day walk with endless coastal views and impressive rock formations as you traverse the ridgeline of the Flinders Peninsula.

Bald Head

This walk is on <u>Minang Country</u>.

WHY IT'S SPECIAL

Many would argue this is one of WA's best one-day walks and it's hard to disagree. Around 1160 million years ago the tectonic plates of Australia and Antarctica collided, causing friction enough to melt the Earth's crust which oozed upwards and cooled into the masses of granite so characteristic of Torndirrup National Park.

Trailing atop the spine of the Flinders Peninsula, this walk flaunts near-constant 360-degree views of King George Sound on one side and the Southern Ocean on the other, while en route to the domed granite headland of Bald Head. The peninsula is equally pounded by frothing seas and hugged by turquoise bays of ridiculous clarity, and its high points make ideal vantage points for spotting migrating whales (May to Oct). Boulder gardens, weathered limestone outcrops and pockets of stunted trees sprinkled with wildflowers means there's something cool at every turn.

WALK IT

Even if you decide not to go all the way to Bald Head, just venturing out for the 30min return walk from the carpark at the end of Bald Head Rd to Isthmus Hill delivers some super impressive views. Push on as far as you feel but whatever you do, resist the urge to deviate off track to return via the beaches as you'll only be thwarted by hidden hazards.

This is a super exposed walk and at times the trail goes over flanks of rock that slip away steeply to the ocean. In strong or gusty winds you'll be really shoved around which is pretty uncomfortable, if not unsafe, so avoid heading out in such conditions. You'll be a sitting duck for the sun too so adequate sun protection is a must.

 Trail talk

- Distance: 14km
- Time: 5-8hr
- Rating: Hard
- Technicality: A mix of compacted limestone and sand trails, boardwalk and sloping granite slabs.
- Puff factor: Make sure you're fit and your battery is fully charged. There are some steep climbs and the terrain can be tiring.
- Watch out for: Be careful around cliff edges. Rocks can be slippery. Watch out for snakes.

 When to go

Sunny days bring out spectacular colours. It's exposed so be prepared, and also avoid hot or windy days and wet conditions when the granite is treacherous. Wildflowers bloom in late winter and spring.

 Resources

Go online to parks.dpaw.wa.gov.au and trailswa.com.au for more information.

Opposite top Searching for whales that pass May to Oct *Opposite bottom* Ocean views are a constant

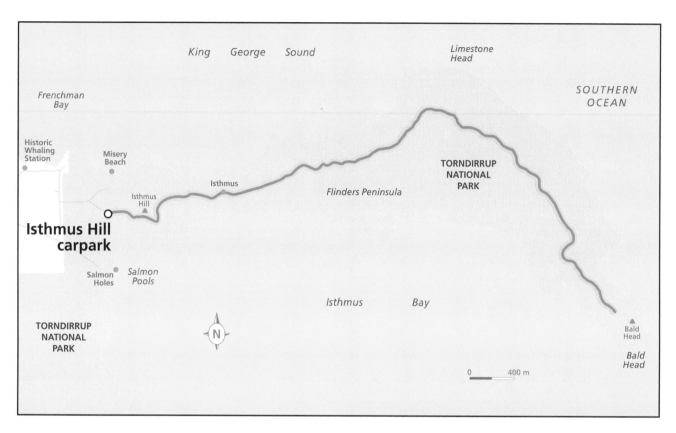

⊙ **LOCAL SNAPSHOT**

The Albany/Kinjarling area has been the land of the Menang Noongar People for over 18,000 years. When Major Edmund Lockyer arrived in 1826 aboard the convict ship *Brig Amity*, Albany became the first colonial settlement on Australia's west coast. With such a large and safe harbour in King George Sound, Albany became an important port for ships from Europe and Australia's eastern shores, as well as a place of strategic military defence. Opportunities for farming and mining were minimal, so whaling became the industry of choice. Albany's history is evident in the dozens of heritage buildings, the whaling station at Discovery Bay, and the replica of the *Brig Amity* on the waterfront. In 2016, the Menang People worked with the British Museum for a temporary return of the full collection of Menang objects from the museum. In 2020, the local council announced a dual-name initiative to have 'Kinjarling' displayed with 'Albany' throughout the town.

Top Colourful flowers along the trail *Opposite* Isthumus Hill and the Flinders Peninsula

ITINERARY

The Flinders Peninsula looks like a dolphin leaping off the end of the Torndirrup Peninsula and the walk begins at its narrow tail. It's a dolphin with kick though. Beginning a hike with a decent climb is no easy way to start but at least it sets the tone for what's to come. Isthmus Hill's granite peak is barely 800m into the trail, but from here walkers are rewarded with the first of many views, stretching back towards Albany and over the dazzling white sand and turquoise waters of Salmon Holes, a popular beach and fishing spot. Really whetting the appetite though is the spectacular view east, down the entire length of the peninsula to come.

Bald Head's granite dome was once an island but when sand collected to form massive sand dunes, later compacting and cementing into limestone, it became joined to the mainland and a peninsula was born. The track descends to cross the isthmus, at its narrowest barely 300m across, before climbing again to a path that undulates at times over 200m above sea level. Such height and unhindered views make for a stunning walk on a trail that drapes like a piece of string across the peninsula's emerald back, giving the sense of walking out into the ocean. In fine weather the near constant 360-degree panoramas are utterly captivating.

The peninsula's flanks fall – sometimes steeply – to the water, calm and turquoise on the northern side and a darker cobalt blue frothing with waves on the Southern Ocean side. Looking back, Isthmus Hill looks like a giant limpet with smooth granite slopes sliding into the water.

Much of the greenery out here is low heath but the track does slip in and out of thickets of banksia and stunted eucalpyt, providing a change of pace and a chance to soak up a myriad variety of wildflowers and orchids. Where the route hugs the northern edge of the peninsula, the enormous blue expanse of King George Sound dominates the view stretching all the way to Albany and Gull Rock National Park on the far side. At Limestone Head, walkers meander through jagged limestone outcrops, before continuing on across a swathe of sand, slabs of granite tinted orange-pink and then an extensive boulder garden.

The last stretch is deceptively long and tiring, descending steeply on sandy tracks, only to climb once more to finally crest the smooth granite of Bald Head. A stone cairn marks the end of the line but getting here is only halfway. Walkers must retrace their steps and things look totally different heading in the other direction but it's equally spectacular.

BEST EATS

- **The Store on Frederick:** Sit at a table or on the couch at this comfy vintage cafe. Ideal for brekkie, lunch or cream tea. 55 Frederick St, Albany; (08) 9841 2635.
- **Majuba Bistro:** You'll get chic décor and fancy cuisine, ranging from French bouillabaisse to homemade pasta at this wine bar and restaurant. One of Albany's best. 132 York St, Albany; (08) 9841 1852.

BEST SLEEPS

- **Emu Point Motel & Apartments:** Located at peaceful Emu Point, this place is ideally located for swimming at Middleton Bay or wandering the local bike trails and footpaths. Cnr Medcalf and Mermaid Ave, Emu Point, Albany; (08) 9844 1001; emupointmotel.com.au.
- **Spencer Suites Albany:** Oozing with character, these spacious and modern suites have kitchenettes and are located in a circa-1890 heritage building, just a few streets back from the action. 69 Spencer St, Albany; 0402 419 039; spencersuitesalbany.com.au.

WHILE YOU'RE HERE

- **The Gap & Natural Bridge:** Also in Torndirrup National Park are these spectacular rock formations pounded by the Southern Ocean and accessible via a short walk from the carpark at the end of The Gap Road. The highlight is peering over the crashing sea from a cantilevered viewing platform while waves surge between 40m high cliffs. parks.dpaw.wa.gov.au/site/gap-natural-bridge.
- **Historic Whaling Station:** Okay, it's a bit gruesome but this whale processing factory, restored whale chasing ship and assortment of whale skeletons, are a fascinating insight into Albany's whaling industry, which operated from 1800 until 1978. 81 Whaling Station Rd, Torndirrup; (08) 9844 4021; discoverybay.com.au.

The peninsula's granite formations flow directly into the ocean

Climb the highest mountain in the state's south in the spectacular Stirling Range.

Bluff Knoll

This walk is on <u>Ganeang</u>, <u>Goreng</u> and <u>Minang Country</u>.

WHY IT'S SPECIAL

The state's second highest peak rises from a rocky range that stretches for over 65km and it's an imposing vision. Like the prow of a ship, Bluff Knoll gazes out over the surrounding Stirling Range and lowlands.

The Stirling Range has its origins in the layers of sediment deposited by a shallow sea that existed here some 2000 million years ago (ripple marks are occasionally visible in the rock). Continents collided and the land buckled, tilted and eroded to leave a range with impressive sheer cliffs on one side and sliding gently into the lowlands on the other.

From its forested lowlands, dotted with grass trees and goannas, to its rocky, lichen-encrusted peak at 1095m, this route takes walkers through a range of habitats with ever increasing views that provide ample excuse to pause for a breather. Bluff Knoll is one of the few places in WA to get snow – usually a few times a year – and wildflower displays in spring are spectacular.

WALK IT

This is one of those walks that can be a vastly different experience each time you do it. On some days, blue skies and carpets of wildflowers can make it feel like a Sunday picnic, but it can just as easily turn into an alpine-esque battle against wind and hail. Some hikers like to get up there for sunrise, when you might be lucky enough to see banks of cloud swirling around the summit while the sun's golden orb rises in the sky.

These mountains are cloud catchers and near the summit the rocky trail is often loosely defined, requiring extra care to stay on track in low visibility. But even if you don't make it all the way to the top, there are excellent views to be had anywhere in the top half of the trail.

Trail talk
- Distance: 6km
- Time: 3-4hr
- Rating: Moderate-hard.
- Technicality: Mix of rocky trail, well-defined track and steps.
- Puff factor: It's uphill all the way to the summit (around 650m in elevation), so expect to give your lungs and legs a good workout.
- Watch out for: The track is exposed and weather changes can be rapid and unpredictable at any time of year, so pack a jacket and something warm just in case.

When to go
It's doable year-round but during Oct-Dec the mountain is carpeted in wildflowers. Avoid walking on high fire danger days.

Resources
Download the Stirling Range National Park Visitor Guide from parks.dpaw.wa.gov.au/park/stirling-range.

Opposite Spot the goanna on the trail to Bluff Knoll

⊙ LOCAL SNAPSHOT

The south-west corner of WA has been recognised internationally as one of the world's top 35 hotspots for biodiversity, and around 80 of the 1500 species of flowering plants in Stirling Range National Park are found nowhere else on Earth. Multiple factors are believed to have contributed to the region's diversity, beginning with the fact that there is an unusually high number of bird and mammal pollinators that distribute pollen further and more indiscriminately than insect pollinators. In addition, this corner of the state is remote and the land outrageously old - dated at around 2000 million years. With minimal outside interference and little volcanic or glacial activity, there's not been much to disrupt evolutionary processes here.

Bottom Views of the Stirling Range increase with ascent
Opposite Cloud hanging over the summit

ITINERARY

There's plenty of time for the anticipation to build before setting foot on this trail. For a good half-hour on the drive in, the mountain range grows in size and awe-factor until I'm standing at Eastern Lookout at the foot of Bluff Knoll, wide-eyed and salivating at the prospect ahead.

It starts as a sealed path from the carpark at Eastern Lookout, soon turning into an ascent of honey-coloured rocky track, all the while overlooked by the Bluff whose sheer-edged, grey summit rests like a crown on top of rippling folds of green. Traditional Owners call Bluff Knoll 'Bular Mial', meaning 'many eyes' and I can feel them on me as I climb. For Traditional Owners, the Stirling Ranges represent a giant old Noongar man left lying on his back after a bloody battle between two tribes, his body – the mountains – now separating the two tribal grounds.

It's slightly intimidating to think that a track a mere 3km each way can take up to 4hr to complete. Picking a slow and steady pace that can be sustained over the distance is wise. Trail markers flag your progress as each kilometre passes.

Devastating bushfires swept through here in the summer of 2019/2020, but regrowth is happening. Stunted eucalypt mingle with grasstrees and wildflowers, and the track switches between rough ladders of rocks and formed steps. At one point I pause to allow a metre-long goanna swagger slowly across my path.

As height is gained, spectacular views increase, spreading down the jagged band of mountains that form the range, lapped at their base by velvety green folds. Trees give way to low scrub hardy enough to survive the exposure of altitude, and the path becomes a lick of pale crushed rock.

I climb a gap through the cliffs, then emerge above the trees where the unhindered mountain views are seriously impressive. I walk a little further to reach a small rock ledge perched on Bluff Knoll's sheer northern rim that marks the summit lookout. There's a real sense of height as the ground falls away steeply, overlooking the carpark and spaghetti thin line of trail 650m below. The Traditional Owners call the Stirling Ranges 'Koi Kyenunu-ruff', meaning 'mist rolling around the mountains', and at Bluff Knoll's summit the ranges live up to their name. Mist and clouds descend over me like a white veil and though I started the walk in a T-shirt, I now need the storm hood of my jacket to keep the icy wind at bay.

The non-stop descent is easy on the lungs but relentless on the quads. As I retrace my steps I look back and see Bluff Knoll wearing a 'hat' of fluffy white cloud, while blue skies and a warm afternoon sun bathe me from overhead. Such is the Stirling Range.

Descending near the summit

BEST EATS

- **Six Degrees:** You'll get top-shelf pub food and a cool vibe at this restaurant, bar and laneway beer garden. With views looking out over Princess Royal Harbour, it's an Albany favourite. 7 Stirling Terrace, Albany; (08) 9841 1466; albanymotelwa.com.au.
- **Gourmandise & Co:** Step into a little piece of France at this bakery-cafe producing everything from pastries, gateaux and quiche to more substantial fare. The wood-fired oven adds another dimension. 56 Stirling Terrace, Albany; (08) 9847 4005; gourmandiseandco.com.au.

BEST SLEEPS

- **Best Western Albany:** You'll find stylish renovated rooms at this motel and apartment complex in the heart of Albany and some rooms have sea views. It's just a short walk to bars, restaurants and the waterfront. 41 Frederick St, Albany; (08) 9842 7670; albanybestwestern.com.au.
- **Beach House at Bayside:** Located just behind the dunes at Middleton Bay, this boutique B&B hotel is famous for its warm welcomes and bountiful breakfasts. Ideal for quick access to Albany's main beach. 33 Barry Ct, Collingwood Park, Albany; (08) 9844 8844; thebeachhouseatbayside.com.au.

WHILE YOU'RE HERE

- **Keep exploring:** Once you witness the beauty of the Stirling Range, you'll be in no rush to leave. Five other hikes (each about 3hr long) lead up other spectacular peaks in the range, plus there are a handful of lookouts and scenic drives that show off Stirling's craggy cliffs, as well as in the adjacent Porongurup Range. Download the Stirling Range National Park Visitor Guide from parks.dpaw.wa.gov.au/park/stirling-range.
- **National ANZAC Centre:** In 1914, 30,000 ANZACs set sail from Albany to join World War I. At this award-winning war museum overlooking the sea, you are given the 'identity' of one of them to follow their journey - and it's a powerful experience. 67 Forts Rd, Mount Clarence, Albany; (08) 6820 3500; nationalanzaccentre.com.au.

Expansive cliff-tops, perfect beaches and a chance of whales and wildflowers make this a delightful coastal hike.

Cape to Cape Track

This walk is on <u>Wardandi Country</u>.

WHY IT'S SPECIAL

Bookended by two lighthouses – Cape Naturaliste in the north and Cape Leeuwin in the south – this glorious coastal route trails along beaches and cliff-tops, with just a dash of forest thrown in. It follows the ancient Leeuwin-Naturaliste Ridge whose layers of granite and limestone have weathered into some pretty impressive rock formations.

Nowhere does beaches better than Western Australia and this walk involves hours of either gazing at its famously baby blue water and white sand or setting foot on it, so definitely factor in swimming time. The fact that you can plan your hike to include a few comfy nights in hotels and indulge in the odd cafe meal is a decadent bonus. It all makes for a spectacular hike in the Margaret River region.

WALK IT

With dozens of access points, this track really lends itself to section hiking or day hikes. Unfortunately the section between Boranup Beach and Redgate Beach was hit by bushfires in December 2021 but regrowth is slowly regenerating.

While there are free national park campsites and paid camping en route, you can also nab yourself a hotel bed or cabin along the way. You can pretty much walk to accommodation at Yallingup, Prevelly, Gracetown and Hamelin Bay, but there are dozens more places to stay in the Margaret River region that will collect you from the trail and whisk you somewhere nice for the night. All these options mean that, unlike most multi-day hikes, there is not one standard itinerary, so study the map and choose your own adventure.

Southbound or northbound? You can hike either direction but note that the sun will be in your face when travelling north. If wind is your nemesis, you'll be more likely to have it at your back heading northbound in summer or southbound in winter. Most people seem to head 'SOBO' (southbound) but this itinerary describes the walk heading north (as I did it), from Cape Leeuwin to Cape Naturaliste.

 Trail talk

- Distance: 136km
- Time: 6-8 days
- Rating: Moderate-hard
- Technicality: Generally well-graded tracks with long stretches of sand.
- Puff factor: There are few major climbs, but long beach walks in soft sand can be exhausting.
- Watch out for: The track is very exposed so you'll cop whatever the elements throw at you - whether it's rain, storms or relentless sun. Carry a fly head-net, keep an eye out for snakes and take special care when crossing the Margaret River Mouth or use the land detour instead.

 When to go

It's doable anytime, though summer can be sizzling hot. Wildflowers are spectacular in spring. Whale season is Sep-Nov.

 Resources

Visit capetocapetrack.com.au for planning details. *The Cape to Cape Track Guidebook* by Jane Scott and Ray Forma is really helpful and includes detailed directions, small maps, and notes on flora and fauna, as well as plenty of short walk suggestions. The fold-out Cape to Cape topographic map is also useful.

Opposite top **Wilyabrup Cliffs**
Opposite bottom **Cape Clairault**

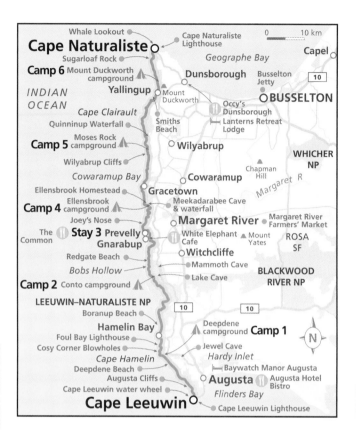

LOCAL SNAPSHOT

The Margaret River region has got a lot going for it. Surfers discovered it back in the 1960s (there are around 75 surf breaks) and now, every May, the world's best come here for a bout of the World Surf League Championship Tour. Equally renowned is its reputation as a hotbed of gastronomy and there are more than 200 wineries and cellar doors in the region, dozens of craft breweries and award-winning eateries, plus it's the heartland of Australia's truffle industry. If you visit the Margaret River Farmers' Market, held every Sat, you'll get a pure foodie extravaganza bursting with fresh local produce and artisan goods, such as fresh bread, pasta, homemade nougat, olive oil and cheese.

Top Blue tongue lizard *Opposite* Sugarloaf Rock

ITINERARY

DAY 1

Cape Leeuwin to Deepdene campground, 18km, 6hr

Most people walk north to south on this track, but since I was already down south I head out from the trail's southern terminus, the country's tallest mainland lighthouse, Cape Leeuwin (39m tall and 56m above sea level), which was built in 1896. A rock hop across coastal rock platforms soon takes me to an 1895 wooden water wheel at Quarry Bay, once used to supply spring water to the lighthouse but now frozen forever in calcified lime.

The track pulls away to climb above the Augusta Cliffs, diving through coastal heath, peppermint and a smattering of spring wildflowers, including the south-west's famous orchids, later to descend to a rugged coastline. Long stretches of rocks are as porous and textured as honeycomb, and I spot a fat python coiled like rope, incongruously framed by pink pig face flowers and the blue ocean.

Around half of the day's route is spent on the remote and unsullied sands of Deepdene Beach before retreating to camp for the night, tucked in forest behind the dunes.

DAY 2
Deepdene campground to Conto campground, 32km, 8–10hr

I leave early, knowing I've a big day ahead, but blue skies and still air lure me into lingering at Cape Hamelin where brown kelp swirls lazily in dark blue bays. At the Cosy Corner Blowholes rock platform, chemical weathering in the limestone has created jagged peaks and holes several metres deep through to the sea below. In more lively conditions, water charges through the solution tubes sending water erupting like geysers, but on my shift it sloshes and gurgles beneath the rock like a subterranean beast.

Sandy tracks head inland past a lighthouse and then down to Hamelin Bay and its beachfront caravan park – popular with fishermen and families who come to snorkel with friendly stingrays – but I push on for 6.5km along the stunning Boranup Beach. Its pale aqua water is lighter than the blue sky but the soft white sand is slow going and to say it's blindingly bright is an understatement. Walkers heading north cop the sun head-on and it makes temperatures feel considerably warmer. A welcome reprieve from the heat comes as the trail veers inland past grass trees and into towering karri forest where I spot an emu peeking out at me from behind a tree. Beautiful peppermint woodland surrounds Conto camp, but with 116 sites for car campers it's not the most peaceful night.

DAY 3
Conto campground to Prevelly, 18km, 8hr

What was one of the trail's most spectacular sections was sadly hit by bushfire in December 2021. During my visit, the 100m high cliffs were carpeted in coastal heath and wildflowers, however regrowth here may take some time. In any event, you'll still enjoy peering over arcs of white sand and the sapphire Indian Ocean, and from the high vantage point I managed to spot a pod of 20 odd dolphins splashing in circles on the hunt.

A steep descent down craggy white limestone cliffs passes Bobs Hollow, an open cave, and then it's on to Redgate Beach. Surfers and sunbathers flock to these sheltered waters and gentle waves but I foolishly haven't scheduled in enough time to join them. I stagger instead another 2km through soft sand and a few more through dunes alongside Boodjidup Brook which flows tannin brown out to sea. Sun bounces off the sand and my face feels close to exploding with heat so I make

an unscheduled early stop and splash out on a motel room in Prevelly plus dinner at The Common, a cool local's bistro. It's definitely a good move.

DAY 4
Prevelly to Ellensbrook campground, 12km, 4hr

The town of Margaret River is 9km inland but its famously good food spills all the way to the coast, and breakfast at the southern end of Gnarabup Beach's White Elephant Cafe (see p. 187) gets me stoked for the day. It's 1km west from the trail but a convenient and stunning diversion after my overnight in Prevelly.

I merge back onto the trail and the first glimpse of the actual Margaret River comes from a string of high lookouts, an impressive sapphire snake meandering between vegetated dunes and spilling out to sea. Hikers usually wade across the river mouth, but if water levels are high there is a land detour around it. I manage the crossing getting wet only up to my knees.

After climbing over a headland, the trail reaches Joey's Nose, a beach hugely popular with surfers and accessible by 4WD, and there's about 30 vehicles parked up in the sand when I pass it. The trail climbs again to undulate gently across coastal heath accompanied by expansive ocean views until it reaches Ellensbrook camp, a shady area nestled in the trees.

DAY 5
Ellensbrook campground to Moses Rock campground, 22km, 6–7hr

It's not huge but after all the sandy trails and ocean views, the moss covered Meekadarabee Cave and waterfall (less than a kilometre north of camp) makes a nice contrast. Nearby is National Trust owned Ellensbrook Homestead, built around 1857 for the Bussell family who established a dairy and later ran the property as a home for Aboriginal children. In 1876, 24-year old Noongar man Samuel Yebble Isaacs was working for the Bussells when he spotted a steamship, carrying 54 passengers, struggling on the rocks offshore. Legend has it, he raced back to the homestead to raise the alarm and returned to the bay with 16-year-old Grace Bussell and the two of them began rescuing survivors of the *SS Georgette* from the surf. In 2021 the new locality of Yebble was established in honour of Samuel's efforts, incorporating Ellensbrook and parts of Gracetown and Burnside.

The track soon gravitates back to the coast, undulating on coastal heath that slopes gently toward the ocean. Sleepy Gracetown shelters in Cowaramup Bay, a safe spot for a dip, and there's a handy general store and takeaway with yummo homemade pies if you need to stock up.

While the southern end of the track is characterised by the Leeuwin-Naturaliste Ridge's limestone formations formed from wind-blown sand, the north of Gracetown is where its much older granite and gneiss is revealed. The track follows high rock ledges tinged with orange lichen that overlook the sea – a perfect vantage point for whale watching (June to Nov).

The day is spent going from one world-class surf break to the next and I'm regularly sharing the trail with buff men jogging with a board tucked under one arm. A steep descent of stairs to cross Biljedup Brook is overlooked by the impressive, rust orange Wilyabrup Cliffs, often draped in rock-climbers.

Moses Rock camp is perched high above the coast, perfectly situated to watch the sun sink into the Indian Ocean.

DAY 6
Moses Rock campground to Mount Duckworth campground, 24km, 9hr

About an hour in to today's walk is a short side trip through soft dunes to Quinninup Waterfall. Quininup means 'place of the Zamia Palm' and the site is of huge importance in Wadandi culture. After heavy rain there can be quite a decent flow gushing over the orange rock but today it's a couple of thin milky lines of white.

The onward cliff-top track overlooks sandy beaches and black neoprene-clad surfers that look like seals in the aqua blue. Views from Cape Clairault are some of the best I've seen in a long time. I sit on a profusion of orange rocks bubbling from the green heath, mesmerised by the contrasting colours of pink flowers, blue ocean and frothing white waves. It's another perfect vantage point for whales but there aren't any so I watch the surfers instead, riding neat curling tubes. The water is so clear they cast shadows on the sandy ocean floor.

For a while the route follows a coastline seeming carved from rock. Sizeable cuttings in the pink granite lead through to the ocean, and giant boulders line sandy paths. Eventually the track spills onto Smiths Beach, and Supertubes surf break, towards the little town of Yallingup.

Mount Duckworth camp is a few kilometres further north, tucked in the trees above the cliffs.

DAY 7
Mount Duckworth campground to Cape Naturaliste, 10km, 4hr

Razor-sharp limestone formations line the track as it winds along jagged cliffs falling steeply to the water. Perched on the edge of the ocean, I cop hot sun and wind but, for the first time all week, there are darkly bruised clouds and they mean business. By the time I reach Sugarloaf Rock, a granite island rising from the water like a gigantic fin, great belts of rain are sweeping across the ocean. Between Sept and Feb, red-tailed tropicbirds nest here after spending months at sea.

The spectacular sea views continue as I walk the final kilometres and though thunder rumbles and thick daggers of lightning pierce the water, I'm lucky that the storm stays offshore. It's one thing to be fried by the sun, quite another to be fried by other means. Guided tours of Cape Naturaliste Lighthouse (built in 1903) depart every half hour and take in commanding ocean views from its top balcony, as well as the history and present day functions of this working lighthouse. My arrival here heralds the end of my Cape to Cape journey, but I'm reluctant to end my connection with these capes and keep walking on the 2.4km return Whale Lookout trail. It takes me to a cliff-top overlooking Geographe Bay, a resting spot for humpback, southern right and even blue whales during their southern migration, and though I don't see any it feels the perfect place to wrap up an epic week of hiking.

Opposite Cliff top walking between Conto and Prevelly

Dazzling Boranup Beach

BEST EATS

- **Augusta Hotel Bistro:** Come here for pub food classics and primo views overlooking Hardy Inlet, where the Blackwood River flows out to the ocean. 53 Blackwood Ave, Augusta; (08) 9758 1944; augustahotel.com.au.
- **The Common:** Mingle with the local crowd at this cool bar and bistro dishing up good vibes and yummo food. 1 Resort Pl, Margaret River; (08) 9757 1586; thecommonbistro.com.au.
- **White Elephant Café:** Sit indoors or at the plentiful outdoor tables at this cafe situated virtually on the beach. It's barefoot dining with great food and even better views. Gnarabup Rd, Gnarabup; (08) 9757 1990; whiteelephantcafe.com.au.
- **Occy's Dunsborough:** Sit outside with the crowd and enjoy a craft brew or cocktail or tuck into wood-fired pizza, burgers and ribs. 34 Dunn Bay Rd, Dunsborough; (08) 9756 7777.

BEST SLEEPS

- **Baywatch Manor Augusta:** Named for its ocean views, rather than a fondness for red swimsuits, Baywatch Manor has everything from multi-bed dorms with a communal kitchen to queen rooms with private bathroom, and it's just a 10min drive from the southern trailhead. 9 Heppingstone View, Augusta; (08) 9758 1290; baywatchmanor.com.au.
- **Lanterns Retreat Lodge:** This luxury B&B is set in lovely gardens and is within easy walking distance to town and the beach. 16 Newberry Rd, Dunsborough; (08) 9756 7542; lanternsretreat.com.au.

WHILE YOU'RE HERE

- **Go underground:** There are over 100 limestone caves beneath the Leeuwin-Naturaliste Ridge and while many require a hard-hat and caving skills, anyone can marvel at the underground chambers and crystal formations of Lake Cave (complete with underground lake), Jewel Cave and Mammoth Cave. margaretriver.com.
- **Busselton Jetty:** The longest timber-piled jetty in the southern hemisphere is a destination in its own right. Walk or take a train down its 1.8km length, visit the underwater observatory, or do a dive, snorkel or undersea walk to appreciate the myriad marine life it harbours. Busselton beachfront; (08) 9754 0900; busseltonjetty.com.au.

Northern Territory

*The NT's outback trails celebrate mountains, gorges,
and an ancient and spiritual land.*

Swim beneath heavenly waterfalls and discover ancient rock art while following the Arnhem Land Escarpment.

Jatbula Trail

This walk is on <u>Jawoyn Country</u>.

WHY IT'S SPECIAL

Possibly the best thing about this walk is when you're not walking. Every campsite is situated next to a water feature so incredible that you'll relish long afternoons spent swimming under waterfalls, floating on your back in waterholes overhung with palms, or kicking back like a boss in natural spa pools.

The trail spans between Nitmiluk Gorge and Edith Falls/Leliyn, shadowing the western edge of the Arnhem Land escarpment as it shifts from dry sandstone plateau to pockets of woodland and monsoon forest, lush palms and riverine land. Of major significance is the abundance of the Jawoyn People's rock art hidden throughout. This piece of outback is only accessible on foot and, with limited numbers allowed, it's easy to slow down, forget the modern world exists and connect with the land – as the Jawoyn People have always done.

WALK IT

Only 15 lucky hikers are let loose on this trail each day – a good thing as it never feels crowded, but it does mean spaces are in hot demand. Bookings open on 1 Nov for the following season and usually sell out within a few days. Waitlists for walking this trail sometimes clear, but another option is to consider going with a guided walk company as they have their own allotments.

Campsites are au naturel. There are drop-toilets, but you'll be collecting your drinking water from rivers and waterholes, and there is no mobile coverage at all. Long stretches of this walk are exposed to the searing sun so a broad-brimmed hat is a must.

The trail is walked in one direction but transfer operators in Katherine can drop you off at Nitmiluk and collect you from Edith Falls/Leliyn when you're done.

 Trail talk

- Distance: 62km
- Time: 5 days
- Rating: Moderate
- Technicality: It's very remote so hikers should be confident and self-sufficient. Occasional sections of rocky and unformed track require care to stay on route, plus there are a few creek crossings (easy in normal conditions).
- Puff factor: With short days and reasonably flat terrain, your only puffing might be from the heat.
- Watch out for: Give freshwater crocs (i.e. the frog and fish-eating variety) their space. Salties (i.e. the human-eating variety) aren't an issue, until you descend off the escarpment at Edith Falls/Leliyn. Heed all signs and read the 'Crocodile safety: Be Crocwise' section of nt.gov.au. Take care on slippery rocks and never dive or jump into creeks and waterholes.

When to go

Hiking season is June to Sept. Outside of these times can be super hot (over 40°C), and the trail may be flooded.

Resources

Visit nt.gov.au/parks/find-a-park/nitmiluk-national-park/nitmiluk-national-park-jatbula-trail for detailed planning information, a comprehensive maps booklet, and to book trail permits and campsites. An excellent guide by Peter Eve, *The Jatbula Trail*, includes maps, detailed trail notes and info on flora and fauna. Book the ferry (7am and 9am) to cross the Katherine River at the start of the walk through Nitmiluk Tours; nitmiluktours.com.au.

Opposite Swimming is a highlight of this trail

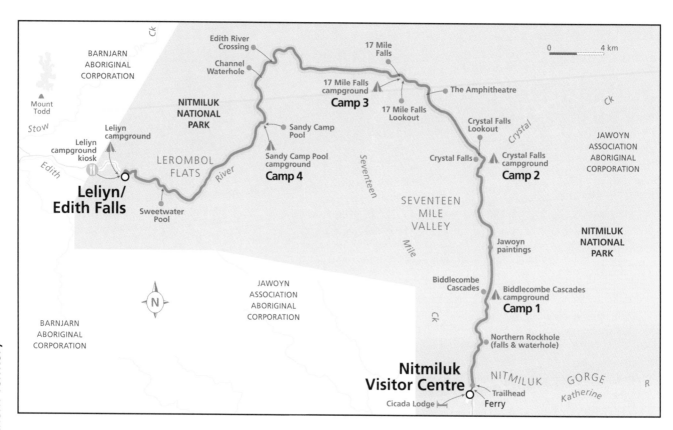

◉ LOCAL SNAPSHOT

For thousands of years the Jawoyn People have walked across this land. Peter Jatbula, a Jawoyn Traditional Owner, was instrumental in securing land rights for his people but he also wanted to share his Country and culture with others, and so in 1989 (the same year the government returned the land to the Jawoyn People), the Jatbula Trail was launched. All 292,008ha of Nitmiluk National Park are now 100 per cent Jawoyn-owned and jointly managed with NT Parks and Wildlife. Nitmiluk Tours - the park's main tourism provider - is also fully owned and operated by the Jawoyn People, a venture that seeks to provide employment, training and economic independence for its people, as well as maintaining the crucial connection to heritage.

Right Gazing out from the escarpment *Opposite* Cooling off in Biddlecombe Cascades

ITINERARY

DAY 1
Nitmiluk Gorge to Biddlecombe Cascades campground, 8.3km, 3hr

Over 250,000 visitors flock annually to Nitmiluk Gorge – to cruise up the Katherine River and witness the gorge's sheer orange walls – but once I'm dropped off by ferry at the trailhead on the river's far side, I'm suddenly in another far more remote world.

I'm walking with a group – five hikers plus a guide – and we take our lead from Seventeen Mile Creek, a major waterway that has branched off the Katherine to carve a vast valley by the same name. The rocky earth and golden grass are parched but a smattering of eucalypts adds a touch of green.

The biggest draw of the first short day is Biddlecombe Falls. It's usually flowing early season (after the Wet) but on my shift the 60m cliff-face is dry, though the decent-sized pool at its base makes a good spot for a dip.

Further on, camp at Biddlecombe Cascades is a short walk from the cascades themselves where frothy water rushes over a series of rock shelves to an inviting base pool. The water temperature is a perfect 25°C and so clean that we can drink it while swimming. It's tempting to scramble all over the playground but it's worth noting a saying around these parts: 'rocks kill more than crocs'.

It's late June and 32°C during the day but nights in the desert are cold. Though I swelter in a T-shirt at 8pm, by midnight the air chills to around 10°C and my neighbours, sleeping without a flysheet on their tent, are freezing, despite wearing thermals.

DAY 2
Biddlecombe Cascades campground to Crystal Falls campground, 11km, 5hr

The 'alarm clock' is the call of the honeyeater – 'not the kookaburra', says our guide. 'He's about half an hour too early.' Arising with the birds is a good move if we want to avoid the worst of the day's heat.

At first glance, the land seems as dry as a dog biscuit but it's more complex than that. Flooding wet season rains filter through Precambrian sandstone, topping up the Tindall Limestone Aquifer and filling springs, creeks and ultimately the mighty Katherine River. Our day alternates between dry savannah marked by spear grass, spinifex, and dozens of termite mounds rising from the ground like pointed grey spears, to lush pandanus-filled gullies and swampy areas that call for a tightrope walk of strategically placed tree branches.

Blue triangles flag the route but on long stretches of rock the way is less obvious. Likewise, finding the Jawoyn People's paintings hiding in an outcrop of sunburned orange rock and Livistona palms where three panels feature human-like figures.

Under the shade of a gnarled and ghostly-pale gum tree, we down packs and venture a few hundred metres off trail to the left, leading us to a rocky outcrop with vast panoramic views out west over Seventeen Mile Valley. The final leg of today's walk reveals a white rock-art site set in a cliff-face.

We reach camp at Crystal Falls in time for lunch, leaving all afternoon free to enjoy this heavenly spot. Tent sites are scattered amongst the trees next to a deep and dark swimming hole in Crystal Creek, fringed in lilac water lilies. Freshwater crocodiles inhabit these parts and though I'm assured they're no danger to humans, it's hard not to let the imagination run wild, and every time the trailing roots of a water lily brush my ankles I stifle a little squawk of alarm. More relaxing is lazing on the rocks with the water monitors in between swims.

DAY 3
Crystal Falls campground to 17 Mile Falls campground, 10km, 5hr

There's mist rising off Crystal Creek when we rock hop across it in the early morning. An impressive lookout peers over Crystal Falls as it pours between walls of rock on its way to lower ground, but the track stays high across a grassy plain scattered with eucalypt. It's hot and dry but suddenly the land falls away as though sliced by a giant cookie cutter, and we descend into a cool oasis of monsoon forest and jigging butterflies. The Amphitheatre's walls are sheer, dripping with ferns and pocked with caves where pythons live, but most impressive are the galleries of Jawoyn paintings, over 2000 years old. One stretches for about 20m and features emus, kangaroos, crocodiles, catfish, and other designs.

Our camp for tonight at 17 Mile Falls is visible from a lookout on the edge of the escarpment long before reaching it. Situated at the top of the falls, this campsite is one of the best, and views

from the waterfall's orange rocky heights to the ink-dark pool fringed in palms 30m below are utterly spectacular.

Hiking is officially finished by lunchtime today, but I walk kilometres more barefoot to explore upstream, clambering over rocks and swimming from pool to pool. It's not until dark that we spot on the far shore the red eyes of a freshwater croc, reflected in a torch beam.

DAY 4
17 Mile Falls campground to Sandy Camp Pool campground, 16.8km, 6hr

It's a decent rocky scramble to traverse the head of the falls. We leave in the cool twilight before dawn and when the sun peeks over the horizon, golden light and long shadows wash across grassland peppered with rust-coloured termite mounds.

The day is considerably more lush in its scenery than others – a succession of creeks, waterholes and marshes that are a magnet for birds, from red-tailed black cockatoos to flocks of varied lorikeets and the rare Gouldian finch.

Interspersed with the damp is the dry, in flat, open woodland, dotted with pandanus or broad rocky slabs, such as at Channel Waterhole. Around the crossing of Edith River, waterholes are thick with water lilies and crowded by grevilleas and peeling paperbarks.

Sandy Camp is another scene of perfection, a sandy beach shaded by melaleucas on the edge of a large waterhole. My tent is almost an 'overwater bungalow', less than a metre from deep water almost level with the earth. Hot property here is the round natural spa bath set in shallow cascades.

Unsurprisingly, with no light pollution, stars on the Jatbula are insane at night and at Sandy Pool they glitter magically in its millpond calm. In the midnight hours, the howl of a dingo drifts into my dreams.

DAY 5
Sandy Camp Pool campground via Sweetwater Pool to Leliyn/ Edith Falls, 15km, 5hr

Sandy trails leave behind the ghostly white melaleucas of camp for open woodland dotted with pandanus. Marshy grassland draws the birds in again and the air rings with their songs.

I walk alone for a while across a grassy plain known as Lerombol Flats, dotted with what appear to be fresh mounds of buffalo poo, and although wallaroos are known to graze here, all I can think about is what my strategy is should I happen to come face to face with one of the tank-like horned beasts (answer: stay still and let them pass).

The Edith River swells at Sweetwater Pool, inky blue and with a smattering of low burnt-orange rocks scattered in the water like tiny islands. The flat shelves that cascade towards the water's edge are ideal for lazing about on, and there's a campsite here too, but we skirt around the ledges and push on for the final leg across red dirt and a descent off the escarpment.

Leliyn/Edith Falls marks the end of the trail. It's flanked by rocky walls and pours into a huge swimming hole but it's worth noting this is saltwater crocodile territory (they're not known to climb up to the escarpment). Although the chances of one slipping past the annual season-start trappings is extremely slim, the 'low risk crocodile area' sign can be off-putting. I make it a quick one and then head for a celebratory burger at the Leliyn campground kiosk.

After hiking a spectacular 62km, it seems only fitting to treat myself to a bit of luxury on a sunset dinner cruise up Nitmiluk/ Katherine Gorge. I sit on deck as the boat glides quietly between red rock walls and indulge in a three-course meal with sparkling wine. It's another view of Nitmiluk National Park and there could be no better way to finish.

Bottom Red earth outback trails *Opposite* Water lillies at Crystal Creek

Swimming above 17 Mile Falls

BEST EATS

- **Leliyn Campground Kiosk:** Walk straight off the trail and sit down at this outdoor cafe, where you can fill up on homemade pies, burgers and milkshakes. Leliyn Campground; (08) 8972 2884.
- **Pop Rocket Cafe:** It's an idyllic setting under the trees at this al fresco cafe next to the Katherine hot springs. Probably the best food in town for breakfast, lunch, and a coffee fix. Riverbank Dr, Katherine Hot Springs, Katherine; 0427 348 915.

BEST SLEEPS

- **Cicada Lodge:** Located right in Nitmiluk National Park, this luxury lodge is just a minute's walk from the ferry departure point to the Jatbula trailhead, and perfectly situated if you want to spend a day or two exploring Nitmiluk Gorge before hitting the trail. Gorge Rd, Nitmiluk National Park; 1300 146 743; nitmiluktours.com.au.
- **Beagle Motor Inn:** Slap bang in the middle of Katherine town and with the popular Stormy's Bar and Bistro onsite, this clean and comfy place should tick most of your boxes. 2 Fourth St, Katherine; (08) 8972 3998; beaglemotorinn.com.au.

WHILE YOU'RE HERE

- **Katherine Hot Springs:** Soak in a string of natural thermal pools (25-30°C), overhung with greenery on the edge of Katherine township. Riverbank Dr, Katherine.
- **Top Didj:** Spending a few hours with award-winning Aboriginal guide Manuel Pamkal is a profound opportunity to learn about culture from someone who grew up with traditional ways. Learn how to make fire, throw a spear and paint Rarrk (cross hatch) designs. The Top Didj Cultural Experience is available May to Oct. There's also an art gallery onsite. 363 Gorge Rd, Lansdowne, Katherine; 0414 888 786; topdidj.com.
- **Nitmiluk Gorge:** Glide between the towering orange walls of Nitmiluk Gorge (there are 13 separate gorges within it) on a 2hr cruise, sunset dinner cruise, or by canoe. Nitmiluk Tours, Nitmiluk Gorge; 1300 146 743; nitmiluktours.com.au.

Explore the sheer orange walls, sandstone domes and hidden oasis of an outback canyon.

Kings Canyon Rim Walk

This walk is on <u>Luritja Country</u>.

WHY IT'S SPECIAL

Kings Canyon/Watarrka in Watarrka National Park is an enormous v-shaped incision in a sandstone plateau, part of the George Gill Range which was laid down over 400 million years ago. Wind and water have carved sheer orange cliffs 30m high, beehive-shaped sandstone domes and a lush Garden of Eden filled with rare cycads and a waterhole, while ghost gums sprout from a valley floor 100–150m lower.

This circuit walk leads hikers on a rocky adventure up to the plateau, around the rim of the canyon via numerous lookouts, and back down to the valley floor. If you happen to be in the area after heavy rain, when water spills over the cliffs, you can add the spectacular Kestrel Falls to the list.

WALK IT

This is an exposed walk and heat exhaustion is not cool, so wear sun protection and carry plenty of water. They don't close the track in summer, when temperatures easily reach into the high 30s°C or even into the 40s, but hikers are required to start walking before 9am. A better idea is to time your arrival on the plateau with sunrise when the early light sets the red walls alight. Plus, you're more likely to spot wildlife in the early hours.

The track is walked clockwise, starting from Kings Canyon carpark. If you don't fancy climbing up to the plateau, an easier option is the 1hr Kings Creek Walk, following the valley floor.

Bring a face net to keep the flies at bay if you have one – they can be a bit annoying.

 Trail talk
- Distance: 6km loop
- Time: 3-4hr
- Rating: Moderate
- Technicality: Mix of trail, stairs and rock hopping.
- Puff factor: The first 500 steps to the plateau is the hardest bit, with a few more steps in and out of the Garden of Eden.
- Watch out for: Keep well clear of cliff-edges and note they're prone to being unstable. It's exposed so don't underestimate the heat, and make sure you carry plenty of water.

 When to go
May to Sept is coolest. On days forecast to be 36°C or above, walkers are required to start before 9am.

Resources
Download the Kings Canyon Walking Tracks guide from nt.gov.au.

Opposite Climbing the stairs up Kings Canyon

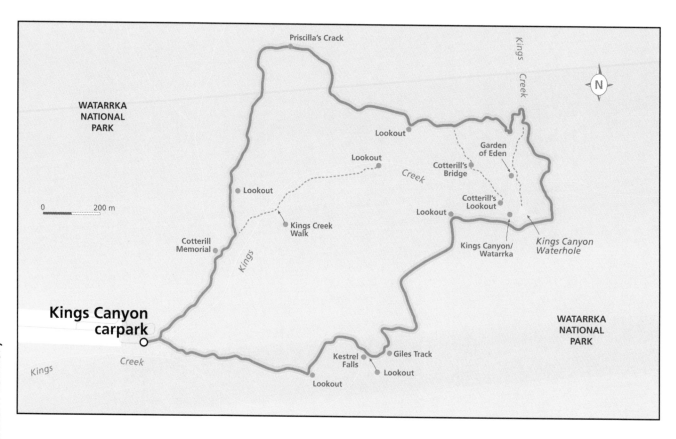

👁 LOCAL SNAPSHOT

Jack Cotterill arrived in Australia from England in 1952, within a few years launching Alice Springs Tours Ltd and running camping trips to Palm Valley and later Uluru; he built the rock's first permanent tourist accommodation - an iron shed with 12 beds. Through a friend he heard of a magnificent oasis on Tempe Downs Station at a place called Kings Creek and, with his son, went to investigate. Even in drizzling rain, Kings Canyon made an impression. 'We couldn't believe how beautiful it was', said Jack. 'It was out of this world. The colours were so varied, bold and pastel...' Jack set his sights on offering it as a new destination for his tour company and, with the help of a Luritja man named Leslie, from Docker River station, built a bridge over a crevasse on what is now the Rim Walk. Though the original bridge collapsed in 1991 after nearly 30 years of service, a new metal walkway called Cotterills Bridge now crosses the gap.

Opposite The canyon's sheer walls are impressive

ITINERARY

From Kings Canyon carpark, you only get a brief warm up on the flat alongside Kings Creek before the biggest climb of the entire walk. It's considered a bit of a test – if you're fit and nimble enough to manage it, you'll be right for the rest of the walk. Rocky steps rise steeply around the inside of the canyon to gain around 100–150m in elevation (takes about 10min), offering increasing views over the distant surrounding plains and the streak of trees along the valley floor that marks the path of Kings Creek.

The climb works its way through Priscilla's Crack (so-named because it featured in the movie *Priscilla Queen of the Desert*) and once on the plateau, the spectacular outlook over the canyon really opens up. A short climb leads to a striking 'lost city' of striped sandstone domes reminiscent of the Bungle Bungles in the Kimberley. Kuninga is the Luritja name for the Western Quoll and to the Luritja People the domes are young Kuninga men who travelled through here during the Dreaming.

The track is at times a rock hop over slabs of fractured orange sandstone eroded by wind and water and dotted with tufts of spinifex and a few stunted trees. With no visible ground trail, care is needed to stick to the path which is marked with blue triangles.

There's a string of lookouts on this walk and the next one shows off the gorge's expansive orange walls, so sheer and smooth in places it's as though a bricklayer has rendered them. All cliffs are unfenced and plummet like the edge of a skyscraper, so take great care and don't go near the edge. Chunks of sandstone are prone to occasionally calving off the cliffs – as you move around the rim you'll notice house-sided blocks on the canyon floor – so maybe don't linger for long.

A short 300m side-track leads via Cotterills Bridge to reach Cotterills Lookout for a peek over the Garden of Eden waterhole, to which the trail soon visits.

Upstream of the main gorge, Kings Creek has gouged another cutting in the top of the plateau, and the trail dips in and out of it via several zig-zagging wooden staircases and a bridge

to pass through a lush oasis – the Garden of Eden. This land is essentially comprised of two layers of porous sandstone, sandwiching a layer of impermeable mudstone, and when rainwater hits the mudstone it creates a water table that vegetation thrives on. A side track leads past ghost gums and cycads that are 300–400 years old to a waterhole shaded by sandstone walls. It might look inviting but swimming is not permitted, as it's the only drinking hole for wildlife for miles around.

A flight of wooden stairs climb back onto the escarpment, bringing hikers to the canyon's South Wall where the trail winds between more impressive rock domes and scattered cycads, cypress pines and eucalypts.

Kestrel Falls only flows after heavy rain but even if the waterfall isn't working, you might spot some of the kestrels that nest in the cliffs. It's a flight of stone steps back down to the carpark to complete the loop, wrapping up a spectacular outback hike.

Crossing Cotterills Bridge

BEST EATS

- **Kings Canyon Resort:** There are options here, from the Thirsty Dingo Bar to Outback BBQ hall, pub-style food at the Desert Oaks Bistro, and a la carte dining at Carmichael's Restaurant. Luritja Rd, Watarrka National Park; (08) 7210 9600; kingscanyonresort.com.au.

―

BEST SLEEPS

- **Kings Canyon Resort:** Just a 10min drive from the trailhead, this freshly renovated resort offers camping, glamping and hotel rooms to suit all budgets. Luritja Rd, Watarrka National Park; (08) 7210 9600; kingscanyonresort.com.au.
- **Kings Creek Station:** This cattle station, 36km from Kings Canyon/Watarrka, offers a range of options, from basic camping to super swish glamping tents. While you're there, take a tour of the station by buggy. 12725 Luritja Rd, Petermann; (08) 8956 7474; kingscreekstation.com.au.

WHILE YOU'RE HERE

- **Karrke Aboriginal Cultural Experience & Tours:** Learn about Luritja and Pertame (Southern Aranda) culture on a one-hour walk and talk covering everything from bush tucker and bush medicine to dot painting and wood craft. This is an authentic experience. Tours operate in peak season, Feb to Oct. Wanmarra Community, Kings Creek; (08) 8956 7620; karrke.com.au.
- **The Giles Track:** Kings Canyon/Watarrka is a long way from anywhere so if you fancy stretching your legs a bit further, step out on the 22km Giles Track, a relatively easy 1-2 day hike that follows the southern rim of the range between Kathleen Springs and Kings Canyon/Watarrka. Finish at the canyon end for a suitable grand finale. Download track notes and map from nt.gov.au.
- **Professional Helicopter Services:** From up above, you get an appreciation of the rock formations of Kings Canyon/Watarrka, that just isn't possible at ground level. With flights lasting anywhere from 8-30min, there's an option to suit most budgets. (08) 8956 7873; phs.com.au.

An epic outback traverse of the West MacDonnell Ranges/Tjoritja, featuring red rock gorges, waterholes, and starry starry nights.

Larapinta Trail

This walk is on <u>Arrernte Country</u>.

WHY IT'S SPECIAL

There's a real spiritual energy in Australia's Red Centre that is unmistakable on this epic journey weaving along the West MacDonnell Ranges/Tjoritja, between Mount Sonder/Rutjupma and Alice Springs/Mparntwe. It's desert but that doesn't mean its beauty is subtle. The route is jam-packed with striking features, from towering narrow gorges and dry riverbeds lined with palms, to steep mountain scrambles with panoramic views across vast plains. A smattering of waterholes attract birds, wallabies and dingoes, and wildflowers add extra colour.

At times, the trail is loosely formed but this only adds to the sense of wildness and connection with this ancient land.

WALK IT

West to east or east to west – either way is good. While some people knock it out in 12 days, a more leisurely 15-18 days allows time to fully appreciate the landscape. With a number of car access points en route, you can also hike it in four-day sections. Mount Sonder/Rutjupma and Ormiston Pound make for great day walks.

There are over two-dozen campsites to choose from en route. Major ones have a shelter, water tanks, toilets and even USB charging points but you'll probably want to plan for a few nights at basic wild camps too, at choice locations like Hugh Gorge Junction or on high points such as Brinkley Bluff where sunrise and sunset views are truly epic. There are hot showers (woohoo!) at Ormiston Gorge/Kwartatuma and the commercial campground at Standley Chasm/Angkerle Atwatye.

Although it's long, you don't need to carry more than 3-5 days of food at a time. As well as offering transfers to and from Redbank Gorge (Mount Sonder/Rutjupma end), you can arrange for operators in Alice Springs (*see* Resources opposite) to drop off your pre-prepared food boxes to four locked storage sheds en route, at Ormiston Gorge, Serpentine Gorge, Ellery Creek South and Standley Chasm/Angkerle Atwatye.

You'll be camping on sand so carry sand pegs or peg out your tent fly by adding large elastic loops to hook over rocks.

 Trail talk
- Distance: 226km
- Time: 12-18 days
- Rating: Hard
- Technicality: Terrain is often rough and rugged with rock scrambling, loose shale, soft sandy riverbeds and some long climbs. The track is mostly well marked, though some places require attention. Extremes in temperature and the trail's overall length add to the challenge.
- Puff factor: Challenging terrain, plus a few long steep climbs means you'll burn a decent amount of energy on this one.
- Watch out for: Keep food secure in airtight containers or deep within your pack to avoid tempting mice and dingoes. Flies can be a real pain so pack a face net. Heat stress can be deadly so drink heaps (electrolytes are good) and rest in the shade if you start to overheat. In the unlikely event of heavy rain, be wary of flash flooding in riverbeds. Never jump or dive into waterholes as submerged rocks and logs can cause serious injury.

 When to go
Anytime between May and Aug, with June/July being peak time. Summer is dangerously hot.

 Resources
For detailed planning days and to purchase the Larapinta Trail Info Pack (comprising maps and trail notes), go online to larapintatrail.com.au and nt.gov.au/parks/find-a-park/tjoritja-west-macdonnell-national-park/larapinta-trail. Trail and camping fees apply. Campsites need to be booked well in advance. For trail transfers and food drops, contact local operators in Alice Springs such as Larapinta Trail Trek Support (treksupport.com.au).

The Larapinta Trail guidebook by John and Monica Chapman is an excellent and very detailed resource.

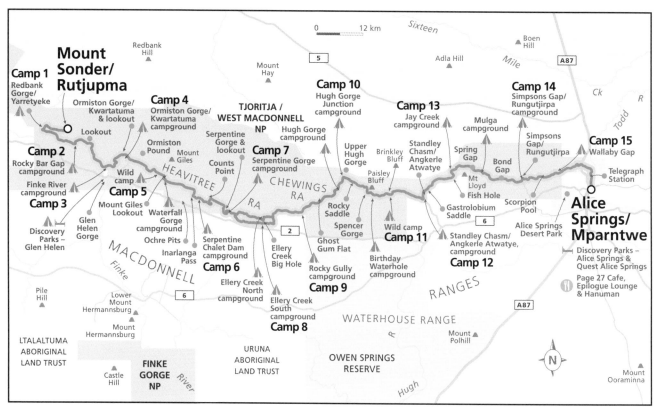

LOCAL SNAPSHOT

With around 228mm of rainfall annually (most of which falls in summer), the West MacDonnell Ranges/Tjoritja are officially desert, though they're still rich with life. Around 200 bird species and 100 reptile species live here, along with mammals such as echidnas, wallabies and dingoes. All life needs water and a few permanent waterholes provide a vital supply along with the vast Finke River system which flows on rare occasions. Even when riverbeds are dry, enormous old river red gums still drink from water captured deep beneath the sand. Meandering for almost 700km, the Finke has been critical to all life here for eons. Translating to 'salty river', the Arrernte People call it 'Lhere Pirnte' (or 'lara pinta').

ITINERARY

DAYS 1–4, MOUNT SONDER/RUTJUPMA TO ORMISTON GORGE/KWARTATUMA AND FOOD RESUPPLY

DAY 1
Mount Sonder/Rutjupma to Redbank Gorge/Yarretyeke, 16km, 5–6hr

At 1379m, Mount Sonder/Rutjupma is the loftiest point of the entire trail and from its rocky peak I get a glimpse into the landscape I'll be walking for the next few weeks. Australia's central heart is dusted in soft pinks and oranges. Long mountain ranges ripple across vast desert, as though something has tunnelled beneath the dirt – the Arrernte Dreaming says they were created by giant caterpillars – and in the distance, salt lakes shimmer.

After being dropped off at Redbank Gorge/Yarretyeke, at the western end of the trail, the round trip to Mount Sonder/Rutjupma takes five hours. I'd dumped most of my gear at camp beforehand, setting my tent up on the appealing soft sand of a riverbed, surrounded by gnarled river red gums, a short walk from the official campsite. Camping in a riverbed is normally a no-no, however these rivers run once a year if they're lucky.

Even before the sun's light fully fades from the skyline, a billion stars start showing up for a night of heavy twinkling. It's nice of them to arrive so early, because by 8pm I'm fast asleep.

DAY 2
Redbank Gorge/Yarretyeke to Rocky Bar Gap campground, 12km, 3hr

My second day on the trail begins with breakfast at Redbank Gorge, a 20min side trip that follows along the creek to a rocky amphitheatre with an icy pool at its base. It seems surreal to see a lonely orange life buoy hanging over the rocks fringing it.

After retracing my steps and packing up camp, I begin my journey east towards Alice Springs/Mparntwe, on earth packed as hard as tarmac, past mulga scrub, blonde grass and spears of termite mounds. It's only a short walk but my focus today is to slow down – both body and mind – and once my tent is set up at Rocky Bar Gap camp, I spend a peaceful afternoon feeling the smooth white trunks of ghost gums and contemplating how a few of them have managed to sprout from the red rock walls of the gap. The desert isn't an easy place to live, yet plenty of flora and fauna here manage it. When I fill my bottles at the water tank there's a treeful of opportunistic honeyeaters loitering next to it, waiting for a free drink. Thankfully hikers don't need to do it quite so tough. This land is largely parched dry, but rangers check the tanks regularly to avoid any unwelcome surprises.

DAY 3
Rocky Bar Gap campground to Finke River campground, 14km, 6hr

Mount Sonder/Rutjupma glows orange in the early morning sun and I can't help turning around every 5min to stare at it receding behind me as I walk east on Day 3. It's the mountain that inspired Albert Namatjira to paint it in 1954. Born in the MacDonnell Ranges, Namatjira was a talented watercolour painter – his career began in the 1930s – and the first Aboriginal artist to achieve acclaim and popularity for his outback scenes of mountain ranges and ghost gums.

It's a gradual climb to a hilltop lookout on low rocky ridge but out here, even the slightest elevation offers uninhibited views. I spy a break in the adjacent range that marks the entrance to Glen Helen Gorge, an optional 7km return side trip that leads to a resort and campground with a restaurant (see p. 213). Some hikers drop in for a night, a shower or a decent feed but I carry on, descending to Davenport Creek which is largely dry – except for a few pools fringed in reeds. It's one of the great joys of hiking that you're permitted to get dirty without judgement, so I lay against my pack in the dusty creek bed and eat lunch.

An hour and a half further, Finke River camp sits on the edge of a wide and dry riverbed, the sand scattered with rocks and red gums choked with the flotsam of earlier floods. The Finke is often cited as the world's oldest river and though it rarely runs these days, its general path has remained unchanged for about 100 million years.

Left Most camps have three-sided shelters *Previous* Climbing Mount Sonder/Rutjupma

Nights are so clear here I can make out the emu, an Indigenous constellation defined by its darkness rather than light, set amongst the billions of stars that light up the sky. I attempt to sleep al fresco on the sleeping platforms provided in the shelter so I can continue my stargazing, but the minute I turn my head torch off mice start scurrying about around me. Hey, it's warmer inside a tent anyway.

DAY 4
Finke River campground to Ormiston Gorge/Kwartatuma campground 9km, 2–3hr (plus Ormiston Pound Walk)

When you're on hiker-time, early to bed means early to rise. On Day 4, I watch a thin line of orange swell on the horizon with the rising sun, spilling light across the land. It's a short walk to Ormiston Gorge/Kwartatuma that takes in a hilltop lookout, rolling lowlands and a crossing of the dry Ormiston Creek. The highlight for this day though (and one of my favourite parts of the entire walk) is a side trip around Ormiston Pound.

I set up my tent, dump my gear, fill a water bottle and head off on the 3–4hr circuit (anticlockwise is best). Enclosed by a circle of mountains, the Pound reveals rocks embedded with the ripples of an ancient shallow sea. After traversing the valley floor, the track returns via the gorge where white ghost gums defy nature, sprouting from between cracks in the towering red rock walls. It finishes with a rock hop around the permanent waterhole in Ormiston Gorge. You can swim here but the water is cold enough to freeze the balls off a brass monkey.

Ormiston is one of a few areas on the trail accessible by car (it's also where you can collect a pre-organised food resupply), so make the most of the visitor centre, kiosk and showers because they're the last bit of comfort for about 120km.

DAYS 5–8, ORMISTON GORGE/KWARTATUMA TO ELLERY CREEK – FOOD RESUPPLY AT ELLERY CREEK SOUTH OR SERPENTINE GORGE

DAY 5
Ormiston Gorge/Kwartatuma campground to wild camp Heavitree Range, 12km, 4hr

Day 5 begins following the south side of the Heavitree Range, before climbing up steep and layered red rock to a ridgeline. The views are vast and I feel as though I can see the entire MacDonnells – the Heavietree Range where I am and the Chewings Range running in distant parallel.

This morning I set out with 6l of water; my plan is to wild camp high on top of the Heavitree Range. I'd received a tip-off about a few tasty tent sites at the '17km marker' and it's a good

one. My tent perches just a few metres from the edge of the range and the views are almost 360-degrees, taking in the long and rippling Chewings Range opposite and an ever-shrinking Mount Sonder/Rutjupma to the west. Sunset sends long shadows sweeping across the valley, highlighting every dip and fold, before the sky fades through burnt orange and blue.

DAY 6
Wild camp Heavitree Range to Serpentine Chalet Dam campground, 17km, 4–5hr

At sunrise, the rocky landscape is so bright orange it looks on fire. I start Day 6 walking east again atop the range, passing Giles Lookout which gazes across at Mount Giles (1389m) opposite, before a long and rocky descent to Waterfall Gorge camp, about 3km in. There's not a drop of water in the pool at its base during my visit and no water tank or toilet. A long stretch through a wide valley makes for easy and beautiful walking but, without any of the breezes altitude offers, it's also hot and I'm an easy target for flies. My water is running low but it has to do until I reach camp tonight.

Inarlanga Pass cuts a way through the Heavitree Range, once a boundary line that wasn't crossed without permission from Land Custodians on either side. Red rock walls squeeze a route of boulders dotted with ancient cycads, cone-bearing plants that once shared the earth with dinosaurs. At the southern end of the pass, a 2.5hr side trip leads to the Ochre Pits – a quarry where minerals have been dug up for thousands of years by the Western Arrernte People and used for painting and ceremonies. A 10m-high cliff reveals swirls of white, yellow and red-brown minerals. Though women and children are not permitted to dig, they may use minerals provided by the men.

It's a few more hot kilometres to Serpentine Chalet Dam camp, spread across either side of a creek.

DAY 7
Serpentine Chalet Dam campground to Serpentine Gorge campground, 13km, 5–6hr

Day 7 begins on easy singletrack through mulga woodlands, before climbing a rocky staircase to the top of a ridge. It's a 20min side trip to Counts Point, another trail highlight overlooking a long valley lined either side with mountains like a gigantic halfpipe, a sprinkling of tiny trees in its base. It's an astounding view and one of many that I wasn't expecting to find in this outback desert.

Temperatures fluctuate wildly. If the relentless sun was threatening to turn my skin as red as the land on the valley

Fish Hole

floor, up on these exposed ridgelines, cold winds have me scrambling for a jacket.

It's a long descent down rocky steps to arrive at Serpentine Gorge camp where wind whips red dust into the air, so fine that it penetrates the mesh of my tent inner and settles on my sleeping bag. In the late afternoon, I follow a 30min side trip up a steep track to an epic lookout over the gorge and surrounding ranges.

There's a food drop storeroom here for those planning on camping at Ellery Creek North camp.

DAY 8
Serpentine Gorge campground to Ellery Creek South campground, 13km, 4–5hr

There are two routes between Serpentine Gorge and Ellery Creek on Day 8, one skirting the northern side of the Heavitree Range and the other on the south. Both are great, however the new camp at Ellery Creek North keeps walkers separate from the hordes of car visitors who flock to Ellery Creek South and its swimming hole. The northern camp has its own swimming gorge area or you can access the southern hole via a 2hr track over the saddle.

During my visit only the southern route is an option, a pretty walk that undulates along a low ridgeline through a valley. Ellery Creek offers some of the most appealing swimming on the Larapinta and I camp next to a large pool framed by orange rock walls and a small sand beach. It's idyllic. Idyllic that is, until a big black crow breaks into a long-awaited bag of Twisties retrieved from my latest food drop here.

DAYS 9–12, ELLERY CREEK SOUTH TO STANDLEY CHASM/ ANGKERLE ATWATYE AND FOOD RESUPPLY

DAY 9
Ellery Creek South campground to Rocky Gully campground, 15km, 5hr

On Day 9 the route begins its transition from the Heavitree to the Chewings Range. I climb over a saddle from the southern side of the Heavitree and descend to cross a vast valley floor of red sand and dirt, and sprinkled with a few sad looking trees. It's boiling hot and the flies buzzing around my face are really annoying but a slight reprieve comes when I sit down for lunch in a dry riverbed, beneath the cooling shade of a river red gum.

Rocky Gully camp is a dustbowl and I spend the afternoon moving my tent around to chase the shade.

DAY 10
Rocky Gully campground to Hugh Gorge Junction campground, 19km, 7hr

I leave at 7am on Day 10 in an effort to avoid the worst of the heat. In the hot, broad valley bridging the two ranges, I really get the sense of being in the outback. I spot my first cloud in ten days, a tiny wisp no bigger than my thumb held against the sky. When I stop moving, the silence rings in my ears but the flies are persistent. I pause briefly at Ghost Gum Flat, with one magnificent ghost gum for shade, then push on to reach Hugh Gorge campground. It's a major campsite but I max out my water-carrying capacity (8l) and push on another 3km along a challenging creek bed littered with boulders and tree trunks to reach Hugh Gorge Junction campground.

It's nice having the facilities of a big camp but even nicer sometimes to find a plot all for yourself. With my tent erected beneath a few ghost gums towered over by a burnt red bluff, I head off on the 1hr return side trip to Upper Hugh Gorge, scrambling between its red walls, until a pool of water prevents me going any further. Finally I can plonk myself in the cool sand in the shade, surrounded by a few cycads and flowers, and relax without the flies.

DAY 11
Hugh Gorge Junction campground to wild camp at Stuarts Pass, 12km, 7hr

Things get far more rugged in the Chewings Range. Uniformity and flat open spaces are replaced by dynamic and constantly undulating land, and it's a tad greener too with low shrubs and clumps of spinifex, but the terrain's challenges are matched by its visual rewards. On Day 11, I crest Rocky Saddle and traverse the inside of a steep-sided valley, before digging in for a long scramble up to Razorback Ridge. It's aptly named, a narrow route trailing atop jagged layers of tilted orange rock that ripple into the distance. Today it's cold (I barely remove my long-sleeved thermal all day) and with the winds of altitude, it's even more so. The views are spectacular in all directions, across steep-sided and jagged orange ridges with a smattering of green.

A steep switchback descent funnels into a rough rock-hop along the dry creek of Spencer Gorge, stuffed with wildflowers. Back on the lowlands the flies are waiting to greet me, but thankfully a passing French hiker generously donated a spare face net to preserve my sanity.

Birthday Waterhole is the next camp but I fill up with water here and push on to a wild camp at Stuarts Pass enabling me a head start on a big day tomorrow. It's a cold afternoon and I relish the last of the sun warming the side of my tent.

DAY 12
Stuarts Pass wild camp to Standley Chasm/Angkerle Atwatye, 13km, 6hr

It takes me two hours to scramble up the one in four ascent that kicks off Day 12 to scale Brinkley Bluff. It's followed by 3km of ridgeline, punctured with shards of rock and offering unhindered views of scree slopes, mountain ranges and distant plains. It's one of the most spectacular days of the trail and

Ghost gums sprout in the walls of Ormiston Gorge

so full of dramatic mountainous terrain that I almost feel as though I'm in New Zealand – just with a different colour palette.

By the time I reach camp at Standley Chasm/Angkerle Atwatye, I'm long overdue for the waiting shower and cafe. The small private settlement here is owned and operated by the Arrernte community, and after a week of ramen noodles and dehydrated potato mash, a hearty serve of lasagne and salad goes down quickly. My clothes are so cardboard stiff from salt and dust I almost have to bend them to get them in the washing machine.

DAYS 13–16, STANDLEY CHASM/ANGKERLE ATWATYE TO ALICE SPRINGS/TELEGRAPH

DAYS 13–14
Standley Chasm/Angkerle Atwatye to Jay Creek campground, 13km, 6–7hr

A rest day on Day 13 gives me the chance to soak up Standley Chasm/Angkerle Atwatye. Soaring 80m high, yet only 3m wide, it was once a tributary of the Finke River, now dry. At around midday, tour buses flock to see the high sun bathe the narrow cutting in fiery red, but I have the luxury of enjoying it alone in the early morning as well as during its dazzling peak hour.

There's a high route and a low route option on Day 14. I go for the high road, embarking on an energetic climb through a remarkable maze of small pointed peaks, the serrations of a tilted ridgeline. Descending from Gastrolobium Saddle is gnarly, including one decent rock scramble down the side of a dry waterfall. Fish Hole is worth lingering at, hidden between pale orange walls and fringed by sand and smoothly sculpted beds of rock. Such waterholes attract flocks of zebra finches that come to drink with tiny red beaks and twitter like squeaky toys.

Walking in soft sand can be quite the energy suck and the final kilometres to Jay Creek camp are along the dry riverbed. As soon as the sun goes down, my down jacket and beanie are layered over thermals and it's so cold I sleep in them too.

DAY 15
Jay Creek campground to Simpsons Gap/Rungutjirpa campground, 25km, 7hr

Dingoes howl in the night, and about 7km into Day 15 I reach Spring Gap, an impermanent waterhole frequented by these wild dogs, as well as birds. The walk takes me along a series of low ridges, past boulder outcrops and thickets of mulga. I skip Mulga camp and push on to Bond Gap where a 600m side trip leads to a permanent waterhole. By the time I reach Simpsons

Gap/Rungutjirpa, I've seen countless gaps and gorges but these rock walls seem especially impressive, towering over a permanent waterhole and a vast rockfall of boulders that makes an ideal home for a colony of black-footed rock wallabies. Simpsons Gap/Rungutjirpa is accessible by car but a separate hiker campsite offers a degree of seclusion.

DAY 16
Simpsons Gap/Rungutjirpa campground to Wallaby Gap, 10km, 3hr

By car it's only 20min from Simpsons Gap/Rungutjirpa to Alice Springs/Mparntwe, but the Larapinta meanders for another 8hr or so. Most of the big mountains have petered away now but it's still beautiful looking out across the plains. I knock out 3hr of walking, dipping into woodland, skirting ridges, and passing a half-hour return side trip to the excitingly-named Scorpion Pool, although the water scorpions that live here have no sting and aren't considered the real deal. More finches, squeaking around the water, are super cute though.

I could probably have merged Days 16 and 17 together but then I would have arrived in town a day early for my hotel booking, so instead I while away a long afternoon at Wallaby Gap wishing I had better food left in my dwindling supplies.

DAY 17
Wallaby Gap to Alice Springs/Mparntwe, 13km, 4–5hr

The most impressive feature of Day 17 is Euro Ridge, a sloping ridgeline that falls away steeply to a plain stretching all the way to Alice Springs/Mparntwe, now visible in the distance. Euros are the most common kangaroo species in Central Australia's rocky hills, and the two high points of Euro Ridge are said to be the back and head of an Arrernte Euro ancestor. While travelling east from Standley Chasm, he grew thirsty and dug for water, creating the waterhole known now as Alice Springs.

The town of Alice Springs/Mparntwe was born from the establishment of a telegraph station in 1871, built to relay messages on an Overland Telegraph Line between Adelaide and Darwin, and though the Telegraph Station marks the official end point of the Larapinta, I opt to follow the Todd River for another 3.5km back to Alice.

There's something very cool about arriving into a city on foot with the dust and memories of an adventure still plastered across your face. The Larapinta took me away from the modern world and immersed me in an ancient and deeply spiritual country. It's an epic journey, and one I'd love to do again, but after 17 days of dehydrated food, it's time for an epic feast of fresh food.

BEST EATS

- **Page 27 Cafe:** A great vibe, cool décor and a menu that will inspire the tastebuds can be found at this indoor and laneway cafe on Todd St Mall. Head here for breakfast or lunch. 3 Fan Arcade, Alice Springs; 0417 486 464.
- **Epilogue Lounge:** This place is pumping day and night, serving up excellent food and regularly playing live music on the rooftop. Shop 1/58 Todd Mall, Alice Springs; 0429 003 874.
- **Hanuman:** Overseen by renowned chef Jimmy Shu, Alice's pinnacle of fine dining has been serving up divine Asian cuisine since 2001. 82 Barrett Dr, Alice Springs; (08) 8953 7188; hanuman.com.au.

———

BEST SLEEPS

- **Discovery Parks – Glen Helen:** Located in Glen Helen Gorge, a 3.5km detour off the Larapinta Trail, this place offers an alternative place to spend a night mid-trail or to drop in and get a good feed. There's camping and hotel room-style accommodation; discoveryholidayparks.com.au/ glen-helen.
- **Big 4 MacDonnell Range Holiday Park:** Whether you're a party of two or six, you'll get modern budget accommodation to suit at this holiday park on the edge of town. Choose from campsites, cabins, villas or even glamping safari tents, if you can't say goodbye to canvas. Palm Place, Alice Springs; (08) 8952 6111; big4.com.au.
- **Quest Alice Springs:** This studio and apartment complex faces the Todd River and is a 10min walk from the town centre. 9-10 South Terrace, Alice Springs; (08) 8959 0000; questapartments.com.au.

WHILE YOU'RE HERE

- **Pyndan Camel Tracks:** Camels have been walking the outback since the 1800s when they were drafted for transport, and nowadays you can ride with these placid creatures through the West Macs with Pyndan Camel Tracks. Sunset is a particularly special time to roam. 2/15 Jane Rd White Gums, Alice Springs; 0416 170 164; cameltracks.com.
- **Alice Springs Desert Park:** This is a great place to get a deeper understanding of the diversity of desert life and habitats, as well as insights from First Nations' guides on living off the land for thousands of years. The nocturnal house and bird show are highlights. Larapinta Drive, Alice Springs; (08) 8951 8788; alicespringsdesertpark.com.au.
- **Outback Ballooning:** You'll get a totally different perspective of the West MacDonnell Ranges/ Tjoritja from above in a hot-air balloon. Dawn flights reveal sunlight spilling across mountains and plains, followed by bubbles and refreshments; (08) 8952 8723; outbackballooning.com.au.

Opposite Endless outback views

Queensland

From outback gorges to rainforest and tropical island trails, the Sunshine State is a stunner.

Enjoy a spectacular panorama of volcanic peaks in the Glass House Mountains. It's even better at sunset.

Mount Ngungun

This walk is on <u>Jinibara</u> and <u>Gubbi Gubbi Country</u>.

WHY IT'S SPECIAL

It might be short but this walk packs a punch, with stunning summit views that are guaranteed to make the soul soar. Eleven peaks make up the volcanic domes and spires of the Glass House Mountains in the Sunshine Coast hinterland, and from the top of Ngungun (pronounced 'noo noo') you get a 360-degree panorama of them all as they rise boldly from flat plains.

Sunrise and sunset add a spectacular lightshow, backlighting the mountains and sweeping colour and light across the surrounding forest and macadamia and pineapple plantations. There's decent variety on the walk itself too, as the trail shifts through ferns and eucalypt forest to grass trees. It's a popular walk – but for good reason.

WALK IT

It's a 1hr drive south of Noosa or north of Brisbane, or half an hour west of Caloundra to get to the carpark (off Fullertons Rd) at the base of Mount Ngungun. Being just a quick hoof up on well-formed track, this is one of the easiest of the Glass House Mountains to climb.

If you go for sunset, take a torch for the descent. It's tempting to head back from the summit immediately after the sun dips below the horizon, but wait a little longer because the colours will continue to get richer for some time. The walk back down is pretty quick and your night vision should see you through the twilight of the top half at least, before switching on a torch for the easier lower section.

This is one of those walks where you might appreciate a little picnic at the top, perhaps with a glass of something refreshing – so pick up some supplies in the nearby towns of Glass House Mountains, Beerburrum or Beerwah.

→ **Trail talk**
- Distance: 2.8km return
- Time: 2hr
- Rating: Easy-moderate
- Technicality: Well-formed track with some rocky steps and a teensy scramble at the summit.
- Puff factor: It's uphill all the way but it's only short.
- Watch out for: Be careful around sheer drops at the summit and avoid in wet conditions or after rain when the rock becomes slippery. Take a torch if you go at sunset or sunrise.

When to go
Cooler winter months are more comfortable. Avoid weekends if you can, when it can get crowded. Sunrise and sunset are epic.

Resources
Visit parks.des.qld.gov.au for maps and more details.

Opposite Sunset on the summit ridge*Previous* Resting in Carnarvon Gorge

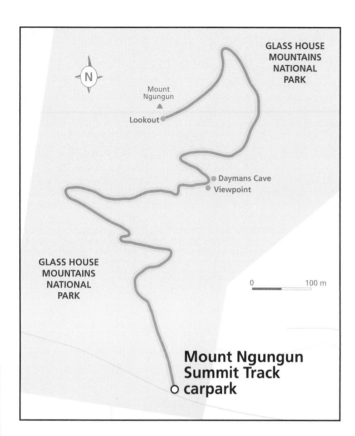

GLASS HOUSE
MOUNTAINS
NATIONAL
PARK

Mount
Ngungun

Lookout

Daymans Cave
Viewpoint

GLASS HOUSE
MOUNTAINS
NATIONAL
PARK

0   100 m

**Mount Ngungun
Summit Track
○ carpark**

◉ LOCAL SNAPSHOT

Around 26 million years ago, magma rose through underground vents and cooled beneath the surface, and it took a few million years more of erosion to wear away the surrounding sandstone to leave the hardened plugs of today's Glass House Mountains. When James Cook cruised through these parts in 1770, he jotted in his journal that the region's hills 'very much resemble glass houses', though we're talking less of the plant hothouse variety and more of the conical brick glass foundries of his Yorkshire home. Of course, these mountains already had names and a history to go with them. According to Jinibara Law, the Glass House Mountains are a family. The broad dome of Mount Tibrogargan is the father, while Mount Beerwah, with its bulbous protrusion on one side, is a pregnant mother. The remaining smaller mountains are their children, and the elongated ridge of Mount Ngungun is a dingo. Because of their sacred importance, Traditional Owners ask that neither Beerwah or Tibrogargan are climbed. Unfortunately people do sometimes still tackle it but it's a near-vertical climb in places and rescues are common. A culturally respectful and safer way to appreciate the mountains is via a viewpoint walk or a circuit around the base.

Left Mount Tibrogargan
from the summit ridge
Opposite The steady climb

ITINERARY

Unlike Mount Beerwah, Mount Tibrogargan or Mount Coonowrin, Mount Ngungun itself is not immediately impressive to look at, but that all changes with a short walk.

I start my hike from the Mount Ngungun Summit Track carpark about an hour before sunset, along with a steady stream of other walkers, gently ascending a wide and zig-zagging path between a sea of green ferns. The canopy of eucalypt trees here harbour koalas and rainbow lorikeets, and at the halfway point, the large rock overhang of Daymans Cave draws the eye south to the bulk of Mount Tibrogargan (the father of the Glass House Mountains family – *see* p. 218).

As the height increases, so does the steepness, and rocky steps become more frequent. Nearing the top, ferns are replaced with grass trees, and the trail becomes a smidge on the rock-hopping side, before one short scramble to the top.

Emerging onto Mount Ngungun's ridgeline peak is like mounting the back of a stegosaurus. A narrow fin of rock rises above the bush, like a jagged spine plate, capturing the golden sun on one flank and casting ever-lengthening shadows on the other side. The views are endless in all directions, and if you add in shifting light in the early morning or late afternoon, the ever-changing scene can keep you occupied for a good hour or two.

Most notable in the south is the massive dome of Mount Tibrogargan, but I follow the ridgeline to perch on a rock facing west for one of the most epic sunset views Queensland offers. From this angle, Mount Beerwah appears like a pyramid, backlit by a golden ball of fire sinking into the horizon. According to the Jinibara Dreamings, Beerwah was the wife to Tibrogargan, father of all tribes, who gave him many children. However, after a great shame was brought to the family by their eldest son Coonowrin (his mountain is a pointed column that brings to mind a giant lipstick) Beerwah's sadness was so great that the stream of her tears flowed all the way to the sea. She stands tallest at 556m and is the 'pregnant mother' of the Glasshouse Mountains.

Though I share the mountain with dozens of others, the stunning panorama goes a long way to quieten the crowd, leaving plenty of space to soak up the serenity. I stay as long as I dare while the sun's light fades, but it's a hard scene to leave. Several times I prepare to descend, but even with the sun well below the horizon, the colours only seem to get richer and more dazzling, and I struggle to draw myself away.

Eventually I slip over the backbone of Ngungun and into the trees, eyes now accustomed to the dim light. By halfway down it's significantly darker but a line of mandarin light persists on the horizon, peeking through the trees at intervals. It's only in the final few hundred metres that I feel the urge to turn on the torch from my phone, but somehow finishing this walk in the dark only enhances the sense of connection and magic of this spiritual mountain.

BEST EATS

- **The Lookout Cafe:** Combine great food with panoramic views of Mount Coonowrin and surrounds at this light and airy cafe, onsite at Glass On Glasshouse luxury cottages. 182 Glass House-Woodford Rd, Glass House Mountains; 0476 623 288; glassonglasshouse.com.au.
- **Bombay Bliss:** This unpretentious Indian restaurant has excellent food and is only 5km from Ngungun - perfect for a quick post-hike meal. 50 Simpson St, Beerwah; (07) 5494 6919; bombaybliss.com.au.

BEST SLEEPS

- **Glass House Mountains Ecolodge:** Nestled between rainforest and fruit orchards, there's accommodation to suit everyone, from standard rooms to an 1800s train carriage or even a church with a loft bedroom. Take a self-guided bush-tucker or orchard walk, or enjoy coffee grown and roasted onsite. 198 Barrs Road, Glass House Mountains; (07) 5493 0008; glasshouseecolodge.com.

WHILE YOU'RE HERE

- **Glass House Mountains Visitor and Interpretive Centre:** Visit here to pick up maps and brochures that will help you explore the Glass House Mountains, and to read the interpretive displays that explain the history, geology and Traditional Owners' culture of the region. Corner of Bruce Pde and Reed St, Settlers Rotary Park, Glass House Mountains; 1300 847 481.
- **Hike Mount Coolum:** This 208m volcanic dome overlooks ocean and hinterland, making for an epic little hike that never gets old. The 1.6km return track climbs fairly steeply - mostly on well-formed rock steps - but the unobstructed views in the top half make it all worth it. Keep an eye out for passing whales between May and Nov. Allow an hour or two.
- **Blackall Ranges Scenic Drive:** The lush, cool heights of the Blackall Range seem a world away from the beaches of the Sunshine Coast (though you can still see them from here). Follow a scenic, winding 55km route, stopping off at the cute and arty towns of Montville, Maleny and Mapleton, where you can get a decent fix of cheese and chocolate shops, art galleries, and artisan gelato.

Sunsets silhouette Mount Beerwah and Mount Coonowrin

Get lost in the land of the giants with towering rainforest, Antarctic beech and lots of waterfalls.

Toolona Creek Circuit

This is on <u>Bundjalung Country</u>.

WHY IT'S SPECIAL

Toolona Gorge in Lamington National Park feels like another time and place. The rainforest is supersized, bursting with waterfalls, and home to rare plants and animals, such as gnarled Antarctic beech trees, giant king ferns, Alberts lyrebirds, and bright blue crayfish that hiss. If it all sounds a bit like *Jurassic Park*, it's not surprising – considering this is a remnant pocket of Gondwanan rainforest, with some of the plants here descendants of those from 200 million years ago when Australia was still part of the ancient supercontinent.

The walk climbs the flanks of a 20-million-year-old volcano, following Toolona Creek to the edge of the Tweed Caldera, where views extend into New South Wales, before skirting the rim and returning to base.

WALK IT

Getting to Toolona Gorge is an adventure in itself. Whether you come from Brisbane or the Gold Coast, the last 36km on Lamington National Park Rd is winding and narrow – sometimes only one lane. It makes for a super pretty drive though, particularly near the top where tall trees grow right to the road edge. Park at Green Mountains day-use area, adjacent to O'Reilly's Rainforest Retreat (*see* p. 227), where picnic tables and electric barbecues are provided.

With a starting altitude of 935m, it can be a good 10°C cooler here than on the coast, so pack something warm to wear. Walking clockwise is best, allowing you to get the more challenging sections done first.

Trail talk
- Distance: 17.4km return
- Time: 6hr
- Rating: Hard
- Technicality: The trail is narrow and rocky at times, plus there are about eight creek crossings (feet should stay dry in low water levels).
- Puff factor: It's reasonably energetic, thanks to overall length, a steady 300m climb and generally rough terrain.
- Watch out for: Rocks are slippery when wet. After rain, be prepared for leeches and take extra care on river crossings.

When to go
Winter is best. Summer is the wet season which means impressive waterfalls, but also potentially impassable or dangerous creek crossings. Summer is also the time when you're most likely to bump into the Lamington spiny crayfish.

Resources
Visit parks.des.qld.gov.au for maps and more information.

Opposite top World Heritage-listed rainforest
Opposite bottom Lamington spiny crayfish

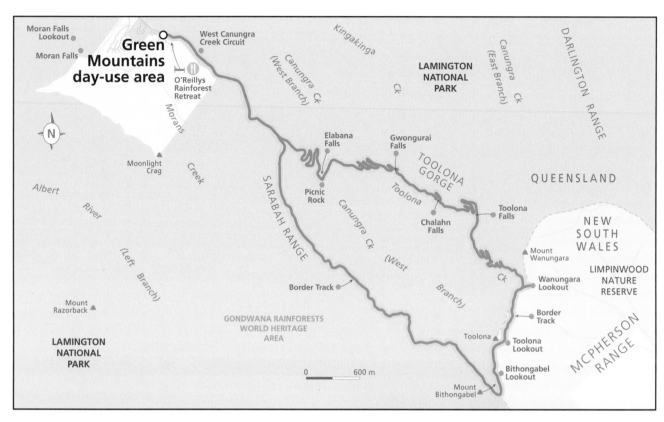

LOCAL SNAPSHOT

On a stormy afternoon in 1937, a Stinson airliner with seven on board was caught in a sudden down current, crashing into the dense forest of the McPherson Range. Rescuers were searching well south of the crash site but local Bernard O'Reilly had other ideas. A conspicuously brown and dead treetop in the canopy led him to find the virtual needle in a haystack, and though four died he was able to save two men. Every year, O'Reilly's Rainforest Retreat runs a guided hike to the wreckage and graves. At 37km long, through dense jungle and with no formed trail, it's no easy walk. You can do the bush-bash independently, if you've got the navigation skills, but guides from O'Reilly's give meaning to the journey, recounting the history of the rescue mission along the way.

Right Strangler fig in the rainforest *Opposite* The caldera rim of the McPherson Range

ITINERARY

I knew the mountains would be colder but I wasn't expecting 7°C when I get out of the car on an August morning wearing only shorts and a light jacket. Power walking is my warm-up plan. Even in the Green Mountains day-use area, the forest is immediately enveloping with earthy smells, birdsong and every shade of green.

On the trail, strangler figs mingle with Black booyong trees, soaring from buttressed bases, while thick wonga vines twist and wrap around tree trunks. A paved path soon slips onto narrow dirt, zig-zagging down through tree ferns and picabeen palms, to reach Toolona Creek which it follows all the way to the headwaters at the top of the crater rim.

It's here that you really start to forget what millennium you're in. The gorge is a dense and towering world of green, occasionally split open by flows of white water. Waterfalls create their own breeze, slowly swinging enormous Tarzan-like vines as thick as tree trunks.

The climb up the ancient caldera is gentle yet steady, crossing the creek numerous times and regularly punctuated by around a dozen cascades and waterfalls. The double cascade of Elabana Falls flows into dark teal pools, Gwongurai Falls gushes spectacularly over a black basalt face, and Toolona Falls spills over a high lip down to a mass of huge blocks that have carved off the rock face. They don't feel landscaped and neatly

presented like some waterfalls can, but rather wild and hidden in a way that sometimes requires a little effort to discover.

In the warmer months, the Lamington spiny crayfish can often be seen here walking between creeks. If encountered, they can be aggressive, snapping claws and hissing, and are best given a wide berth.

Though I took my jacket off for the climb, it's back on again when I reach the caldera rim of the McPherson Range. The land ends abruptly, a steep cascade of green to the valley below. A 50m detour to the left leads to Wanungara lookout with views across to Mount Warning/Wollumbin, the central plug of this ancient volcano.

It's too cold to sit down for a leisurely lunch so I eat on the go, joining the Border Track, following the boundary between Queensland and New South Wales. The trail is dryer up on the ridge, yet still carpeted in green and draping long strands of moss – an indication of the mist and rain that regularly sweeps the area. Antarctic beech trees flourish here, and they look as old as they are – 2000 years, for some specimens – with gnarled and exposed root systems covered in moss and shedding gold and rust-coloured leaves.

My final kilometres are accompanied by the low swoop of a green catbird and the distant calls of a lyrebird, and by the time I return to the car at 4pm it has 'warmed' to a balmy 13°C.

Base of Tooloona Falls

BEST EATS

- **O'Reillys Rainforest Retreat:** Head to the cafe for tea, scones, cakes and more (the views across the mountains are pretty special), or wander upstairs to the Rainforest Bar for sunset beers and pizza. If you're staying overnight, The Dining Room offers something more substantial. 3582 Lamington National Park Rd, Canungra; 1800 688 722; oreillys.com.au.
- **Canungra Hub:** You'll find local and organic food at this cafe, including vegan options. It's mostly healthy, if you don't count the divine homemade cakes. 32 Christie St, Canungra; 0422 894 174.

—

BEST SLEEPS

- **O'Reilly's Rainforest Retreat:** O'Reilly's has been around since 1926 and it's more than just a place to sleep. Onsite activities include hand-feeding crimson rosellas and king parrots, Segway tours, a bird of prey show, flying fox, treetop walk and small botanic gardens. Park your van, pitch a tent or indulge in comfy rooms and spa villas. 3582 Lamington National Park Rd, Canungra; 1800 688 722; oreillys.com.au.

—

WHILE YOU'RE HERE

- **Keep walking:** You could spend days hiking the trails from Green Mountains carpark alone. The 14km West Canungra Creek Circuit is epic, with lots of stunning waterfalls and a pretty wild and ungroomed track. A spectacular lookout over Moran Falls is reached via an easy 1.5hr return path, or pick from the other half-dozen routes on offer. Skirt around to the Binna Burra section of the park for another dozen tasty trails. Download the Lamington National Park guide from parks.des.qld.gov.au.
- **O'Reilly's Canungra Valley Vineyards & Mountview Alpaca Farm:** Grab a stone-baked pizza and wine from the cellar door and settle down somewhere on the property's 15 acres on the banks of Canungra Creek for a picnic, or sit down at the Vintage Restaurant, set inside an 1858 homestead. Onsite alpacas are super cute and you can pat them. 852 Lamington National Park Rd, Canungra; (07) 5543 4011; oreillys.com.au.

Traverse the Cooloola Sand Mass, taking in sand dunes, lush rainforest, sea views and the Noosa River.

Cooloola Great Walk

This walk is on <u>Gubbi Gubbi Country</u>.

WHY IT'S SPECIAL

Easy walking means you can kick back and enjoy the glorious and ever-changing scenery on this coastal route spanning between Noosa and Rainbow Beach. It undulates across the Cooloola Sand Mass, 24,000ha of mostly vegetated dunes that divide the Western Plains and the ocean, and is one of Queensland's largest coastal sand deposits. Hiking across vast sandblows, up to 1km wide and spilling towards the ocean, is a surreal experience. Add rainforest flittering with birds and butterflies, wildflower-dotted plains, and a tannin-stained Noosa River and Poona Lake and there's never a dull moment. It's rich with wildlife too, with birds and goannas common, and between July and Oct whales are often spotted.

WALK IT

You can walk this trail in either direction but as it's a one-way adventure you'll need to do a car shuffle or catch a bus back to your start point. It might take five days to walk but it's only 1.5hr by car! You can leave a car at the Queensland Parks Information Centre in Tewantin and walk onto the ferry that crosses the Noosa River, from where it's a 2km road walk to the trailhead. There is a carpark at the Rainbow Beach end, on the edge of town.

The northernmost section of the trail (Day 5 in the itinerary below) has a choice of inland or coastal route, and though the coastal option adds an extra 14km, and some potentially tiring beach walking, it does take you to the lighthouse at Double Island Point, which has some pretty excellent ocean views.

Walker campsites are nestled in pretty forest and have basic drop-toilets, water tanks and a few picnic tables. On the whole the route is reasonably isolated and you'll mostly only see other hikers and maybe the odd paddler cruising up the Noosa River. However, the trail is set to get busier with the planned addition of new eco tents and cabins to supplement the current basic camping.

With so much walking on sand, short ankle gaiters will help prevent any annoying grains from making their way into your shoes.

 Trail talk
- Distance: 88-102km
- Time: 5 days
- Rating: Easy
- Technicality: Sand and dirt tracks, plus some beach walking. Attention is required while walking across the trackless sand blows, but otherwise it's well marked.
- Puff factor: It's reasonably flat with just a few gentle undulations between sea level and 220m.
- Watch out for: The track is exposed in places and can be hot in full sun. Keep an eye out for snakes and the odd wild dog. Beaches are also shared with vehicles so take care. Be prepared for mosquitoes.

 When to go
Late March to Sept is best. It gets hot in summer and the trail may close due to fire danger.

 Resources
For more details and to make campsite bookings, visit parks.des.qld.gov.au. Purchase the Cooloola Great Walk topographic map and trail notes.

Opposite Rainforest sections are magical

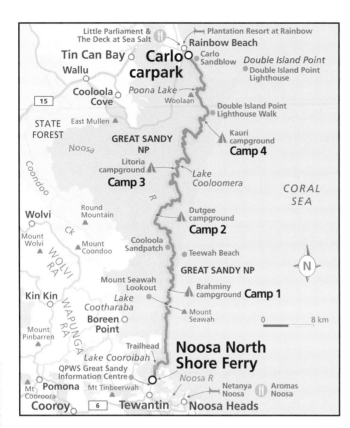

Map labels:

Little Parliament & The Deck at Sea Salt — Plantation Resort at Rainbow — Rainbow Beach

Tin Can Bay — Carlo carpark — Carlo Sandblow — Double Island Point — Double Island Point Lighthouse

Wallu

Cooloola Cove — Poona Lake — Woolaan

15

STATE FOREST — East Mullen — Double Island Point Lighthouse Walk

Noosa — GREAT SANDY NP — Kauri campground — **Camp 4**

Coondoo — Litoria campground — **Camp 3** — Lake Cooloomera — CORAL SEA

Wolvi — Round Mountain — Dutgee campground — **Camp 2**

Mount Wolvi — Mount Coondoo — Cooloola Sandpatch — Teewah Beach

WOLVI RA — GREAT SANDY NP — **N**

Kin Kin — Mount Seawah Lookout — Brahminy campground — **Camp 1**

Lake Cootharaba — Mount Seawah

Mount Pinbarren — WAPUNGA RA — Boreen Point

0 — 8 km

Trailhead — **Noosa North Shore Ferry**

Lake Cooroibah — QPWS Great Sandy Information Centre — Noosa R — Netanya Noosa — Aromas Noosa

Mt Cooroora — **Pomona** — Mt Tinbeerwah

Cooroy — **6** — **Tewantin** — **Noosa Heads**

Queensland

👁 LOCAL SNAPSHOT

Sand dominates this part of the coast, incorporating Cooloola and neighbouring K'gari/Fraser Island, the world's largest sand island. Dune systems here are the oldest in the world. Over a period of two million years, the rocks of eastern Australia have slowly eroded, their quartz and sandstone grains carried via rivers out to sea where wind and coastal currents washed them back onshore to create huge accumulations of sand. It seems incredible that entire forests, including lush rainforest, have managed to grow here but they obtain their nutrients from mineral coatings around sand grains, trace minerals from rainfall, and from decaying plant matter. It makes for a pretty unique landscape.

Opposite Crossing the Carlo Sandblow *Overleaf* Coastal tracks in the south offer expansive ocean views

ITINERARY

DAY 1

Noosa North Shore to Brahminy campground, 17.3km, 6hr

I park my car at the QPWS Great Sandy Information Centre in Tewantin and walk 5min to reach the $1 ferry service that transports me across the Noosa River, and from there it's just a short road walk to the trailhead. Car campers flock to Noosa North Shore but once I've passed them, on a 2km beach walk, I leave humanity behind.

A sandy track carves a line across heath plains dotted with wildflowers, before climbing gently through bracken fern punctuated by the tall spears of grass trees. You don't need much elevation here to appreciate a view and a 300m return side trip to Mount Seawah (90m) provides a 180-degree sweep over ocean beach and inland plains where the vast Lake Cootharaba is backed by the pointed volcanic plugs of Mount Cooroora and Mount Tinbeerwah.

I'm not the only one enjoying the views. Further on, perched on a branch within metres of the track, is a wedge-tailed eagle gazing out. He seems lost in thought, oblivious to my presence until the drive of my camera disturbs him and he launches across the valley, enormous wing tips splayed.

It's mid-spring but a good portion of this first day is spent on exposed white sandy trails that reflect the sun's heat and, despite my new broad-brimmed sun hat, it's hot walking.

Views from Brahminy are the best of all the campgrounds, facing inland over Lake Cootharaba and the low peaks that dot the horizon like the blips of a heart rate monitor. Sunset is spectacular and it's a good birdwatching spot, too.

DAY 2

Brahminy campground to Dutgee campground, 20.3km, 6–7hr

I leave early to try to avoid the worst of the heat that threatened to bake my brain the day before. Coastal tracks in the southern section offer little shelter – the Cooloola Great Walk topographic map (*see* p. 229) highlights areas where you're particularly exposed so you can plan accordingly – but on the plus side they provide great vantage points from which to spot passing whales. Amid the spear-like flower heads of grass trees, I climb a silica white sand track that gives long views of Teewah Beach and the vast blue sea.

Butterflies jig and birds sing in a small pocket of rainforest draped in vines, after which I climb gradually to reach the edge of the Cooloola Sandpatch. Though most of the

42km-long Cooloola Sand Mass is stabilised by vegetation, wind and rain have exploited a gap in the tree cover, allowing coastal dunes to sweep inland and swallow the forest, leaving a sweep of bare sand that takes a good half-hour to traverse. Crossing this Sandpatch provides the biggest navigational challenge of the entire route. It's 1200m across (uphill, if you're heading north), and don't bank on following the footsteps of those before you – the wind is likely to blow them out within half an hour. A sign recommends following a compass bearing, although a dead tree trunk midway provides a pretty good landmark to aim for. The sun is blinding on these stretches, shining relentlessly and bouncing off the sand below.

I start getting hot and tired as the day progresses but it's pretty walking in the afternoon through pockets of grass trees and banksia laden with seedpods. The track descends to shadow alongside the Noosa River, passing through woodland dotted with scribbly gums and blackbutt eucalyptus. 'Dutgee' is a local Aboriginal name for the pink and mauve boronia flowers that bloom here from spring to summer, and it's the name given to camp tonight which sits on the banks of the Noosa River. In the mid-20th century this site was used as a timber landing.

Despite emptying my shoes several times throughout the day, sand managed to work its way in and rub my heat-swollen feet. The river's dark tea-coloured waters are tempting for a swim but the odd bull shark has been known to cruise far upstream, so I opt for a foot soak instead and sit in peace to enjoy the river's mirror reflections of the trees lining it.

DAY 3
Dutgee campground to Litoria campground, 14.8km, 4.5–5.5hr

From Dutgee the trail stays inland, veering away from the river. I begin hiking across open heath plains dotted with purple wildflowers. Clouds sit like puffy balls of cotton wool against a blue sky, and, again I'm a sitting duck for the sun until the track merges into open forests of blackbutt and coastal wattle.

It's exceedingly pretty and provides welcome shade. Sandy tracks are lined with banksia and grass trees, and goannas are plentiful. I come across one huge specimen around 1.5m long, swaggering across my path in his own sweet time before scaling a tree.

There are a few hills on this section but none are long, and the sandy forest tracks are nicely padded with a sprinkling of leaves.

Litoria camp is nestled in the forest, with enough height to capture a cooling breeze and I laze about under trees all afternoon with a book, moving with the sun to catch the shade.

DAY 4
Litoria campground to Kauri campground, 20.5km, 6–7hr

Lake Cooloomera sits just off to the side of the track about 500m north of Litoria campground but don't plan to swim in it, as its waters are mildly acidic and home to the endangered 'acid' frog, Litoria cooloolensis, aka the Cooloola sedgefrog. Trampling the thick reeds that surround the lake causes

erosion and damages what is an important breeding habitat for them. As the night chorus starts up, you might hear the high-pitched sounds of this small green frog.

Every day on this walk is beautiful but this stretch seems particularly so. Much of it meanders on spacious sandy tracks through rainforest, rich with earthy smells and twittering with birds. Light filters through fronds of Picabeen palms, twisting vines dangle from the canopy, and strangler figs encase tree trunks like cast-iron netting. Only a smattering of kauri pines stand alone – with no low branches, climbers aren't able to gain a foothold. Their flanks are so arrow-straight and symmetrical, they appear almost like brown concrete columns.

In places, moss and fungi carpet fallen tree trunks. A wompoo fruit-dove catches my eye, perched on a branch overhead with its striking green plumage, white head and maroon chest.

The undulating sandy tracks continue all the way to Kauri campground, nestled deep in the rainforest. It's a noisy night from all the critters who also call it home. My kit stays safe but another camper has a hole nibbled in his tent. Food here is best securely stored in airtight containers or deep in your pack.

DAY 5
Kauri campground to Carlo carpark, 15.2km, 5hr

The final day begins in woodland carpeted with bracken ferns, before heading into rainforest dense with hoop pines, kauri and slender piccabeen palms. Whipbirds crack and butterflies flitter.

There is an option today for a significant detour out to Double Island Point, including about 9km of beach walking, but I opt for the shorter rainforest track via Poona Lake. Poona is a perched lake (meaning it sits in a sandy depression sealed by layers of organic matter and peat) and its beach is like a finger poking into the lake's belly, a drift of powdery soft white sand dotted with a few peeling paperbarks. With no inflow or outflow, it's best to avoid diving in while wearing sunscreen or insect repellent that would pollute the water, but it's an ideal rest spot regardless.

Only 600m from the finish line is the Carlo Sandblow. It's smaller than the Cooloola Sandpatch but no less impressive, another vast sweep of dunes with views stretching inland to plains and lakes, and out to sea where the golden sand seems to fall away infinity-style to meet a band of blue. Wander down the slope a little and you can catch a peek at Rainbow Beach.

It's an easy 15min walk from the sandblow, through scribbly gum forest, to the trail-end, which is worth bearing in mind if you fancy returning at sunset with a sundowner.

BEST EATS

- **Aromas Noosa:** There's no shortage of excellent dining options in the holiday resort town of Noosa, but this French-style cafe is an institution with chairs spilling onto the pavement and perfect for people watching. 32 Hastings St, Noosa Heads; (07) 5474 9788; aromasnoosa.com.au.
- **Little Parliament:** Cool décor and excellent, locally sourced food awaits at this cafe. 12 Rainbow Beach Rd, Rainbow Beach; (07) 5486 3277.
- **The Deck at Sea Salt:** Open air and facing the ocean, this is a perfect spot to hang out with a drink or a meal, from breakfast through to dinner. 2 Rainbow Beach Rd, Rainbow Beach; 0499 008 624; thedeckrainbowbeach.com.au.

BEST SLEEPS

- **Netanya Noosa:** If you want to do Noosa properly, plonk yourself right on Main Beach with all the shops and restaurants of stylish Hastings Street just out the back door. 71 Hastings St, Noosa; (07) 5447 4722; netanyanoosa.com.au.
- **Plantation Resort at Rainbow:** You can't beat the location of this luxurious apartment property on the corner of the main street and opposite the beach. 1 Rainbow Beach Rd, Rainbow Beach; (07) 5487 9600; plantationresortatrainbow.com.au.

WHILE YOU'RE HERE

- **Whale watching with Noosa Wave:** Between July and Oct, there's a steady stream of humpbacks migrating along the coast, and a 2hr cruise lets you get close enough to see the barnacles on their skin. Swimming with them is an optional extra. Noosa Wave, Noosa Whale & Dolphin Centre, 186 Gympie Terrace, Noosaville; 0458 997 188; noosawave.com.au.
- **Noosa National Park:** Watch surfers, spot whales and swim in remote bays while exploring the beautiful coastal tracks of Noosa Headland, all within easy walking distance of the hub of Hastings St. parks.des.qld.gov.au.
- **Epic Ocean Adventures:** A half-day kayak adventure with Epic Ocean Adventures begins with a beach drive past the multi-coloured sand cliffs of Rainbow Beach to reach Double Island Point (home of Australia's longest surfable wave). Boats are launched here into aqua waters to paddle with dolphins. 1/6 Rainbow Beach Rd, Rainbow Beach; 0408 738 192; epicoceanadventures.com.au.
- **Doors-off heli ride:** Swirls of sand and water, swathes of rainforest, and vast sand blows make for a spectacular landscape to fly over. It's almost certain you'll spot dugongs in the shallows, and maybe rays or a whale too. Rainbow Beach Airfield, Inskip Point Road, Rainbow Beach; 0448 883 442; rainbowbeachhelicopters.com.au.
- **K'gari/Fraser Island:** It's the world's largest sand island and is full of significant natural features, from pristine freshwater lakes to lush rainforest, ever-changing dunes, mangroves, dingoes, sand blows and long, long beaches, earning it UNESCO World Heritage status in 1992. In Sept 2021, the island's name was officially changed to K'gari, following a long campaign by the Traditional Owners, the Butchulla People. Previously it was Fraser Island, named after Eliza Fraser who was shipwrecked on the island in 1836 and whose false stories of mistreatment are associated with the dispossession and vilification of the Butchulla People.

Top Sunset from Brahminy camp *Opposite* Poona Lake

Hike and swim a wild island in the Wet Tropics.

Thorsborne Trail

This walk is on <u>Wargamaygan Country</u>.

Queensland

WHY IT'S SPECIAL

If you want to forget the modern world exists and live like a character from a children's adventure book, Hinchinbrook Island is the place to go. Here, you can walk barefoot on remote beaches, swim in abundant waterholes and waterfalls, camp in stunning locations and gather drinking water from pristine rivers.

The island is wild and mountainous with rocky peaks thrusting to heights of over 1000m. Lush rainforest is cut with streams and gushing waterfalls, and the terrain changes daily from beach to palm swamps, and paperbark and banksia country.

If you could design your own Eden, this would be it.

WALK IT

It's not an overly long trail, but if the challenging terrain doesn't slow you down at times, the endless swimming opportunities will, so allow plenty of time to linger and soak up the serenity. Four days is about the average to walk it but you might require some flexibility once you've taken into account boat transfer times to the island – dictated by the tides – and which of the seven hiker campsites you choose to stay at. I've detailed it in five days here but I've also walked it over six days, which allows for one full day of hanging out and swimming in waterfalls.

Walkers are restricted to a maximum of 40 per day to help minimise impact on the island's fragile landscapes. Campsites need to be pre-booked and they often fill up well in advance. Boat transfers to the island depart from Port Hinchinbrook in Cardwell and Lucinda (further south), often spotting wildlife en route, such as turtles, dugongs and even whales.

It makes little difference which direction you walk, though more people tend to walk north to south (I like to buck the trend and head north, ending with the spectacular mountain-backed beaches). Consult the Lucinda tide table before locking in dates, as tides affect departure times for island transfers as well as the hiking on coastal sections. While there are lots of river crossings, under normal conditions they are only ankle deep but hiking poles really help for balance here.

 Trail talk
- Distance: 33.5km
- Time: 4-5 days
- Rating: Hard
- Technicality: Lots of rock hopping, river crossings and a little graded trail.
- Puff factor: The nature of the terrain means it can be tiring at times, although there are no particularly long climbs to contend with.
- Watch out for: Use the pack racks provided in camp to prevent critters chowing down on your food. Rocks are slippery when wet. Marine stingers wash onshore from Oct-May. At the time of writing, no crocodile attacks on hikers have occurred on the island's east coast. However, this is croc country and it's possible they could pop up at any time so download the fact sheet on how to 'Be Crocwise in Croc Country' from environment.des.qld.gov.au.

 When to go
April to Oct is best, avoiding the overly hot and wet seasons.

 Resources
Visit parks.des.qld.gov.au for map and trail notes, and pre-book campsites at parks.des.qld.gov.au/parks/hinchinbrook-thorsborne/camping. Arrange a water taxi from Port Hinchinbrook in Cardwell or Lucinda to and from the island trailheads. See hinchinbrookislandcruises.com.au or absolutenorthcharters.com.au.

Opposite The rugged interior, from Nina Peak

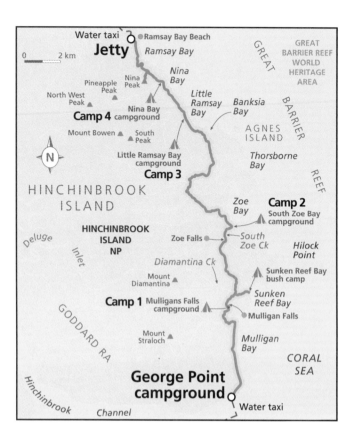

At 393sqkm, Hinchinbrook is one of Australia's largest island national parks, protected since 1932. It sits within the Great Barrier Reef World Heritage Area and, at the time of writing, it remains uninhabited and undeveloped, save for a few drop-toilets and picnic tables - that is, if you discount the small tourism lodge at the northern end of the island that closed in 2010, now all but reclaimed by nature. The Thorsborne Trail was named after key Queensland environmental conservationists and activists, Arthur and Margaret Thorsborne. It was in 1964 when they first camped on Hinchinbrook Island and fell in love with the place, later purchasing adjacent land on the mainland - part of which they donated to Edmund Kennedy National Park. They shone a light on the massacre of Torresian imperial pigeons at their breeding colony on nearby North Brook Island. After Arthur passed away in 1991, Margaret fought to defend Hinchinbrook's waters and wildlife against threats posed by the Port Hinchinbrook marina and resort development. Margaret saw herself as a 'protector, not a protestor', and was well respected by governments and decision-makers for her polite but passionate calls to protect the environment. In 2011 she became an Officer of the Order of Australia. Margaret died in 2018, but she inspired a new generation in the fight for conservation.

Opposite Swimming at Mulligan Falls *Overleaf* Standing at the top of Zoe Falls

ITINERARY

DAY 1
George Point campground to Mulligan Falls campground, 7.5km, 2–2.5hr

You get a good look at this huge and sprawling island from the hour-long water taxi ride from Port Hinchinbrook to George Point, passing its mangrove dominated western side to the ocean beaches of the east, where the trail is. With rocky peaks rising from dense greenery and palm trees fringing its shore, it really looks like the Land of the Lost.

I'm dropped with three friends on a beach patterned with little explosions of sand beads made by burrowing soldier crabs and the first 5km of beach walking gives us further opportunity to size up the terrain ahead. One creek crossing is best done at low- to mid-tide, and there's another five to cross once we head inland through rainforest, each one an obstacle course of river rocks and snaking tree roots, though our feet manage to stay dry.

Camp is tucked in the forest, moments from Mulligans Falls where rock slabs the colour of coffee grounds cascade into an emerald pool so crystalline you can clearly see the boulders that line it. It's the first of many perfect swimming holes and is deemed croc-free (*see* p. 236).

DAY 2
Mulligan Falls campground to South Zoe Bay campground, 7.5km, 4–5hr

The day begins with another swim at the falls, before climbing through grass trees for expansive views over the ocean. After only half an hour of walking we're lured by Diamantina Creek for another dip, its water flowing between a maze of rocks to fill a shallow waterhole so lusciously clear we're powerless to resist. Lolling about on warm rocks afterwards keeps us entertained until lunchtime. Lazy? Maybe. But indulging in this playground is what the Thorsborne Trail is all about.

A half-hour diversion leads to a bush camp at Sunken Reef Bay. I stayed here once, wading a slightly nerve-wracking cloudy and crotch-deep river to reach it but sharing the remote beach with only fireflies at night was a real treat.

An energetic climb over tree roots and rocks through dense rainforest lifts us high onto open heathland dotted with grass trees, offering views of the vast green interior. Rock hopping a few more rivers delivers us at the top of one of the island's most treasured features – Zoe Falls. Flopping fully clothed into the infinity pools at its top (swims are too numerous to keep changing into swimming gear), we relish the sweeping views over the sandy arc of Zoe Bay backed by rainforest and mountains.

It's a steep and rocky descent alongside the falls (a thick, knotted rope helps on one stretch) to reach the large green pool at its base – pure heaven and reason for yet another swim. We share the clear water with jungle perch and yabbies that are prone to nibbling on toes.

Sandwiched between rainforest and beach, South Zoe Bay campground is large enough to cater to the sea kayakers and boat campers that come to visit the island. Flowing out to sea here, sandy-bottomed South Zoe Creek is deep and was home to a 4m croc during our visit. Give it a wide berth. At the time of writing, there was talk of creating an additional campsite at the beach's northern end to separate hikers and paddlers.

DAY 3
South Zoe Bay campground to Little Ramsay Bay campground, 10.5km, 6hr

The day we have to tackle a swamp coincides with torrential rain (80mm over two days) but at least it's warm. We surrender to the wet, wading through a fan palm swamp well over knee deep in places, feeling more than ever like wild forest creatures. Blackened mangrove roots contrast with bright green rainforest and everything glistens under the rain's cover.

There are a string of rock-strewn creeks to cross and one of them actually has a crocodile warning sign next to it but the water is ankle deep and unintimidating. We exchange rainforest for peeling paperbarks and tall grassland, then take a detour down to the pale sandy arc of Banksia Bay – another option for camping although we keep going. Keep an eye out for the golden orchids that grow on the rocks here.

A few kilometres of rock hopping around headlands leads to our camp at Little Ramsay Bay. The giant white-tailed rats are particularly active here. One nudges me awake in the night through the tent wall during a search for muesli bar wrappers, while another chews a hole in my friend's tent. Anything with a scent will attract them – hand sanitiser and toothpaste included – so store everything on the pack racks provided.

DAY 4
Little Ramsay Bay campground to Nina Bay campground, 4km, 2.5hr

It's still raining in the morning and with only a short walk ahead of us, no one's in any rush to get up. When the raindrops on the flysheet lessen we finally rouse ourselves from bed, pack up wet tents and start hiking.

For a short stretch we're on the beach, before heading inland alongside a creek. When the trail descends to the coast again it spills onto a mass of round salmon-coloured rocks, polished smooth and treacherous in the wet. It's our path for a while, and I step from clinking stone to stone, my boots slipping awkwardly a few times.

It's a scramble along charred orange rock platforms between the sea and a rising bank of green punctuated by mist-covered rocky peaks to reach the long, wide sand of Nina Bay. Camp for the night is at its northern end.

Though we haven't walked long today, Nina is an idyllic place to while away an afternoon with a huge beach fringed in palm trees and scattered with orange granite and lumps of pumice. A short walk inland leads to a stream running haphazard through a bed of black rocks sprouting paperbarks, palms and mangroves, and little pools offer a sheltered spot to sit and meditate on the birds and butterflies flitting from tree to tree. Such lazy days, empty of an agenda,

are an intrinsic part of the appeal of this island walk. It allows us to scatter and explore on our own, to kick off our shoes and dig our toes in the sand, to wander aimlessly and breathe in the clean air, far from civilisation

DAY 5
Nina Bay to Ramsay Bay, 4km, 2.5hr

It's another short leg from Nina Bay to our finish point at Ramsay Bay today, but finish times need to coincide with the water taxi back to the mainland. We leave at first light with plans for a half-hour side trip to summit Nina Peak on an unmarked but reasonably well-defined goat track. Keep an eye out for a turning not long after camp. From 312m, Nina Peak is an utterly breathtaking 360-degree lookout. The ocean appears endless, the sun's golden orb rising from it to spill light across the island's green interior and dramatic peaks. To the north, Ramsay Bay Beach is a lick of white sand 8.5km long, backed by emerald plains drizzled in mangrove rivers flowing out to the west coast.

The final kilometres are done barefoot. Ramsay Bay is another vision of perfection worth relaxing on if you have time, particularly when you consider it's inaccessible to all except the odd few who arrive by boat. Keep an eye out for the fossilised remains of crabs that wash up in the sand, over 5000 years old.

It's a short walk inland to a small jetty hidden in the mangroves where our taxi to the mainland awaits. Our island escape lasted only five days but it may as well have been two weeks for all the restorative power it had. Hinchinbrook is a hard place to leave but we're soon motoring through narrow passageways in the mangroves while the island's dramatic peaks fall away behind us. Civilisation awaits, leaving our wild adventure to our memories.

Top Rocky trails can be challenging at times *Bottom* Ramsay Bay Beach *Opposite* From Nina Peak, mangrove-lined rivers flowing to the west coast

BEST EATS

- **Seabreeze Café Lounge:** Sea breezes and sea views go very nicely with the hefty burgers and fish and chips at this mainland cafe. 105 Victoria St, Cardwell; (07) 4066 8818.
- **Cardwell Beachcomber Restaurant:** Looking out across to Hinchinbrook Island, this indoor/outdoor restaurant has a menu with something to please everyone. 43a Marine Parade, Cardwell; (07) 4066 8550; beachcombersrestaurant.com.

BEST SLEEPS

- **Kookaburra Holiday Park:** All budgets are catered to at this property nestled in tropical gardens, one street back from the beach. Choose from camping, dorm beds, cabins, and villas. 175 Bruce Hwy, Cardwell; (07) 4066 8648; kookaburraholidaypark.com.au.
- **Cardwell Beachfront Motel:** Absolute beach frontage and prime views across to Hinchinbrook Island make this motel a popular choice. 1 Scott St, Cardwell; (07) 4066 8776; cardwellbeachmotel.net.

WHILE YOU'RE HERE

- **Etty Bay:** If you want an almost guaranteed chance of spotting wild cassowaries, descend off the rainforested Moresby Range into the tiny settlement of Etty Bay. If you're driving to Cardwell from Cairns, you'll pass it en route at about halfway. These enormous horned birds wander along the beach in the late afternoon and early morning, and sometimes in the middle of the day too.
- **Wallaman Falls:** It's a 90min drive south-west of Cardwell to visit the highest permanent single-drop waterfall in the country which gushes 268m off a seriously impressive rocky escarpment in the rainforest of Girringun National Park, on the Traditional Land of the Wargamaygan People. A 2hr return walk descends from the lookout to the bottom of the falls.

Towering sandstone walls hide an outback oasis of palms, moss gardens, waterfalls and rock art.

Carnarvon Gorge

This walk is on <u>Bidjara</u> and <u>Garingbal Country</u>.

WHY IT'S SPECIAL

Over 30 million years, the meandering Carnarvon Creek cut a cookie-cutter slice into one of Queensland's highest plateaus, located in the outback. It's seriously old country, the accumulating river sediment that formed the rock laid down around 200 million years ago. The gorge's sheer, 200m-high sandstone walls contain something of a time capsule of ancient rock and plants. It is a place of Bidjara and Garingbal culture and the Dreaming story tells of how Mundagurra, the Rainbow Serpent, carved the sandstone of the gorge as he traversed the creeks.

One main trail follows the gorge floor, sprouting numerous short diversions into damp and cool side-gorges, each with their own unique appeal. Varied microclimates support ancient king ferns, cycads, wildflowers and waterfalls, plus there are massive rock chambers, and thousands of First Nations' engravings, stencils and paintings (*see* p. 246).

WALK IT

This is an out and back walk, crisscrossing the Carnarvon Creek en route to the turnaround point at Big Bend (although you can turn around before that if you run out of puff). If you only walk the relatively flat path through the gorge floor you'll still be impressed, but it's in the side-trips where things get really interesting. There are seven in total, and most are around 1km return in length. The more you tick off, the longer the walk, so head out early to avoid the worst of the heat. Note that swimming is not permitted in Carnarvon Creek.

While the Carnarvon Highway that leads to the park is sealed, there are two culverts to tackle across Carnarvon Creek which can flood after heavy rain (call the Carnarvon Gorge Discovery Centre on (07) 4984 4652 to check current road conditions). The gorge is a long way from anywhere (6–8hr from Bundaberg, Brisbane and Longreach, 4.5hr from Rockhampton). While you can get very basic supplies from the few resorts here, it's best to come prepared with everything you'll need for your visit, including food if you're camping.

 Trail talk
- Distance: 19.4km return + side trips
- Time: One full day
- Rating: Easy-moderate
- Technicality: Generally well-formed trail along the gorge floor with a little rock-hopping across creeks. Side trips may involve rocky steps or even ladders.
- Puff factor: Reasonably flat while following the main track along the gorge floor, but side-trips involve climbing.
- Watch out for: Take plenty of water. Check conditions and don't walk in hot weather or on days of extreme fire danger, or after rain as access can be restricted and flash flooding occurs (*see* Walk it section opposite).

 When to go
Best from April to Sept. Summer swelters at around 35-45°C.

 Resources
Visit parks.des.qld.gov.au for more info and to download a park guide and map.

Opposite The track crosses Carnarvon Creek numerous times

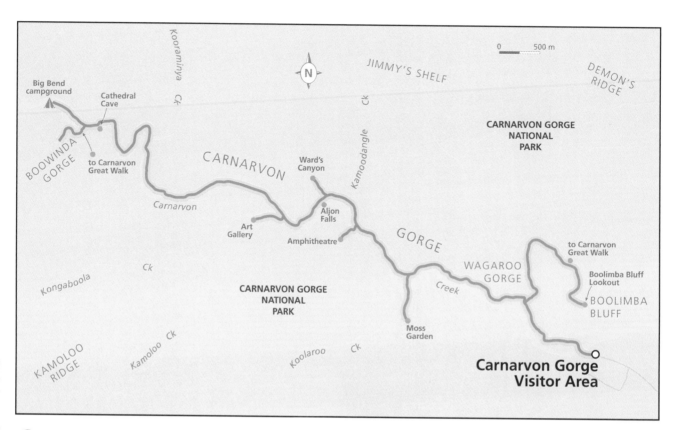

LOCAL SNAPSHOT

Excavations of campfire sites record that habitation of Bidjara and Garingbal Peoples in Carnarvon National Park goes back at least 19,500 years. Thousands of engravings, ochre stencils and freehand paintings adorn the gorge itself and are around 3500 years old. The Art Gallery is an extraordinary example of engravings and stencils (*see* p. 247) but these weren't created for art's sake.

In the mid 1800s, European settlers arrived and ceremonial ways of Traditional Owners haven't been practiced here since the late 1870s. However, the gorge is still a place of great spirituality and a wonderful place to learn more about First Nations' cultures.

Up Wagaroo Gorge, en route to Boolimba Bluff

ITINERARY

I'm always amazed at the diversity the outback manages to hide. I break my journey from Brisbane to overnight in the country town of Roma and after driving nearly 3hr from there across flat and barren land, setting foot in Carnarvon Gorge feels like arriving in Wonderland. Towering white sandstone walls harbour abundant Carnarvon palms, like giant green dandelions with tall thin trunks ending in an explosion of fronds. Pink and yellow hibiscus sprinkle themselves between Sydney blue gums, and the sound of whooping currawongs fills the air.

I begin walking from the Carnarvon Gorge Visitor Area in the cool just after dawn, soon coming across the first side trip, a 4.4km return jaunt to Boolimba Bluff. It's by far the longest diversion and a steep climb too, involving steps and a few ladders through Wagaroo Gorge to a panoramic bluff lookout. If you're anything like me, FOMO will require that you tackle it, but if energy or time is lacking, save yourself for the shorter side-trips which offer the best time-effort-reward ratio.

Back on the main trail, the Moss Garden is the first of many short side trips that veer off to hidden delights. It's only a 650m detour to reach this cool and damp hideaway with a little water cascade. It takes thousands of years for rainwater to filter through the sandstone, but where it meets a layer of impermeable shale it trickles out from the wall, feeding a profusion of moss and ferns.

The Amphitheatre is the next deviation and it's the star attraction here. At first it appears as though the 630m side trail ends in a wall of sandstone, but then I spy a series of metal ladders trailing up to the base of a narrow fissure splitting the cliff. I climb past the ferns that spill from its dark recesses and emerge on the other side in a cool chamber encircled by 60m walls opening to blue sky. The stillness of the space is enough to quieten anyone who enters and I sit on a bench seat for a while to soak it up.

The main trail is excessively pretty on its own, constantly accompanied by palms, highlighted by the white gorge walls. The gorge is a haven for wildlife and I spot wallabies and notice the marks left on tree trunks by yellow-bellied gliders who feed on sap in the night. In summer, lorikeets and swallows hide in cool hollows in the cliffs.

The 270m side track to Ward's Canyon involves climbing a series of rock steps past a waterfall, to eventually slide between the canyon's cool walls. The first chamber is home to tree ferns and the second to giant king ferns. Both are remnants from a time when Queensland's wet rainforests weren't just restricted to the coast.

The Art Gallery shelters under a rock overhang – 62m of emu feet, boomerangs, nets, hands, goanna, emu eggs, and hundreds of vulvas, a record of the women's business that took place here. All up, there are 1300 engravings and 700 stencils here. Further on, Cathedral Cave has yet more impressions.

Almost at the end of gorge is a spectacular deviation and as soon as you turn into it, you're in Boowinda Gorge. Curved and smoothed walls sweep left and right, dripping ferns and tree roots, the base lined with river pebbles. It's easy to imagine the water that once rushed through here – I'm basically walking in the steps of an ancient river – although it's still prone to flash flooding. The six-day Carnarvon Great Walk bears off here, en route to the plateau, but just wandering a kilometre up Boowinda showcases the most speccy bit.

Big Bend is the turnaround point for most and it's a much quicker return if you've already ticked off the many side gorges and can just cruise back along the gorge floor. Big Bend has a campsite set beneath the walls of an unsurprisingly large bend in the river; rather than head back, I spend a night here in readiness to continue the next day on the 87km Carnarvon Great Walk. Carnarvon Gorge is absolutely jam-packed with one magical surprise after another, and as I settle down contentedly for a night immersed within its walls, I drift off to the sound of rushing water, while the full moon silhouettes a Carnarvon palm on the side of my tent.

Steps climb to the Amphitheatre

BEST EATS

- **Takarakka Bush Resort:** Very limited takeaway is available here during the day, but on Tues, Thurs and Sun nights you can join a popular two-course spit roast dinner. O'Briens Rd, Carnarvon Gorge; (07) 4984 4535; takarakka.com.au.
- **Wilderness Restaurant:** Offering dishes such as goats curd tart with roasted beetroot or beef cheek with celeriac remoulade, you might forget that you're out in the middle of nowhere. Carnarvon Gorge Wilderness Lodge, O'Briens Rd, Carnarvon Park; (07) 4984 4503; wildernesslodge.com.au.

BEST SLEEPS

- **Big Breeze Holiday Park Carnavorn Gorge:** Just a 5min drive from the gorge is this sprawling property on the banks of Carnarvon Creek, previously called Takarakka Bush Resort. It has camping through to glamping and cabins. There's also a platypus viewing area with sightings pretty much daily (early morning and late afternoon are best). O'Briens Road, Carnarvon Gorge; (07) 4984 4535; breezeholidayparks.com.au/park/carnarvon-gorge.
- **Carnarvon Gorge Wilderness Lodge:** The closest accommodation to the gorge has 28 luxurious safari style cabins, a swimming pool and licensed restaurant. O'Briens Road, Carnarvon Park; (07) 4984 4503; wildernesslodge.com.au.

WHILE YOU'RE HERE

- **Carnarvon Great Walk:** If you want to get the full Carnarvon experience, head out on the 6 day/87km Great Walk. It's a pretty remote circuit heading through the gorge, up onto the Consuelo Tablelands and back down again. The scenery is more subtle up on the plateau, with most of the trail's highlights jammed into the first two days and last day of the route, but it's enjoyable for the sense of solitude, spectacular views of the gnarled fingers of the gorges from above, and for the forests of macrozamia (cycads) that are the biggest I've ever seen - up to 6m tall; parks.des.qld.gov.au.
- **The Rock Pool:** This is the only place within Carnarvon National Park where swimming is allowed. From the Rock Pool carpark (4.6km from the national park entrance), follow a 300m track and enjoy the refreshingly cool water, pebble beach and shaded picnic tables; parks.des.qld.gov.au.
- **Mickey Creek:** A 3km return walk follows Mickey Creek to reach a fork in the trail. Follow it right into the spectacular Warrumbah Gorge, a cool and slot canyon worn by eons of rushing water, and so narrow in places that you can touch both walls with arms outstretched. Start from Mickey Creek carpark, 4km from the park entrance; parks.des.qld.gov.au.

Tasmania

Australia's smallest state punches above its weight for epic hiking, from wild mountains to dazzling coast.

Mountains, glacial tarns, and epic views of the Southwest Wilderness Area.

Hartz Peak

This walk is on <u>Mellukerdee Country</u>.

WHY IT'S SPECIAL

Step onto the Hartz Peak Track and you could imagine you've been dropped into Tasmania's wild interior, yet it's only a 90min drive from Hobart. Three to four hours on the trail gives a bite-size snapshot of everything that is great about hiking in Tassie: rugged mountain vistas, scattered glacial tarns, a craggy summit climb and uninterrupted views over the Southwest Wilderness Area. It's a reasonably strenuous climb to the park's 1254m peak, but even just a dip of the toes on this route – as far as Lake Esperance – yields massive rewards.

Hartz Peak is the highest point of the Devils Backbone which stretches almost the entire length of Hartz Mountains National Park. It began as molten lava deep below the surface, later morphing into a hardy band of dolerite that pushed its way into existence around 165 million years ago. A little molding of the land, courtesy of a couple of ice ages, has resulted in the dramatic cirques, troughs and horn peaks so spectacular today.

WALK IT

Choose your own adventure: 1.5hr return will get you as far as Lake Esperance, 2hr will earn you views into the Southwest Wilderness Area from Hartz Pass (including gnarly Federation Peak), or go the full distance to Hartz Peak for an epic 360-degree panorama across mountains and ocean.

There's 11km of unsealed road to reach the carpark at the end of Hartz Road – easily done in a 2WD vehicle in good conditions, but in rain, ice or snow a 4WD would be recommended.

Inclement weather can hit alpine regions at any time of year, so hikers heading out in anything less than perfect conditions should go prepared with suitable clothing and supplies. There's an impressive fully enclosed shelter at the trailhead if you need to retreat.

 Trail talk
- Distance: 7.7km
- Time: 4hr
- Rating: Easy-hard
- Technicality: Easy boardwalk and rocky trail to Lake Esperance. Some more difficult scrambling and loose scree on the climb to Hartz Peak.
- Puff factor: Reasonably flat to Lake Esperance, then a lung-busting climb to the summit. Total elevation gain is around 400m.
- Watch out for: Check the forecast before you go and carry warm clothes and a rain jacket, even in summer.

 When to go
Spring to autumn is best. Blooming wildflowers in spring are spectacular.

 Resources
Visit parks.tas.gov.au/explore-our-parks/hartz-mountains-national-park for more details. A Tasmanian National Parks pass is required, available from passes.parks.tas.gov.au or at any parks office.

Opposite Descending towards Hartz Lake

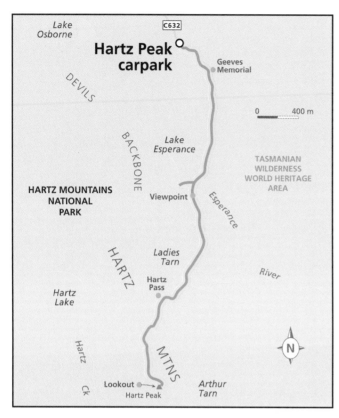

◉ LOCAL SNAPSHOT

The Hartz Mountains was one of Tasmania's first regions to become popular with bushwalkers, thanks largely to the cutting of an access track from nearby Geeveston in the mid 1800s by the Geeves family. Back then, new trails meant access for getting timber and minerals, but in 1897 a prospecting expedition by Osborne Geeves, his three sons and nephew, near Federation Peak, went tragically wrong. A blizzard thrashed them as they crossed the Hartz Range and son Arthur and nephew Sydney died from hypothermia. There's a memorial to the two men close to where they perished, just 5min into the Hartz Peak walk. It's a reminder as to how changeable and dangerous alpine weather can be. Declared a scenic reserve in 1939, the size of Hartz Mountains' protected area has fluctuated over the years in a tug of war with logging interests, before Hartz Mountains National Park was finally ushered into the Tasmanian Wilderness World Heritage Area in 1989. Logging still continues on its periphery.

Top It's a rough and rocky route near the summit *Overleaf* Views from the summit extend into the Southwest Wilderness

Stretches of boardwalk weave in and out of small groves of stunted trees, climbing an incline so gentle as to be barely noticeable. Lake Esperance is another creation of the glaciers that scraped their way through here 20,000 years ago and it ripples blue-green in the breeze, cupped by the Devils Backbone plunging into its far shore and a rising patchwork of rust, green and gold shrubs. Lizards sunbathe on a boardwalk and birdsong rings clear across the water. Several bench seats provide an opportunity to sit and soak up the serenity, if the wind isn't too cold. If you're looking for a short and mellow walk, turning around here (or at Ladies Tarn, a little further on) is an option.

From the vantage point of the trail, Hartz Peak doesn't exactly shout out that it's the highest mountain in the neighbourhood, rather it's a gradually rising continuation of the undulating Backbone, peaking at 1254m and ascending again for the small and pointed Mount Snowy behind it. After passing the smaller Ladies Tarn, I'm ready to begin the ascent to Hartz Pass, an energetic climb up a jumble of uneven rocks and tree roots squeezed by stiff shrubs and pandani. It's short-lived though, and once over the lip the immense Southwest Wilderness Area beyond fills the frame. Unmistakable are the distant jagged grey spires of Federation Peak in the Eastern Arthur Range. Only proper badasses tackle this notoriously remote and challenging mountain, but just looking at it is enough to feel connected with Tassie's wild interior.

Low orange triangles mark the climb to the summit and it's rock-hopping all the way. The final push is a mix of scrambling and a rock scree slope that clinks like rusty nails underfoot.

Hartz Peak doesn't have a lot of room to move, although a few flat rocky areas provide good perching points from which to take in the 360-degree views. From here, the mountains and valleys of the Southwest Wilderness Area ripple into the distance, to the east is a blue lick of sea, and below, Hartz Lake sits like a sapphire jewel set in green. It's a lot to soak in, so I rug up in a windproof jacket and linger for a while to absorb it all.

With the return entirely downhill, I am free to enjoy the trail and its scenery without my lungs and legs complaining. Hartz Lake, behind me on the climb, now sits front and centre in my field of view, growing larger with every step until I veer right to scramble back down off the backbone. I may have lost sight of the Southwest Wilderness Area but these flatter trails weave between tarns, waratahs and flowering red scoparia, wrapping up an unbelievably pretty hike.

ITINERARY

The Devils Backbone is in your face within minutes on the trail, rippling off to one side above a sea of green. I've lucked out with a mild, sunny day in spring when the track is lined with an eruption of wildflowers, most dazzling are the red Tasmanian waratahs. It's a photographer's field day.

BEST EATS

- **Michelle's Roadhouse Kitchen:** This place is renowned for its homemade pies and pasties. 50 Arve Rd, Geeveston; (03) 6297 1433.
- **The Old Bank of Geeveston:** You can get everything from artisan pastries and coffee through to fresh pasta and Tasmanian wine at this stylish bistro. 13 Church St, Geeveston; (03) 6297 9922.

BEST TOWNS

The Huon Valley and surrounds is full of cute towns and gourmet produce - it's famous for its apples and cider. Here are some of my recommended places to explore:

- **Cygnet** is set on sheltered Port Cygnet Bay and is a magnet for creative types and in the heart of farming country. Visit Fat Pig Farm - of *Gourmet Farmer* fame - for a long lunch, a workshop or tour of the property; fatpig.farm.
- **Franklin** is one of the oldest towns in the region and has quaint streetscapes to match. It's also known for its picturesque wooden boats floating on the Huon River, and The Wooden Boat Centre teaches traditional boat building methods; woodenboatcentre.com.
- **Geeveston** is a place to linger if you want to wander the streets of 'Rosehaven' (of the TV show fame). The visitor centre is an interesting stop, with displays on the history of the region's timber industry and local crafts. Geeveston Visitor Centre, Church St, Geeveston; (03) 6297 1120.
- **Bruny Island** is just a ferry ride away from the town of Kettering; sealinkbrunyisland.com.au. This is the place if you want to escape offshore for some wild natural beauty, rugged sea cliffs and gourmet food: the oysters are a specialty, and the cheese, chocolate and berries are delicious too.

WHILE YOU'RE HERE

- **Tahune Adventures:** A 20min detour off the road to Hartz Mountains leads to this immersive forest experience. People come for the Airwalk, a 600m elevated walkway amid giant treetops that ends in a cantilevered lookout 50m above the Huon and Picton rivers, but you could spend a day here if you want to try the hangglider zipline, swinging bridges walking track, or kayak and rafting trips; tahuneadventures.com.au.
- **Geeveston Circuit Platypus Walk:** Early morning or dusk is the best time to try and spot one of the resident platypus that live in the Kermandie River. The walk starts in the Geeveston Heritage Park which backs on to the visitor centre.

Hike a string of glacial tarns on Mount Field's alpine plateau.

Tarn Shelf Circuit

This walk is on Country belonging to the Lairmairrener People/Big River Nation.

WHY IT'S SPECIAL

Tasmania's oldest nature reserve is a pretty special place. Many people come to Mount Field National Park for its famous waterfalls and forests filled with tree ferns and giant ash, but continue driving to the end of the road at an altitude of 1040m, and you'll be launched into a vastly different alpine world. As height is gained, forests of endemic king billy, pencil pines and pandani give way to a rocky wonderland scattered with photogenic tarns. There's even a historic hut stocked with possessions from the backcountry skiers who hung out here in the 1930s. Overlooked by the imposing Rodway Range, epic views are pretty much a constant.

WALK IT

This circuit walk is often tackled anti-clockwise to finish with the most spectacular scenery, however note that route finding is a tad easier heading clockwise. If you're pushed for time, forgo the circuit and make a beeline directly for the Tarn Shelf. The return hike takes 3hr. Alternatively, there's an easy yet beautiful 40min Pandani Grove circuit around Lake Dobson at the very start.

The road is sealed as far as Mount Field Visitor Centre but expect 8km of dirt and gravel to reach Lake Dobson carpark; it's perfectly doable in a 2WD in good conditions but slippery when wet.

 Trail talk
- Distance: 15km
- Time: 5-6hr
- Rating: Moderate-hard
- Technicality: It's a mix of dirt, boardwalk and lots of rock hopping. A couple of sections require attention to stay on track.
- Puff factor: It's quite an energetic hike, with steady climbing and uneven terrain.
- Watch out for: Much of it is above the tree line so check the forecast and always carry warm and waterproof clothes.

 When to go
Spring through to autumn is best. Snow can happen anytime but avoid winter when the track can be hidden beneath it - and even closed. Autumn showcases the spectacular changing colours of Nothofagus beech.

 Resources
Visit parks.tas.gov.au for more details. Check ahead for road closures, phone (03) 6288 1149. A National Parks Pass is required from passes.parks.tas.gov.au or at any Parks & Wildlife Service office.

Opposite Looking out over Lake Seal

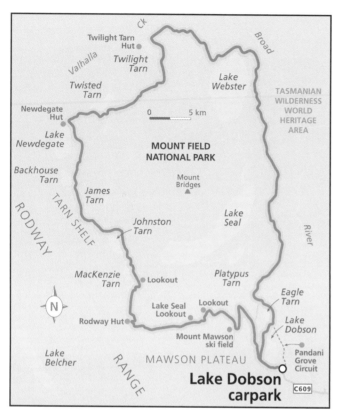

👁 LOCAL SNAPSHOT

Over a century ago, it was recognised that Mount Field should be 'not merely a reserve marked on the map, but a thoroughly valuable and useful and popular feature of Tasmania for residents and tourists alike'. It was Tasmania's first nature reserve in 1885, first national park in 1916 (along with Freycinet) and is now part of the Tasmanian Wilderness World Heritage Area. Of course, it was treasured long before that. The Lairmairrener People/Big River Nation lived here for tens of thousands of years, seeing its transition from a land buried beneath glaciers to one rich in rainforest and giant eucalypt. A significant record of the Lairmairrener People/Big River Nation's traditional way of life exists in caves on the fringe of the park and in nearby rock art, ochre mines and stone tool quarries.

Top Curled fronds of a pandani *Opposite* Historic hut at Twilight Tarn

ITINERARY

I start walking from Lake Dobson carpark, just metres from the lake itself, and as I make my way around its shores, I encounter the world's tallest heath plant. Endemic pandani cast shaggy figures with crowning 'manes' of fronds brushing against rare king billy and pencil pines. Some sprout at ground level, while others look down over me from heights of three or four metres. It's an impressive start.

The track peels away to climb gently and, like a carefully choreographed performance, it really knows how to build drama and anticipation, regularly drip-feeding visions that keep me reaching for my camera. Platypus Tarn, Lake Seal and Lake Webster lead to the serious treat that is Twilight Tarn. Patchwork greens meets the russet water's edge and at its western end sits an impossibly cute wooden hut with roughly hewn walls capped in rusted corrugated-iron. Its construction in 1927 was a labour of love. Back then a hardy bunch of skiers carried in supplies for what became a cosy base for skiing, ice-skating on the frozen lake or just partying on (it's rumoured a gramophone made it in too). Nowadays, the remote hut is part museum, managed by Parks & Wildlife Service Tasmania, and full of memorabilia from its heyday. Wooden skis and bamboo ski poles lean against the fireplace, sepia photos of skiers line the walls and vintage metal food boxes sit stacked in the corner.

Rivers of ice sculpted this terrain – the last ice age ended 10,000 years ago – gouging valleys and leaving the land scattered with random boulders and scree fields. As the trail gently climbs, vegetation becomes sparser. Boardwalks hover over fragile heath dotted with bleached skeletons of trees burned in the 1934 fires. Beyond Lake Newdegate, I'm officially on the Tarn Shelf but, from the chorus of 'ribbits' in the air, it could also be the shelf of a million frogs. One pool leads to the next, mirror-like dollops of mercury reflecting the flat grey skies above (sunlight would paint a different picture but either way is beautiful), and shadowing the plateau is the long backbone of the imposing Rodway Range.

Though the trail is reasonably popular there is a real sense of remoteness to it, thanks to its unformed nature and rugged views. The higher I climb, the better they get. Near the trail's highest point at 1265m there is a prime view east over

Lake Seal, which looks like its namesake flopped in a deep valley far below.

After what seems like an eternity of uphill (albeit mostly gentle), Rodway Hut marks a welcome turning point. It's also the loading point for a volunteer-operated rope tow stretching up Mount Mawson – there are still some diehard skiers in the 'hood.

I ease off the Tarn Shelf and bear east for the descent. It's gentle at first, a mix of boardwalk and an obstacle course of jagged rocks marked by timber poles. As on the shelf, the views are unimpeded until the route drizzles into the trees, where pale trunks contrast against green undergrowth and boulders smeared in orange and black lichen. After hours of climbing and rock hopping, it's a bit of a relief to hit a gravel road where I can make easy progress downhill through the forest. It takes me back to Lake Dobson where my shaggy friends, the pandanus, wait to greet me. I realise looking at them, that when you first pass a point on a walk, you have no idea how much you'll experience, before returning to that point. This experience has been amazing.

A small pool among alpine grasses

BEST EATS

- **Waterfalls Café and Gallery:** This is your closest option to fuel up on hearty burgers, pulled pork rolls or savoury tarts. Mount Field Visitor Centre, 90 Lake Dobson Rd, Mount Field; (03) 6288 1526.
- **Possum Shed Cafe:** This cute indoor/outdoor riverside cafe serves homemade scones through to vegie burgers, nachos and more. Keep your eyes peeled for the resident platypus. 1654 Gordon River Rd, Westerway; (03) 6288 1364; thepossumshed.com.au.

BEST SLEEPS

- **Government Huts:** These unpowered wooden huts are basic but perfectly situated for exploring Mount Field and just moments from the trailhead on Lake Dobson Rd. Built in the 1940s, the huts have bunk beds for up to six people, cold water and wood-fired heaters. Book via parks.tas.gov.au or call (03) 6491 1179.
- **The Woodbridge:** If you fancy playing lord or lady of the manor for a night, stay at this meticulously restored country house (circa 1825), perched on the shores of the Derwent River with distant views of Mount Field. 6 Bridge St, New Norfolk; 0417 996 305; woodbridgenn.com.au.

WHILE YOU'RE HERE

- **Russell Falls:** The three-tiered cascade of Russell Falls is an easy 15min walk from Mount Field Visitor Centre through the rainforest (at night you'll see glow worms). Continue on from here for the 6km Three Falls Circuit and its giant ash trees.
- **Maydena Bike Park:** This epic gravity-based bike park spans 820m of vertical elevation (shuttle buses whisk you to the top) in the Derwent Valley, with scores of trails that offer spectacular mountain and forest views. Suitable for all comers but a downhiller's dream. 34-36 Kallista Rd, Maydena; 1300 399 664; maydenabikepark.com.
- **Styx Tall Trees Conservation Area:** Come here to see some of the fattest and tallest eucalypt in the world, the giant ash. A few short walks wander between specimens over 80m high. The Conservation Area is a 45min drive from Mount Field National Park and there is no mobile phone coverage. It often rains here so carry wet weather gear and be careful on roads which can be slippery. Big Tree Reserve, Styx Rd, Styx Valley; parks. tas.gov.au/explore-our-parks/styx-tall-trees-conservation-area.
- **New Norfolk:** Less than an hour's drive from Mount Field National Park is the charming town of New Norfolk in the Derwent Valley. It has become a hub for antiques stores, like The Drill Hall Emporium (thedrillhall.com.au), and artisan stores like FlyWheel Stationery & Letterpress Studio (flywheel.net.au) and Miss Arthur Home Goods (missarthur.com.au). The renowned restaurant, The Agrarian Kitchen (theagrariankitchen.com) is also here.

A touch of luxury with hut-to-hut walking around Australia's tallest sea cliffs.

Three Capes Track

This walk is on <u>Paredarerme Country</u>.

WHY IT'S SPECIAL

Forget counting the grams in your backpack. With fully equipped huts en route, this is a walk where you can swap tents and stoves for more important things like wine and antipasto. Lassooing a chunk of the Tasman Peninsula/Turrakana, the trail meanders a dramatic coastline, including Australia's highest sea cliffs, as well as heathland, moors and forest. Whale spotting is a bonus.

Australia's slickest hut-to-hut walk launched in 2015, with architecturally designed cabins complete with sleeping mattresses, kitchens, yoga mats and even board games. With USB charging points and mobile reception widespread, it's not a place to fall off the radar but at least your socials will be up to date.

For those wanting to embark on their first multi-day hike, carry a little less weight, or simply wallow in the luxury of a well-crafted trail, there can be few better choices.

WALK IT

For a walk that is neither guided nor supported, the price tag of $495 might initially seem high but it's actually good value. The track starts and ends at Port Arthur Historic Site – Australia's best-preserved and perhaps most infamous convict-era site – and walk fees include entry to its buildings and ruins. Access to the trailhead is provided via a 1hr scenic cruise with Pennicott Wilderness Journeys and at the end of the hike, a bus transfer returns walkers to Port Arthur.

Numbers are capped at 48 and there's no deviating off the standard anti-clockwise, three-night itinerary. Bunkrooms have anywhere from four to eight beds and friendly rangers at each camp are fonts of knowledge on the natural history.

If you don't have four days to spare, then dedicate four hours for the spectacular hike from Fortescue Bay to Cape Hauy and back.

 Trail talk
- Distance: 48km
- Time: 4 days
- Rating: Easy-moderate
- Technicality: The track is well-formed dirt, boardwalk and steps.
- Puff factor: Elevation changes are frequent but rarely fluctuate beyond 100m, though the thousand steps leading to Cape Hauy will test the lungs and knees.
- Watch out for: Take care close to precipitous sea cliffs.

 When to go
The track is open year-round and huts are heated for cold winter nights. Spring brings wildflowers, while autumn is when migrating short-tailed shearwaters pass through and orchids bloom. Whales pass through in both spring and autumn.

 Resources
Visit threecapestrack.com.au and pennicottjourneys.com.au/three-capes-track for information and bookings. A comprehensive guidebook, including maps, is given to walkers on arrival.

Gear rental and yummy dehydrated food can be sourced from Three Capes Gear & Gourmet; 3capesgearandgourmet.com.au.

Opposite Looking out over Arthurs Peak

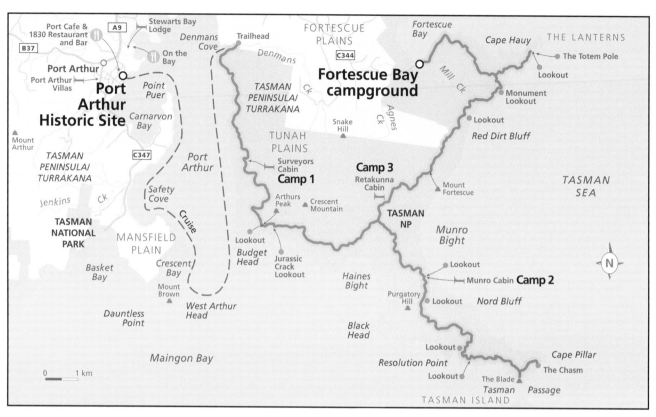

◉ LOCAL SNAPSHOT

For such a stunning region, the Tasman Peninsula/Turrakana has had a brutal past. Connected to mainland Tasmania by an isthmus, Eaglehawk Neck/Teralina, only 30m wide, it was once considered as the ideal place to isolate convicts. From 1830 until 1877, they slaved away at Port Arthur and punishments for bad behaviour were severe. Lashings inflicted by the cat o' nine tails were problematic, due to infection and occasional death, and were eventually replaced with solitary confinement in pitch-black cells, causing lasting trauma of a different kind. The nearby Coal Mines Historic Site was a virtual hell on Earth, with convicts working half-naked 100m underground in damp, dark and confined conditions. The ruins here are unmanned and far less well defined than at Port Arthur, but are worth checking out for the sense of discovery and beautiful setting at Norfolk Bay.

Opposite Munro cabin

ITINERARY

DAY 1

Port Arthur to Surveyors Cabin, 4km, 1.5-2hr

The first day's walk is short but, like everything else on this track, there is a carefully curated method to it. A good few hours are needed to wander the grounds of Port Arthur before you even begin hoisting your backpack. Then there's the exhilarating cruise-cum-transfer onboard *The Blade* boat to the trailhead, giving a close up of the rugged sea cliffs and caves soon to be explored from above. On the day I set out, the clean sapphire waters are unusually calm and our boat noses inside a high-roofed cavern where the gentle swell swirls great ribbons of kelp clinging to its insides.

By the time we're deposited onto the trail at Denmans Cove, it's already mid afternoon – but there's no rush. Rangers pre-allocate sleeping cabins, removing any temptation to hurry ahead and bags a bed.

The trail starts gently, skirting the coastline and climbing through heathland, with regular glimpses out to sea. One of the trail's great features is the scattering of 'story-seats' at regular intervals, a prompt to pause and read interpretive information relevant to the area from the guidebook given to all walkers. There are 40 all up, each with their own imaginative and artful design, and stories provide insights on anything from flora and fauna to geology and convict history. Aside from being super interesting, they also provide a very valid excuse to stop and rest every half an hour.

Eucalypt woodland and buttongrass plains lead to Surveyors Cabin, actually a series of cabins surrounded by tiered timber decks. In the world of multi-day hiking, huts are a rare treat, and these ones strike a fine balance between being cool and relatively luxurious, yet in keeping with the environment.

The distant ocean and the jagged profile of Cape Raoul is the focal point this evening, and if you haven't brought your own stash of wine and nibbles you'll spend sunset drooling over everyone else's. Despite the trail's name, this is the closest hikers will get to the third cape.

DAY 2
Surveyors Cabin to Munro Cabin, 11km, 4–4.5hr

One of the perks of having a light pack and a fully equipped kitchen to work with is the ability to create meals that would otherwise be a wistful hiker's dream. I've upgraded my usual peanut butter and crackers breakfast to pancakes from local supplier Three Capes Gear & Gourmet (*see* p. 265), plus I've added raspberries and it sets a good tone for the day.

I'm feeling refreshed and eager when I launch into eucalypt forest and boardwalks lined with wildflowers. A 100m climb up Arthurs Peak passes briefly through moss and lichen-filled forest, watered by the upwelling of cold damp air hitting the adjacent dolerite wall rising from the ocean. It's visible in all its glory from a rock platform lookout further up, along with the sandy arc of Crescent Bay, Cape Raoul and any pods of dolphins that happen to be passing by.

Open heathland undulates across the cliff-tops with panoramic ocean views. It's a patchwork of colour from wildflowers in

spring, but for hikers who can't tell their Tasman hairy boronias from their golden bushpeas, an instalment from the guidebook has a handy ID guide.

Munro Cabin leans into swamp gum forest while gazing out over Munro Bight, 242m below. It's another masterpiece of design, a thoughtful cluster of cabins and open-air spaces, shielded from the wind by sliding doors that are reminiscent of a Japanese teahouse. A telescope perched at a lookout allows close inspection of the wall of sea cliffs, and there are even two outdoor showers enclosed by curls of corrugated-iron. Steaming water from a hoisted bucket is a dream ending to a day's walk.

DAY 3
Munro Cabin to Retakunna Cabin, 19km, 6-7hr

The trail's longest stage can be done mostly carrying just a daypack (carry a lightweight compactable one or a cheap cloth bag with strings for straps), and you can leave your larger pack at Munro Cabin. From Munro, walkers head out to Cape Pillar and return to collect their packs, with just an additional hour further to reach Retakunna Cabin. It's a day of high drama, skirting Australia's highest sea cliffs, around 300m tall.

The start is mellow. Birds twitter in a forest scattered with red Tasmanian waratahs, before the trail emerges onto open heathland and possibly Australia's longest boardwalk at 2.5km long.

About an hour in is the first opportunity to peer over a cliff edge and it's the kind of sheer and seemingly endless descent

to frothing blue water that makes you want to hang onto a bush, in case vertigo strikes. The fact that nearly all cliffs on the track are unfenced only amplifies the feeling of exposure.

The views come thick and fast and, though the trail itself is wide and secure, there are regular opportunities to peer over vertiginous walls – but take great care and don't get too close to the edge. Around 185 million years ago, magma worked its way through cracks in sedimentary rock that later wore away to leave the striking column-like formations so predominant now. Even offshore, the enormous plateau of Tasman Island is skirted by 280m cliffs and features one lonely lighthouse (c. 1906) and hundreds of thousands of seabirds.

A short side-scramble leads to The Blade, a narrow prow of rock reaching for the sea, from where I spy several whales splashing in the distance. The Chasm is another impossibly sheer and deep cutting, before a zig-zag of rocky steps leads to Cape Pillar's end of the line. I retrace my steps back to Munro but, as always, the views are totally different when you turn 180 degrees, and I find my attention drawn to Munro Bight across to the north.

Every camp has a different style and setting and Retakunna is situated in low eucalypt scrub and moorland at the base of Mount Fortescue with deck chairs scattering long verandahs. I pass a happy afternoon 'baking' a chocolate brownie in my cooking pot, stretching on a yoga mat in the sun, and chewing the fat with new friends.

The route trails over Australia's tallest sea cliffs

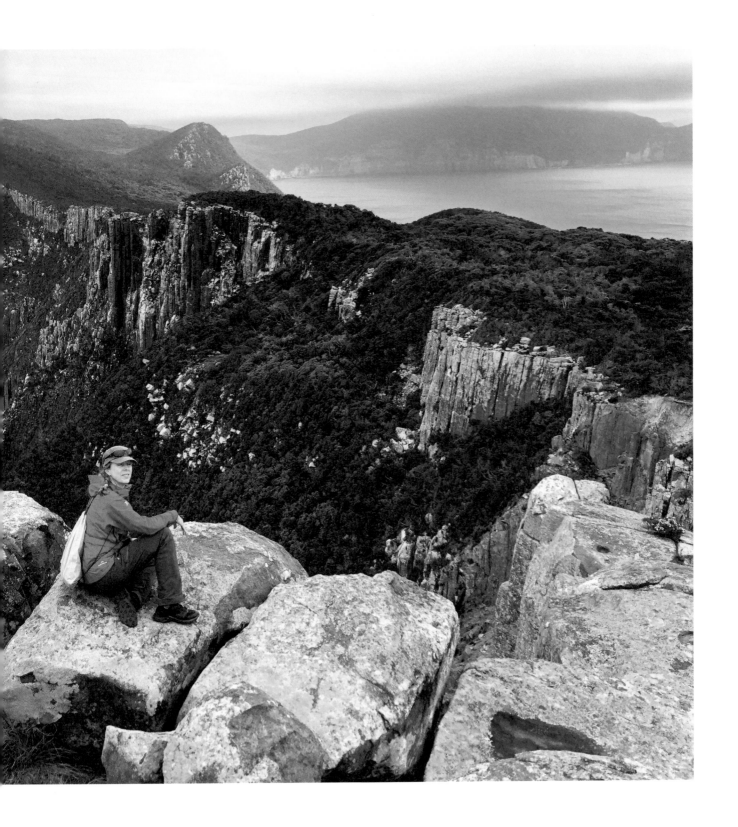

DAY 4
Retakunna Cabin to Port Arthur, via Cape Hauy and Fortescue Bay, 14km, 6-7hr

What's billed as the hike's toughest day starts with a 300m haul up Mount Fortescue, but by now packs are almost depleted of food and far lighter than when we started. Here, dolerite boulders in the rainforest are carpeted in moss and surrounded by tree ferns.

After walking for 3hr, a side-trail branches out towards Cape Hauy and though the nearly 1000 steps descending and climbing again is enough to put some off attempting it, the 2hr side trip is not to be missed. At its end, a rare fence provides enough security to happily stand with toes almost broaching the cliff-edge to peer over. Dolerite columns appear like organ pipes and one, the Totem Pole, stands as a lone sentinel in the ocean. Experienced rock climbers sometimes climb its 65m height, but on my visit the cape is left to wailing seabirds and a colony of fur seals basking on rock platforms pounded by foaming waves.

Fortescue Bay's aqua waters and silky arc of white sand marks the end of the track and despite a rash promise to dive in once my pack is downed, the thought quickly evaporates when I hear the shrieks of other swimmers braving the cold Tasman Sea. Think I'll wait for a hot shower instead.

A cheery bus driver meets our group of hikers to transfer us back to Port Arthur (organised as part of the trail booking), wrapping up an exceptional and slickly run walk. From go to whoa, the scenery, pace, interpretation and campsites offer a walk so perfectly balanced and beautiful I feel more enriched, informed and uplifted than tired. Still, the evening's hot shower, chicken parmi and wine goes down well.

BEST EATS

- **Port Café:** Situated within the Port Arthur Historic Site, this cafe has an excellent range of food; (03) 6251 2310; portarthur.org.au.
- **1830 Restaurant and Bar:** This is arguably the best food and wine you'll find in the area, and it offers sweeping views of the Port Arthur Historic Site too. 6973 Arthur Hwy, Port Arthur; (03) 6251 2310; portarthur.org.au.
- **On the Bay:** Waterfront at Stewarts Bay Lodge, this is the place for a steak and seafood fix. 6955 Arthur Hwy, Port Arthur; (03) 6250 2771; stewartsbaylodge.com.au.

BEST SLEEPS

- **Port Arthur Villas:** These immaculate motel-style self-contained apartments are set on two acres of gardens, just across the road from Port Arthur Historic Site and within staggering distance of pub food and drinks. 52 Safety Cove Rd, Port Arthur; (03) 6250 2239; portarthurvillas.com.au.
- **Stewarts Bay Lodge:** These log cabins and deluxe spa chalets are set around the emerald waters and white sandy beach of Stewarts Bay. 6955 Arthur Hwy, Port Arthur; (03) 6250 2888; stewartsbaylodge.com.au.

WHILE YOU'RE HERE

- **Cape Raoul & Shipstern Bluff:** Early plans for the Three Capes Track included the possibility of ensnaring Cape Raoul, however funding constraints meant it never eventuated. This spectacular outlier can be tackled separately as a 5hr return day-hike. A side-track leads to a lookout over Shipstern Bluff, that infamous surf break where monster waves up to 9m tall develop gnarly 'stepped' formations; parks.tas.gov.au.
- **Tasmanian Devil Unzoo:** Come face-to-face with feisty Tasmanian devils, as well as hand-feed Forrester kangaroos, Cape Barren geese and rosellas. The philosophy here is less about fencing animals in and more about creating a place so inviting the animals come to visit of their own free will (devils are restrained for safety reasons). 5990 Arthur Hwy, Taranna; (03) 6250 3230; tasmaniandevilunzoo.com.au.
- **Rock on:** There's a string of 'wow' moments around Eaglehawk Neck/Teralina where the ocean and elements have carved fractured rock platforms and enormous sea caves and arches. The Tesselated Pavement, Blowhole, Tasman Arch and Devils Kitchen require just a short walk to each.

Top The forest nearing Munro Cabin *Opposite* The cruise to reach the trailhead is half the fun

Salmon-pink granite mountains, clear aqua water, crusted orange rocks and two of Tasmania's most enticing beaches – what's not to love?

Wineglass Bay & Hazards Beach

This walk is on <u>Paredarerme Country</u>.

WHY IT'S SPECIAL

Some landscapes are so perfect they don't seem feasible. This walk slides between two of the five rounded granite mountains that make up The Hazards, before descending to the justly famous Wineglass Bay. Forest and wetlands give a brief change of pace before returning via Hazards Beach – another stunner – along a coastal track.

Two enormous bands of granite formed the foundation of the Freycinet Peninsula around 400 million years ago – The Hazards at the northern end and Mount Freycinet and Mount Graham at the southern – and their pink hue comes from a feldspar mineral that is particularly rosy in the early light of the day or at sunset. The peninsula is a haven for wildlife such as echnidas, Bennetts wallabies, blue-tongued lizards and Tasmanian pademelons. Stick around for dusk and you could be lucky enough to spot a quoll, wombat or even a Tasmanian devil.

WALK IT

The action starts from the huge carpark at the end of Freycinet Drive and though you can walk the circuit in either direction, heading clockwise, to Wineglass Bay first, means you'll get all the climbing out of the way at the beginning and can linger on beautiful Hazards Beach towards the finish. For a shorter walk, head to Wineglass Bay Lookout and back (takes around 1–1.5hr) or a little bit further to stand foot on the dazzling beach itself. It still involves a steep climb and descent over a saddle but the well-formed track and steps should make it a 2.5hr return walk.

Exploring Freycinet in the afternoon might mean you miss some of the morning crowds, but avoid driving through the park after dusk when wildlife is particularly active. I had to slow down for an echidna and blue tongue lizard on the road even at midday.

If photography is your jam, consider an early start up to Wineglass Bay Lookout (or the summit of Mount Amos, 240m higher, if you really want the goods – the track starts from the same carpark) to catch the morning sun beaming across the mountains and bay. The Hazards pinken with sunrise and sunset, and you'll get a good wide-angle view of them from Coles Bay before reaching the trailhead.

Trail talk
- Distance: 11km
- Time: 4–5hr
- Rating: Moderate
- Technicality: Generally well-formed track with a dash of beach walking and one long section of steps.
- Puff factor: Reasonably flat with a few gentle undulations, except for the 200m climb over a saddle to reach Wineglass Bay.
- Watch out for: Insect repellent is recommended for mosquitoes. Beaches are unpatrolled so take care if swimming.

When to go
This walk is good year-round but sunny days bring out the dazzling colours. Going in winter will help avoid the crowds.

Resources
Visit parks.tas.gov.au for more details. A Tasmanian National Parks pass is required, available from passes.parks.tas.gov.au or on entry to the park.

Opposite top Crossing the isthmus
Opposite bottom Hazards Beach

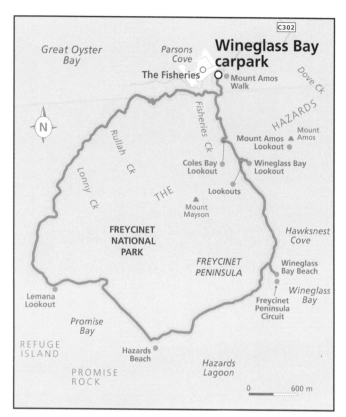

👁 LOCAL SNAPSHOT

It looks pristine now but the Freycinet Peninsula has taken a hammering over the years. The Moomairremener Clan, who lived on the Oyster Bay side of the Derwent River, were the first to be impacted when European settlers arrived. Then in the 1930s Silas Cole dug up shell middens to make lime for brick mortar; two Italian brothers quarried the mountains' pink granite for construction (some of which was used for a Hobart bank); sheep and cattle were let loose to graze; and whales were slaughtered en masse. On arriving into Wineglass Bay in 1840, Skinner Prout noted that the bay's waters were 'thickly spread with oil', with 'occasional chunks of fat and entrails' swimming on the surface. 'From the vast mass of meat, a wide stream of dark blood ran down slowly to the sea,' he wrote. Thankfully the tide turned and in 1916 Freycinet, along with Mount Field (*see* p. 258), was declared one of Tasmania's first national parks.

ITINERARY

I nip in at Coles Bay to pick up some supplies for my hike from the bakery and get distracted by my first good look at the Hazards, a string of rocky nubs dominating on the far shore of the bay. They're mesmerising and seem particularly pink in the early light. I can't wait to get amongst them and it's only another 7min drive to the trailhead where I can unleash.

My walk begins with a steady climb through dry eucalpyt forest and past giant 'marbles' of rock, to crest the saddle between Mount Mayson and Mount Amos, from where a short detour leads to several lookouts over Wineglass Bay. It's the scene that has graced countless calendars and coffee table books – a perfect crescent of white sand cupping a peacock blue bay and backed by green mountains.

Today the cup of Wineglass Bay seems to glow with light but in the early 1800s it was more shiraz in colour from whale blood, which is reputedly how the bay got its name. Southern right whales were nearly hunted to extinction, but in winter migrating humpbacks can still occasionally be seen offshore from these high points.

The rush of gentle waves beckons me down a 200m descent (almost entirely steps) to the beach where I rip my shoes off for a gentle foot massage, courtesy of the coarse sand. These heavy grains are what helps keep the water so gin clear and its azure colour contrasts starkly against the orange that daubs the rocks at the bay's northern end – a lichen that incredibly gets some of its sustenance from chemicals in the rock.

Water temperatures here are always pretty fresh but this big blue is so alluring that, despite being the world's biggest wimp, I once peeled off a down jacket and beanie to swim here. Not today though.

The trail heads inland across a sandy isthmus separating the two granite ranges, through bracken ferns and past a lagoon and wetland chirruping with frogs. Hazards Beach is long and lined with tiny shell fragments – it's not called Great Oyster Bay for nothing. The Toorernomairremener People once feasted on abundant oysters and mussels here and now the remains of these cultural living sites spill from compacted dunes onto the beach.

More sheltered than Wineglass, Hazards Beach has plenty of peach-coloured rocks to drape yourself over. The water might be tempting but take great care if you plan to swim here as it's unpatrolled and rips occur. A dip in the more protected shallows around the rocks at the northern end is probably your best bet. The return track undulates through she-oak forests and coastal woodland, with regular opportunities to perch on outcrops of sloping granite and gaze out to sea.

Even when I'm finished, I'm not ready to say goodbye to the Hazards. I head back to Coles Bay and The Ice Creamery that offers prime views of the mountains, turning pink again in the afternoon light. They look even better with a waffle cone and macadamia ice-cream in my grip.

Right Wineglass Bay from the lookout *Opposite top* The track as it hugs Great Oyster Bay *Opposite bottom* Wineglass Bay

Hazards Beach

BEST EATS

- **Granite Freycinet:** This one has all your bakery favourites and great coffee. Coles Bay Esplanade Shop 2, Coles Bay; (03) 6257 0358.
- **Geographe Restaurant + Espresso Bar:** Views of the Hazards are epic at this licenced cafe, serving wood-fired pizza and tasty dishes made from locally sourced ingredients. 6 Garnet Ave, Coles Bay; (03) 6257 0124.
- **The Ice Creamery:** Perfect for a post-hike scoop of locally-made ice-cream, or fish and chips while watching the sun set over the Hazards. 4 Garnet Ave, Coles Bay; colesbayicecream.com.au.

BEST SLEEPS

- **BIG4 Iluka on Freycinet:** You can choose from camping, cabins or units at this holiday park opposite Muirs Beach. 15 Reserve Rd, Coles Bay; (03) 6257 0115; big4.com.au.
- **Saffire Freycinet:** Multi-award winning and definitely the best place in the 'hood, this all-inclusive luxury hotel offers super swanky digs and views across to The Hazards. 2352 Coles Bay Rd, Coles Bay; (03) 6256 7888; saffire-freycinet.com.au.

WHILE YOU'RE HERE

- **Keep on walking:** The 2-3hr return hike up Mount Amos (450m) is steep and a bit of a scramble at times but from the summit is where you'll get the best views over the Freycinet Peninsula. If you have camping gear and two or three days to spare, the Freycinet Peninsula Circuit will give you a far more secluded experience of the park; parks.tas.gov.au/explore-our-parks/freycinet-national-park/freycinet-peninsula-circuit.
- **Freycinet Marine Farm & Oyster Bay Tours:** This is oyster and mussel territory so if you fancy trying some super-fresh seafood, drop in for a feed at Freycinet Marine Farm. Alternatively, pull on some waders and head out with a farmer (Oyster Bay Tours are partners with Freycinet Marine Farm) to learn about how marine farming works and to prise some oysters and mussels straight off the rack. 1784 Coles Bay Rd, Coles Bay; (03) 6257 0261; freycinetmarinefarm.com; oysterbaytours.com.
- **Freycinet Paddle:** Some places just lend themselves to kayaking and Freycinet is one of them. You get a totally different perspective of the bays and granite mountains from the sea, and the chance to stretch your legs on an isolated beach is a bonus; freycinetadventures.com.au.

Head into a land beyond taming on this iconic traverse across the heart of Tasmania's World Heritage Wilderness.

Overland Track

This walk is on Big River Nation Country.

WHY IT'S SPECIAL

Pause at any high point on this trail and all you'll see is wilderness as far as the eye can see. The famous Overland Track carves a line through a dramatic landscape gouged by glaciers across two million years and six ice ages, and every day brings something new, from craggy dolerite peaks to alpine lakes, moss-filled rainforest, buttongrass plains and staggering waterfalls.

The history of the Earth is on show here, from Precambrian quartzite to Permian sandstones (shell and fish fossils can be found near Pelion Hut), to the Jurassic dolerite columns of Mount Oakleigh. Gondwanan beech trees, endemic pandani, red scoparia, wombats and Tassie devils enhance this unique wonderland.

Shifting seasons, fast changing weather, and up to 10 optional side trips mean you can do this walk many times over and have a completely different experience each time.

WALK IT

The Overland is walked in a southerly direction, from Cradle Mountain to Lake St Clair. The standard six-day itinerary is impressive enough but numerous optional side trips reveal truly spectacular sides of the national park and may have a few less people too. You could easily spend 10 days if you explored them all, checking out waterfalls, mountain summits with epic views and hidden valleys. Plan all you like but know that Tasmania's volatile weather will have the final say on what you end up *actually* hiking.

Nearly half of the Overland Track is above 1000m and much of it is exposed. Tackling steep mountainous side trips in inclement conditions is unwise and, though hut rangers aim to share current forecasts (your mobile phone won't get much coverage out here), alpine weather changes very quickly. Every campsite has a hut, though not always with enough beds for everyone so carry a tent and all the standard gear required for a multi-day hike. Rangers do a briefing at the Cradle Mountain Visitor Centre prior to setting out and will check that you have all the necessary gear.

For a quick taster of this region, hike the 2-3hr Dove Lake Circuit beneath Cradle Mountain.

 Trail talk
- Distance: 63km + side trips
- Time: 6 days +
- Rating: Hard
- Technicality: Everything from boardwalk through to unstable rock hopping. Side tracks sometimes involve very exposed rock scrambling.
- Puff factor: Undulations are pretty consistent but the first day has the steepest climb of about 400m.
- Watch out for: The weather changes quickly and can be harsh so be flexible with your plans. Take extra care on slippery wet rocks or exposed sections. Thieving currawongs will break into unattended packs (and they know where you keep your snacks and how to undo zips), so take precautions to secure unattended gear.

 When to go
Peak season is Oct to May with Dec to Mar having the most stable weather (note, snow can fall any time). Wildflowers bloom Dec to Feb, and in autumn the Nothofagus beech transforms into spectacular red, orange and gold. Winter is for the super-experienced only.

 Resources
For trail information, costs and bookings see overlandtrack.com.au. Bookings open 1 July each year and the Christmas/New Year/Easter periods can sell out within minutes, so book well in advance. You'll need a National Parks Pass, available from passes.parks.tas.gov.au. It's worth purchasing Tasmap's Cradle Mountain - Lake St Clair map and trail notes. Transfers to the Cradle Mountain trailhead depart from Launceston, with walkers returning from Lake St Clair to either Hobart or Launceston. Overland Track Transport is one of the main transport providers to and from the trail; overlandtracktransport.com.au. Book the ferry service at the end of the hike, from Narcissus to Lake St Clair, through lakestclairlodge.com.au.

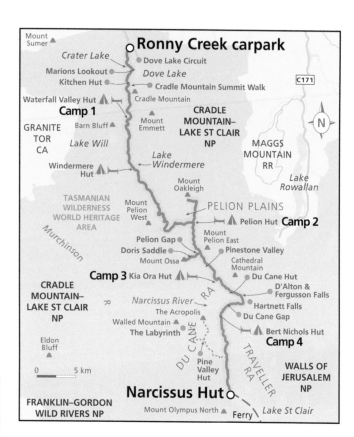

Ronny Creek carpark

Mount Sumer

Crater Lake

Marions Lookout

Dove Lake Circuit

Dove Lake

Kitchen Hut

Cradle Mountain Summit Walk

Waterfall Valley Hut

Cradle Mountain

Camp 1

CRADLE MOUNTAIN–LAKE ST CLAIR NP

GRANITE TOR CA

Barn Bluff

Mount Emmett

MAGGS MOUNTAIN RR

N

Lake Will

Lake Windermere

Lake Rowallan

Windermere Hut

TASMANIAN WILDERNESS WORLD HERITAGE AREA

Mount Oakleigh

Mount Pelion West

PELION PLAINS

Pelion Hut **Camp 2**

Murchison

Pelion Gap

Mount Pelion East

Doris Saddle

Pinestone Valley

Mount Ossa

Cathedral Mountain

Camp 3 Kia Ora Hut

Du Cane Hut

CRADLE MOUNTAIN–LAKE ST CLAIR NP

Narcissus River

D'Alton & Fergusson Falls

Hartnett Falls

The Acropolis

Du Cane Gap

Eldon Bluff

Walled Mountain

The Labyrinth

Bert Nichols Hut

Camp 4

Pine Valley Hut

WALLS OF JERUSALEM NP

0   5 km

Narcissus Hut

FRANKLIN–GORDON WILD RIVERS NP

Mount Olympus North

Ferry   *Lake St Clair*

C171

LOCAL SNAPSHOT

At 1.38 million hectares, the Tasmanian Wilderness World Heritage Area is enormous, making up about 20 per cent of Tasmania's total land mass, and Cradle Mountain-Lake St Clair National Park forms part of it (along with neighbouring Walls of Jerusalem, Franklin-Gordon Wild Rivers, Southwest, Hartz Mountains, Mole Creek Karst and Mount Field national parks). While many World Heritage sites meet only two or three of the possible 10 criteria required to gain status, the Tasmanian Wilderness World Heritage Area is one of only two places in the world that ticks seven! Not only is it gobsmackingly beautiful, it showcases the Earth's evolutionary history and ongoing biological processes, contains important habitats with unique plants and animals, and illustrates significant stages in human history. The cultural heritage is rich for both its physical sites and its intangible knowledge, and there are numerous known Aboriginal heritage sites within the Tasmanian Wilderness World Heritage Area. Tasmanian Aboriginal People have lived on this land for at least 35,000 years. It's big-time special. The vast area of the south west landscape was carved by ice and shaped by fire. Tasmania's First People believe that they were here since the beginning of time and the area is extremely culturally significant to Aboriginal people today. Cultural living places and ceremonial/sacred places hold the memory of the ancestors that is etched in the landscape.

ITINERARY

DAY 1

Ronny Creek carpark to Waterfall Valley Hut, 10.7km, 4–6hr

It's two weeks shy of summer when I head out on a boardwalk from Ronny Creek carpark across peaty plains, but the fog and icy temperatures are a reminder that I'm heading into an unforgiving wilderness where Mother Nature has no regard for my plans.

A steady climb through mossy forest drops me on the shores of Crater Lake with its picturesque boatshed from 1940. The longest and steepest climb of the entire track then takes me up a rocky ridgeline around Crater Lake to Marions Lookout. Today though, Crater Lake's steep-sided rock walls and cobalt water is hidden behind belts of rain, and the view from the top – looking out across some of Tassie's most photographed

icons, Crater Lake, Dove Lake and the jagged cirque wall of Cradle Mountain – is buried in fog.

I make my way across the plateau and skirt behind Cradle Mountain, and the weather lifts enough to appreciate its spiked wall of rock lapped by green. Beyond the emergency shelter of Kitchen Hut, a 2–3hr side trip leads to Cradle Mountain's summit, an exposed and mildly technical scramble that won't suit everyone. Even more exposed is a 3–4hr side trip to Barn Bluff whose steep-sided rocky nub of a summit looks like a giant nipple on the landscape.

It's a mix of boardwalk and rough rocky track down to the new hut at Waterfall Valley. I wasn't planning on staying the night but the palatial retreat – three sleeping quarters, heated common area and large double-glazed windows framing Barn Bluff – is too tempting to refuse.

Opposite Doris Saddle, en route to Mount Ossa *Previous* Mount Oakleigh from Pelion Hut

DAYS 2–3
Waterfall Valley Hut to Windermere, 7.8km, 2.5–3.5hr
Windermere to Pelion Hut, 16.8km, 5–7hr

It's only a short hike to the next hut and I've got side-tripping goals so I'm pushing on to Pelion Hut. Light drizzle and mist accompany me across undulating buttongrass moorlands so I skip the 3km return side trip to Lake Will, fringed in ancient pencil pines, and push on to Lake Windermere. It's vast and croaking with frogs and makes a popular swimming spot in fine conditions. There's a basic hut and campsite nearby but a flashy new one, of the standard at Waterfall Valley, is set to open late 2022.

This trail can lull you into a false sense of security with long stretches of easy boardwalk, before suddenly dumping you in the middle of ankle-twisting rocks, tree roots and mud. The terrain too is ever-changing. Buttongrass moorlands turn to forest carpeted with moss, and when the fog lifts it unveils a vast and dramatic landscape marked by the distant Mount Oakleigh, Mount Pelion East, Mount Pelion West, Mount Ossa and the Du Cane Range.

By the time I reach Pelion Hut, I'm in a T-shirt with actual sunbeams on my skin. Surrounded by grazing wallabies, the large hut sits on the edge of Pelion Plains with a huge deck facing the dolerite spires of Mount Oakleigh which looks so impressive I make an impromptu decision to spend two nights there and climb it the next day – a 4–5hr side trip.

The resident ranger at Pelion Hut knows the Overland inside out, sharing insights on wombats (they're most likely spotted in the forests of the first few days and they can run almost as fast as Usain Bolt at 40kph), and the thieving habits of rogue possums (she also once saw a possum steal underwear from under a man's head as he slept on Pelion's deck). Of the climb up Mount Oakleigh, she describes a section referred to as the 'car wash' and the next morning I discover why. Endemic pandani plants crowd the steep and rocky track like cylindrical tufty brushes. Once on the summit plateau, the route is vague across boulders and shrubs until the final exhilarating view over the columns and spires of Mount Oakleigh's jagged tip. From here, the panorama extends east into the Walls of Jerusalem National Park.

DAY 4
Pelion Hut to Kia Ora Hut, 9km, 3hr

I set out early, climbing moss-filled rainforest to Pelion Gap – my mission, to climb Tasmania's highest peak at 1617m – but I'm not even halfway to Mount Ossa's steep and rocky summit when rain and mist closes in and I'm forced to turn back. The attempt is still worth it for the red and orange flowering scoparia and Kermit-green cushion plants on Doris Saddle, and views of surrounding mountains.

Temperatures have barely peaked 11°C since I set foot on the track and I'm glad for the gloves I splurged on in Launceston. There's little shelter on the descent through Pinestone Valley, across long stretches of boardwalk and rocky tracks so sloshy they flow like a creek. The final stretch to Kia Ora Hut pushes through eucalypt forest thick with tea tree flowers and Tasmanian waratahs, and south of Pelion Gap flowering plants grow more prolific, attracting birds.

After splashing about in puddles and rain all morning, the rain decides to stop just as I arrive at the hut. Wet clothes are peeled off and gear strewn across the deck to dry, and I pull on warm and dry replacements and settle in for an afternoon of snacking and reading. It's only when the skies clear mid afternoon that I can fully appreciate the camp's location with views to Mount Pelion East and the tabletop bulk of Cathedral Mountain whose walls glow orange in the setting sun.

Kia Ora was a basic 24-bed hut during my visit but it's another site set to receive a fancy new hut by late 2022.

DAY 5
Kia Ora Hut to Bert Nichols Hut, 9.6km, 3.5–4.5hr

It's a day of rich green forests and gushing waterfalls. Rain enhances the red and amber streaks on alpine yellow gum trees and brilliant carpets of moss. I squelch through puddles of mud, across tangled tree roots and along old boardwalks all but disintegrated. Du Cane Hut, built around 1910 by snarer and miner Paddy Hartnett, sits in a grassy clearing.

A stint through king billy, sassafras and myrtle leads to the first side track, to D'Alton and Fergusson Falls, and the hour-long diversion is well worth the steep zig-zag descent. D'Alton is a standout. The trail ends at a small rock ledge facing a thundering torrent that smashes over giant cubes of rock. Fergusson Falls is in your face, bursting over a rocky lip nested in the rainforest and, further on, the walk to Hartnett Falls leads across stepping-stones and beds of moss amid twisted trees so pretty it looks like a Japanese Zen garden.

The wind rages in the treetops at Du Cane Gap and from here it's pretty much downhill all the way to Bert Nichols hut. Back in the day, Bert was a trapper and ranger and he was instrumental in the creation of the Overland Track in 1935. His hut is a spacious and cosy one with dramatic views of the Du Cane Range.

DAY 6
Bert Nichols Hut – Narcissus Hut– Lake St Clair, 9km, 3–4hr

Morning cloud clears just long enough to see a dusting of snow over the Du Cane Range. I leave Bert Nichols and 5km south is the turn off to Pine Valley. I had ambitions of power-walking the Overland to make time for this side trip that so many rave about. Walkers often allow for two nights at Pine Valley Hut to hike to the maze of tarns in The Labyrinth or to the epic peak of the Acropolis, but in slippery wet conditions and low viz there is little point. Technically it's not part of the Overland Track, and walkers can access the area from the trail's southern end without an Overland Track Pass. It's an adventure I can save for another day.

Rainforest cut with streams merges with dry eucalypt forest and banksia, and as the flowers increase so does the birdsong. Narcissus River is pumping but there's a swing bridge across it to reach Narcissus Hut and its nearby boat landing. You could walk the 17km from here around Lake St Clair to the visitor centre but most walkers opt to finish with a ferry ride instead (pre-bookings required – see p. 279). Sandwiched between the Traveller Range and Mount Olympus, Lake St Clair is Australia's deepest lake at 167m and another product of the glaciers that once scraped their way through. The Big River Nation call it 'Leeawuleena', meaning 'a lake of the mountain', and cruising this calm and sheltered waterway gives you a chance to soak up the skyline of mountains one last time and reflect on the walk that was.

The week offered a stunning display of raw beauty and dramatic weather but there is still so much more to experience here – the side trips to summits thwarted by bad weather, the hidden tarns and mountains of Pine Valley. I want to come back on a week when the fog has cleared, revealing vistas I missed, or in autumn when the Nothofagus beech sheds a confetti of golden leaves across the track. I want to come back.

Opposite top The Overland is a hiker's wonderland
Opposite bottom Moss-filled rainforest near the trail's southern end

Tasmania

Tasmania

BEST EATS & SLEEPS

Those relying on track transport usually spend their pre- and post-nights in either Launceston or Hobart where there are endless options, however if you've got your own wheels you may want to spend a night or two at either end of the trail.

CRADLE MOUNTAIN

- **Cradle Mountain Highlanders:** If you're looking for a super cosy timber cabin tucked in the forest with a wood-burner fireplace, this one's for you. Some have spa baths. 3876 Cradle Mountain Rd, Cradle Mountain; (03) 6492 1116; cradlehighlander.com.au.
- **Peppers Cradle Mountain Lodge:** It's the closest accommodation to Dove Lake and a longstanding luxury retreat right in the national park. There's cabins and suites, a restaurant, tavern and day spa. 4038 Cradle Mountain Rd, Cradle Mountain; (03) 6492 1309; peppers.com.au/cradle-mountain-lodge.

LAKE ST CLAIR

- **Lake St Clair Lodge:** You can wander straight off the trail and into an eco-cabin tucked in the forest, right on the lake. There's a cafe and bar onsite too. Lake St Clair Rd, Lake St Clair; (03) 6289 1137; lakestclairlodge.com.au.
- **Derwent Bridge Wilderness Hotel:** Just a 5min drive from the trailhead is this cosy timber hotel and pub serving hearty post-hike meals. Derwent Bridge, Lyell Hwy; (03) 6289 1144; derwentbridgewildernesshotel.com.au.
- **Pumphouse Point:** You'll have earned a few nights at this uber-cool retreat located in the iconic 1940s pumphouse, perched on the end of a jetty reaching 274m into Lake St Clair. Stays are fully inclusive of meals and a few tipples. 1 Lake St Clair Rd, Lake St Clair; 0428 090 436; pumphousepoint.com.au.

The Overland carves through a dramatic wilderness area

Wander the rich takayna/Tarkine rainforest and rivers in Tasmania's western wilds.

Whyte River Walk

This walk is on <u>Peerapper Country</u>.

WHY IT'S SPECIAL

Tasmania's western wilds is home to the takayna/Tarkine rainforest, the country's largest temperate rainforest and so other-worldly beautiful it could model for a fairytale picture book. These trees have serious character, trailing moss and are dotted in crazy fungi (who doesn't love fungi?), as they crowd the shores of the mirror-like Whyte and Pieman rivers. Platypus sightings are a decent possibility. Over 50 species here are listed as rare, threatened or endangered, yet for all its treasured inhabitants and natural beauty the takayna/Tarkine is, and has been for decades, under threat of logging and mining. The fight to protect it is ongoing and efforts are being made to secure World Heritage status.

It's remote here – be prepared to say goodbye to wi-fi and mobile reception – but this isolation only seems to enhance a sense of connection with the land. Stay at Corinna Wilderness Experience and you'll be sans TV too. Embrace what is a rare chance to really get away from it all.

WALK IT

You could bang the Whyte River walk out in an hour but this isn't a trail you want to rush. A forest this rich has life at all levels and you'll discover more if you pause frequently and look for the details. Beech leaves turn golden in autumn, leatherwood flowers in late summer, and don't let rain put you off – it only enhances colours and adds to the mood.

Whether you access Corinna from the north or south, you'll hit a stretch of scenic unsealed road, made from white silica tailings from the nearby silica mine – fine for 2WD. Access from the south and you'll need to cross the Pieman River on a barge called the *Fatman*. Once you arrive you're basically off the grid, although you can snatch a few bars of reception from the top of nearby Mount Donaldson – another epic walk that is a 10min drive from Corinna.

Tucked away in the remote Western Wilds, Corinna is a bit of a trek to reach, so plan to spend a few days here and have a good look around at this very special part of Tasmania.

Trail talk
- Distance: 3.3km
- Time: 1.5hr
- Rating: Easy
- Technicality: Generally well formed with a few short sections of tree roots to negotiate.
- Puff factor: Mostly flat
- Watch out for: Tree roots and muddy trails are slippery when wet.

When to go
It's stunning in all seasons. You're more likely to spot a platypus in the early morning or evening.

Resources
Grab a mud map on arrival at Corinna Wilderness Experience; corinna.com.au.

Opposite Early morning sun setting the forest alight

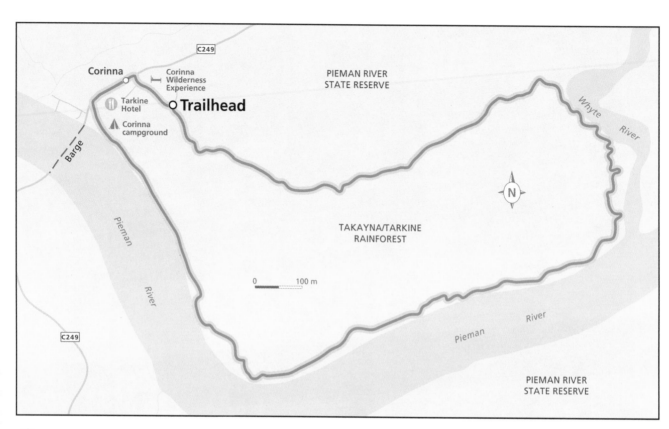

👁 LOCAL SNAPSHOT

In the late 1800s, Corinna bustled with gold prospectors and Tasmania's largest nugget, weighing 7.5kg, was extracted near a small tributary off the Whyte River. There were pubs and a post office, and sailing ships and steamers brought supplies up the Pieman River from the ocean to service the 2500 people who lived here. Some of the old cottages still remain and are now incorporated as part of the accommodation offered at Corinna Wilderness Experience. Today it's a far quieter place with just one pub and a few cabins. It's a true eco experience and a launching pad from which to explore the stunning takayna/Tarkine wilderness.

Right Sections of boardwalk make the walking easy
Opposite Walking around forest giants

ITINERARY

Maybe it's the dirt road to get here, the complete lack of mobile reception, or the tangle of greenery and mirror-like rivers that dominate the landscape. Or maybe it's copping a lungful of some of the cleanest air in the world (the nearby coastline ranks second only after the Southern Ocean). Whatever it is, you can sense the takayna/Tarkine is special long before you set foot on this trail.

I venture out with a few friends not long after dawn – easy to do since the trailhead is about 10m from our cabins at Corinna. The track immediately dives into the trees. Little chimneys of mud sprout from the dark earth, left by burrowing crayfish that store water in underground chambers. The region records an average annual rainfall of up to 2.4m and some of it fell overnight, enriching the intensity of greens around us.

Parts of the takayna/Tarkine have some of the most undisturbed rainforest in the country and the area we walk through has avoided fire for over 400 years. It makes for a fairy wonderland of epic proportions. Myrtle beech, leatherwood, sassafras and the drooping swishy branches of Huon pine combine to create leaves of all shapes, colours and sizes.

Rounds of fungi cling to trunks and fallen logs and swathes of hanging moss swing in the air. Hiding in this forest are quolls, wombats and the world's largest freshwater cray, up to 1m long. Even Tasmanian devils live here – the odd one is occasionally seen poking around Corinna.

The first half of the track undulates gently, crisscrossed with tree roots, but where it meets the Whyte River, at its confluence with the Pieman River, the terrain levels out and opens up. We've timed it perfectly. The early sun shoots beams of golden light low through the trees, setting everything alight. It looks like a painting. The river is mirror calm and the only noise comes from a few birds whose songs ring loud and clear, and a sudden splash at the riverbank, no doubt from one of the platypus that live here. The perfection stills us into silence for a few minutes. For those who really want to soak up the vibe there are a few picnic tables to settle at. It's a much wider and flatter path that follows Pieman River back to Corinna.

With the takayna/Tarkine under threat from logging and mining, I can only hope we'll learn from past mistakes and appreciate and preserve this special wilderness.

BEST EATS

- **Tarkine Hotel:** Grab coffee and snacks to go or sit in the cosy timber tavern for a home-cooked lunch or dinner. The hotel only serves meals Sept to May. 1 Corinna Rd, Corinna; (03) 6446 1170; corinna.com.au.

———

BEST SLEEPS

- **Corinna Wilderness Experience:** Camp on the riverside or stay in cosy cottages built in the style of the old mining village that used to be here. The walk starts from the doorstep. 1 Corinna Rd, Corinna; (03) 6446 1170; corinna.com.au.

———

WHILE YOU'RE HERE

- **Pieman River Cruise:** Hop aboard the *Arcadia II* (built in 1939 out of Huon pine) for a mesmerising journey along the mirror-like waters of the Pieman River, through the takayna/Tarkine forest to the sea. There is also a shorter cruise on the *Sweetwater* to see the wreck of the *SS Croydon* and Lovers Falls. Corinna Wilderness Experience; (03) 6446 1170; corinna.com.au.
- **Kayak to Savage River:** This awesome adventure involves a 90min paddle up the Pieman River to Savage River and the wreck of the *SS Croydon*, followed by a hike through stunning rainforest to return. You can rent boats from Corinna Wilderness Experience; (03) 6446 1170; corinna.com.au.
- **Mount Donaldson:** Views over the takayna/Tarkine, Pieman River and surrounding mountains are spectacular on this 4hr hike that climbs above the forest to an open buttongrass ridge to reach the summit of Mount Donaldson. Start from Savage River Bridge, a 10min drive from Corinna.

Capturing early morning mist on the Pieman River

Keep on Walking

*These trails from around the country give
you more options to keep exploring.*

Bouddi Coastal Walk, NSW

This walk is on <u>Kuring-gai Country.</u>

Skirt rocky headlands, dive into rainforest and linger on secluded beaches on this Central Coast walk.

- **Distance:** 8.5km

- **Time:** 3.5hr one way

- **Rating:** Moderate. There's a pretty steady stream of undulations over sand and dirt tracks, plus some boardwalk.

- **When to go:** It's good year-round but best avoided in peak summer when the track is hot and often exposed.

- **Info:** Visit nationalparks.nsw.gov.au for more info and to download the Bouddi Coastal Walk map. Vehicle entry fees apply in the Putty Beach area.

Is there anything more glorious and uplifting than a coastal walk? This one flows over rocky headlands and dips to caramel-coloured beaches, threads through pockets of rainforest of Bouddi National Park and emerges onto coast-hugging trails that present the vast Pacific Ocean in a way that makes you pause in wonder every few minutes.

It runs between Putty Beach and MacMasters Beach, near Gosford - the skyline of Sydney, 50km south, is visible in the distance. At its western end, the route trails over boardwalk and sandstone, giving prime views of the frothing ocean as it smashes against the coast and washing over huge rock platforms such as the Tesselated Pavement, fractured in geometric patterns. At times the sandstone underfoot is worn in smooth curves, revealing streaks of caramel and cream. It's possible to spot whales at any point on the trail (May-Oct) but the lookout at Gerrin Point is an especially good perch.

There are plenty of steps on this walk to keep the lungs pumping but the trail's regular dips to beaches make for ideal resting spots and many are remote enough to deter the crowds. The long sandy arc of Maitland Bay and its clear green waters are idyllic for a swim. Hit it at low tide and you'll see the remains of the *PS Maitland*, wrecked here in 1898. Little Beach is another good bet for a stop and has gas barbecues.

The track mostly hugs the coast but east of Caves Bay it dives inland on a fire-trail across the perched sand dunes of Bombi Moor, vegetated in heath and banksia and covered in wildflowers in spring. From here, three side trails lead out to expansive coastal lookouts from high rock platforms.

Pockets of forest make for a beautiful and shaded change of scenery, and they get taller and more impressive as you draw to the trail's eastern end, dotted with ferns, grass trees and the rust-coloured flanks of gums.

There are access points midway at Maitland Bay and Little Beach if you just want to walk an hour or two.

Minyon Falls Loop, NSW

This walk is on <u>Bundjalung Country</u>.

Wander through the rainforest to a spectacular 100m-high waterfall in the Byron Bay Hinterland.

- **Distance:** 8km
- **Time:** 3-4hr
- **Rating:** Moderate. Mix of dirt trail and rock hopping, plus there's a decent climb back out at the end. Be careful after rain when the terrain is very slippery.
- **When to go:** Winter makes for pleasant walking conditions. Summer is hot but it's also the wet season when the falls are likely to be at their most impressive.
- **Info:** Visit nationalparks.nsw.gov.au for more info and to download the Minyon Falls walking track map.

The fact that Nightcap National Park receives the highest annual rainfall in NSW is a good thing when your goal is Minyon Falls. Bursting from the rainforest, Minyon free-falls spectacularly 100m over sheer and column-like rhyolite cliffs, once part of the Tweed Volcanic rim (one of the world's largest extinct volcanoes), to land in a dark pool fringed in greenery. A snazzy new viewing platform at the top of the falls makes for a secure perch from which to soak it up and, in clear conditions, views stretch all the way to the ocean - over 15km away.

The falls are definitely the highlight of this walk but it's all part of the Gondwana Rainforests of Australia World Heritage Area - offering a living link to a time when Australia was part of the ancient supercontinent - so the hike in is super pretty too, taking walkers from shrubby dry sclerophyll forest down into the rainforest and back up again. There are two options to walk here, depending on whether you're in the mood for a short or longer walk. From Minyon Grass picnic area, the 2hr return hike to the base of the falls allows you to gaze upwards at this imposing white 'curtain' of water and feel the spray of mist on your face. Bring your swimming gear if you fancy a swim. The alternative is the longer loop track that takes in both the top and base of the falls, and passes boulder-filled creeks (a road section between the top of the falls and Minyon Grass picnic area completes the loop). Keep your eyes peeled for some of the wildlife that call this place home, such as goannas, koalas, frogs and green tree snakes. Bird song is a constant and you may spot superb fairy-wrens, red goshawks and the Albert's lyrebird.

This is a great hike as it is but Minyon Falls is set to be scooped up as part of a new four-day/38km Tweed Byron Hinterland Trail, spanning from Jerusalem National Park to Nightcap. Completion date for this new trail is hoped to be sometime in 2023.

Top Minyon Falls *Opposite* Maitland Bay *Previous* Needles Beach

Great South West Walk, Vic

This walk is on Gundit Country.

An incredibly varied circuit walk that is a haven for wildlife.

- **Distance:** 250km loop

- **Time:** 11-14 days

- **Rating:** Easy-moderate. A mix of well-formed trails with a few gentle undulations, plus quite a bit of beach walking.

- **When to go:** Spring to autumn is best. The coastal stretch is exposed so you'll cop any inclement weather head on.

- **Info:** Visit greatsouthwestwalk.com for planning info.

For such a beautiful route, this one flies under the radar somewhat but that only adds to its appeal since you'll quite possibly see more koalas than other hikers. Wildlife is a major drawcard and koalas, wallabies, emus, seals, echidnas, birds and the odd reptile are pretty much guaranteed. Whales are a maybe.

From its start point in Portland, the trail shifts through inland forests, alongside the mighty Glenelg River with its divine riverfront camps and plentiful swimming, remote ocean beaches and rolling sand dunes, and atop rugged cliffs overlooking capes and bays pounded by the Southern Ocean.

Some of the state's highest sea cliffs are at Cape Bridgewater and colonies of Australian and New Zealand fur seals dive off its coastal rock platforms, drawn by the food provided by the waters of the nearby Continental Shelf. Other highlights include a section of coastal solution tubes - hollow rock 'straws' a metre or two high, as well as Tarragul Cave fringed in stalactites, and Cape Nelson Lighthouse.

Being a loop track, logistics are easy. Portland is accessible from Melbourne by public transport and at the halfway point you'll pass through the tiny town of Nelson, near the South Australian border, with a general store, pub and accommodation. Post a food box to yourself via the Nelson Post Office.

If you want to just hike a three-day section, local operators can assist with transfers. The river and coastal sections are most impressive.

Werribee Gorge Circuit, Vic

This walk is on <u>Wathaurong Country</u>.

An exciting walk through a rugged and forested gorge.

- **Distance:** 10km
- **Time:** 3hr
- **Rating:** Moderate, includes a little rock scrambling.
- **When to go:** Pick a cool and dry day as rocks are slippery when wet. Midweek is less busy.
- **Info:** See parks.vic.gov.au for more info.

It might only be an hour west of Melbourne but it has a distinct feeling of being somewhere very far away (the Northern Territory perhaps?). From the gorge rim are panoramic views across the Pentland Hills and the extinct volcanoes of Mount Blackwood and Mount Cottrell, but the real magic happens when the trail descends a few hundred metres into the gorge itself.

There's 500 million years of geological history here and a lot of it is on show, thanks to the eroding persistence of the Werribee River. Cross sections in the rock unveil wavy synclines and anticlines folded by plate movement in the Devonian period, and layers of clay are embedded with pebbles and scrape marks left behind by melted ice sheets in the Permian ice age.

It's an exciting route alongside the Werribee River, at times a rocky scramble on narrow ledges beneath sheer cliffs, aided by cable handrails, and at other times a rough trail passing waterholes lined with cumbungi (bulrushes) and flitting with dragonflies. The sandy dollop at Needles Beach, backed by towering 'needles' of shale, makes a great spot to linger for a swim. An old water race, built in 1904 for farm irrigation, accompanies the final riverside section, before the trail climbs out of the gorge and over undulating rocky ridges to complete the loop.

Surrounded by cleared land, the gorge has become a haven for wildlife such as black wallabies, koalas, echidnas, platypus, wedge-tailed eagles and many more birds.

This is a popular hike and for good reason. Several other short trails offer alternative ways to explore.

Top A little rock scramble in Werribee Gorge *Opposite* Cliff-top

Waitpinga Cliffs, SA

This walk is on <u>Nagarrindjeri Country.</u>

Walk spectacular cliff-tops with panoramic views on the Fleurieu Peninsula.

- **Distance:** 14.6km

- **Time:** 5hr

- **Rating:** Moderate. Well-defined track, sandy at times with a little bit of rock hopping.

- **When to go:** It's exposed so pick a day when the elements are friendly.

- **Info:** Head to walkingsa.org.au for trail info, and parks.sa.gov.au for details on Newland Head Conservation Park.

It's one of South Australia's best coastal walks and a highlight of the 1200km Heysen Trail that stretches from the south coast all the way to the Flinders Ranges. Between Waitpinga Beach and Rosetta Head (aka The Bluff), this hike skirts the top of the Waitpinga Cliffs whose grey vertical striations shear steeply into a pounding Southern Ocean. At times, the views are so unobstructed and the path so close to the edge it's as though the trail might pour straight off the cliffs and into the blue. At other times, narrow sandy paths drizzle across swathes of coastal heath scattered with wildflowers in a dazzling contrast against the water beyond. In spring, the proliferation of yellow and purple blooms can be quite something.

From up high, the ocean views are truly panoramic, occasionally encompassing migrating southern right whales (Jun-Nov), seals, dolphins and, if you're lucky, rare white-bellied sea eagles. As the trail moves east it showcases the cliffs bending around the coast to Kings Head and the pyramid-like Rosetta Head beyond.

While the walk largely sticks to the coast, a stint through the mallee eucalypt and grass trees of Newland Head Conservation Park, and pockets of woodland dotted with grass trees and ringing with birdsong, make a lovely change of pace. And when the trail is not gazing from up high, it dips to bays littered with orange lichen-covered boulders or beaches cut with streaks of dark rock.

After descending off the cliffs at Kings Beach, the route rolls across grassland to reach Rosetta Head. The epic 360-degree view from its peak makes for an exhilarating finish.

Dales Gorge, WA

This walk is on <u>Banjima Country.</u>

Explore a remote rust-red outback gorge.

- **Distance:** 5km loop
- **Time:** 3-4hr
- **Rating:** Moderate-hard. Rock hopping and a little climbing.
- **When to go:** The cooler and drier months of May to Sept are best.
- **Info:** Download the Karijini National Park guide and read the 'Your safety' boxed text online at parks.dpaw.wa.gov.au/park/karijini.

The Pilbara region is Australia's iron ore central and it shows at Karijini where rust red gorges cut sheer, deep slices into the outback. It's a rugged, spectacular and at times challenging landscape carved from an ancient land, over 2000 million years old. Though Dales Gorge is one of the easier hikes to do here it's still no cake walk.

This walk combines the Gorge Rim Walk and Dales Gorge walk, trailing along the top of the gorge rim and returning via its rocky base, squeezed by 100m-high walls and scattered with cool green pools hung with greenery. From up high, several lookouts offer great vantage points over the rim to the streambed below, and across distant rolling red hills scattered with spinifex.

Negotiating the gorge requires a rock hop in places. Between blocky walls lay rock slabs layered into broad steps, pockets of forest, white-trunked Snappy Gums sprouting from rock, and red boulders tinged dark with iron. At Circular Pool the towering walls wrap around a dark teal pool, while Fern Pool is lined with sedge grasses and fed by a waterfall. Along with the large pool beneath cascading Fortescue Falls, all three make for idyllic, if bracing, swimming spots, but note the Parks and Wildlife Service WA safety warnings.

Karijini is a long way from anywhere so be sure to have a good look around while you're there. The swirling water-smoothed walls of Hamersley Gorge enclose a famously photogenic water hole, and you'll need to 'spider walk' (arms and legs spread wide) to bridge the narrow walls and ledges of Hancock Gorge en route to Kermits Pool. Around a dozen other short trails visit spectacular lookouts, waterfalls and mountain tops.

Cape Le Grand Coastal Track, WA

This walk is on <u>Wudjari Country.</u>

*Granite headlands, aqua bays and kangaroos
lounging on the whitest sand in the country.*

- **Distance:** 15km one-way (or pick one of four short sections)
- **Time:** 8hr (sections take 1–3hr)
- **Rating:** Moderate-hard
- **When to go:** Jan to May or Oct to Dec are ideal.
- **Info:** Visit parks.dpaw.gov.au and trailswa.com.au.

It's a long way from anywhere but that only amplifies the sense of wildness at Cape Le Grand National Park, where rugged granite peaks and emerald heathland nuzzle pristine beaches and bays. In its entirety, the Coastal Track extends from Rossiter Bay at the eastern end to Le Grand Beach at the west, but it's made up of four sections, defined by the bays that divide them, and each is accessible by road, making it easy to just pick a section or two.

Precambrian granite and gneiss bubbles up through the heath, slides into the Southern Ocean and even surfaces offshore in the islands of the Recherche Archipelago. You'll traverse sandplains carpeted in banksia and native honeysuckle that are a magnet for birds. Mount Le Grand, Boulder Hill and Mississippi Hill make for impressive inland views but it's the park's luminescent beaches that it's most famous for.

Lucky Bay is the highlight of this walk and has been measured as having the whitest sand in the country, so pack your swimwear. As if that wasn't enough, Lucky Bay is also home to a mob of kangaroos who are often found lounging on the sand or mingling with visitors.

The hour-long hike between Lucky Bay and Thistle Cove is the easiest stretch and has some of the trail's best scenery. Allow 2–3hr for Lucky Bay to Rossiter Bay. The two sections west of Thistle Cove (via Hellfire Bay to Le Grand Beach) are markedly more difficult, with far less formed trail, more challenging navigation and sections of very steep granite to negotiate.

Top Kangaroos love Lucky Bay *Opposite* Hikers have Lake McKenzie to themselves in the late afternoon

K'gari Great Walk, Qld

This walk is on <u>Butchulla Country</u>.

Walk a tranquil route on the world's largest sand island, sprinkled with stunning lakes and rainforest.

- **Distance:** 90km, including side trips
- **Time:** 6-8 days
- **Rating:** Easy-moderate. Mostly well-formed sandy trails, with a few gentle undulations.
- **When to go:** April to Sept is best
- **Info:** Visit parks.des.qld.gov.au for planning info. Purchase the K'gari/Fraser Island Great Walk map and trail notes.

A wander on the world's largest sand island is full of surprises. It is a World Heritage Site, with half of the world's perched lakes, vast rolling dunes, moss and fungi-filled rainforest, verdant valleys of picabeen palms and strangler figs, and the purest breed of dingoes on the eastern seaboard. You can literally see slow-moving sands swallowing forests whole here, leaving expansive and surreal sand blows punctuated by the skeletal remains of dead trees. Sea views from these sandy lookouts sometimes include migrating whales.

K'gari is a popular tourist destination but hit the trail and you'll see another side of it and without the crowds. This becomes especially handy when camping at highlights such as Lake Wabby, a barrage lake flanked by steep dunes, or Lake McKenzie whose gin-clear blue water and silica white sand makes a heavenly spot for a swim. When the daytrippers leave in the late afternoon, you'll have these gems to yourself.

You can hike the whole thing independently or arrange for a tour operator to collect you at the end of each day and whisk you back to your accommodation. If you only have time for a quickie, the Pile Valley Circuit is a stunning 4km walk along the white sand-bottomed Wanggoolba Creek, overlooked by picabeen palms, kauris, strangler figs and king ferns.

The dingoes of K'gari occasionally cop some bad press but the reality is you'd be lucky to spot one of these wild dogs on the trail. To be on the safe side, every campsite has metal bins to store your food in and more popular campsites have fences too. Be alert and wary, and never feed one.

Warrie Circuit, Qld

This walk is on <u>Bundjalung Country.</u>

A trail through lush rainforest and waterfalls in the Gold Coast Hinterland.

- **Distance:** 17km

- **Time:** 5-6hr

- **Rating:** Moderate. A bit of rock hopping, a few water crossings and around 400m of elevation.

- **When to go:** The dry winter season makes for easiest conditions (not too hot or wet), however if there's been just a bit of rain the waterfalls will look extra impressive.

- **Info:** Download the Springbrook National Park Guide from parks.des.qld.gov.au.

You could spend a few days exploring the epic trails in Springbrook National Park but this one gives a good taste of what it's all about. Tucked in the Gold Coast Hinterland, and part of the Gondwana Rainforests of Australia World Heritage Area, it is dominated by rainforest and dramatic waterfalls. In local language, 'Warrie' means 'rushing water', and you're never far from it on this trail.

It starts with a bang at The Canyon Lookout, overlooking the rainforest and the sheer rock wall of the gorge rim opposite, and what follows is a descent through strangler figs, palms, ferns and twisted vines, crossing creeks and gullies to eventually reach the 'Meeting of the Waters', where all watercourses draining the Canyon meet.

Abundant waterfalls are a highlight and the trail passes behind a few of them, giving walkers a cooling spray of mist and a spectacular illumination of spray against sun. Rainbow Falls truly deserves its name. When the sun hits this one, you'll walk beneath bands of colour so bright you'll be searching for the unicorn to go with it. Deep in the rainforest, the opportunity to soak in a few pools surrounded by giant boulders makes a nice diversion.

The Warrie Circuit begins and ends with a section of the Twin Falls Circuit, another stunning walk beneath rock overhangs and past yet more waterfalls. The Twin Falls Circuit is a shorter (4km, (2hr) and easier alternative that

Walls of Jerusalem, Tas

This walk is on <u>Big River Country.</u>

Explore a stunning alpine wonderland hidden beyond dramatic rock walls.

- **Distance:** Roughly 22-32km+ (depending on side trips)

- **Time:** 2-4 days

- **Rating:** Moderate-hard. It's a well-formed trail, albeit a steep climb to the plateau where a mix of boardwalk and rougher trails explore numerous side trips.

- **When to go:** Hiking season is Oct to May. While Dec to Feb is best for stable weather, spring has wildflowers and autumn offers changing colours. Both are quieter than peak summer.

- **Info:** Visit parks.tas.gov.au for planning details and to register. Note this is remote and exposed alpine country, so come prepared.

Walls of Jerusalem National Park is only accessible on foot but it's undoubtedly worth the effort. A wall of pale fluted dolerite peaks rise from the Central Plateau, surrounded by thousand-year-old pencil pine forests, colourful alpine herb fields, delicate cushion plants, lakes and dozens of magical glacial tarns. It is part of the Tasmanian Wilderness World Heritage Area, but gets a fraction of the traffic of neighbouring Cradle Mountain - Lake St Clair National Park and, combined with its remote and rugged scenery, there's a real sense of wilderness here.

It begins with a well-graded though steep hike to Wild Dog Creek, where you can set up camp in the shadow of King Davids Peak and spend a day or two exploring the inner walls and peaks of this alpine labyrinth. Alternatively, a rough circuit route takes in yet more dazzling terrain and spectacular lakes, with a few wild camps to pitch a tent at.

Inspired by the walls that surround the actual city of Jerusalem, surveyor James Scott named these dolerite walls in the 1800s and the Biblical theme was extended between the 1930s and 1960s to other features within the park. Herods Gate grants access to the central basin, the Pool of Bethesda is an idyllic lake surrounded by pencil pines, Dixons Kingdom mixes pine forest with views of endless lakes and tarns, and Solomons Throne is a highlight with spectacular 360 views from up high.

Index

About the author

Award-winning author, travel writer and speaker **Laura Waters** left a corporate job to pursue a career in media following a life-changing 3,000km hike down the length of New Zealand in 2014. She now writes for major national newspapers and magazines, and her hiking memoir *Bewildered* won Best Travel Book in the prestigious Australian Society of Travel Writers Awards For Excellence in 2021.

Since her 5-month New Zealand epic, Laura has been hopelessly addicted to the blissful simplicity of walking and has hiked thousands more kilometres on trails around Australia and as far afield as Patagonia and Jordan. She is a passionate advocate for getting more people outdoors and connected with nature, as well as caring for the planet. An engaging speaker, Laura trained with Al Gore in 2009 to be a climate presenter, later shifting her focus to give talks about her experiences in the wilds and the lessons learned, as well as hosting events. See www.soultrekkers.com.au

Photography credits

All images © Laura Waters except for the following:

Front cover iStock; back cover Alamy; pp xi, 76 Visit Victoria; pp xv, 283, 284, 285 Marie Barieri; pp xx, 3 (left), 4, 7, 8, 112, 119 (bottom), 131 (bottom), 184, 195, 197, 198, 295, 296 Tourism Australia; p 1 Hamilton Lund/Destination NSW; p 2 Adam Calaitzis / Shutterstock.com; p 3 (right) David Moore/South Australia / Alamy Stock Photo; p 5 EA Given / Shutterstock.com; p 6 aiyoshi597 / Shutterstock.com; pp 13, 158 Christian B. / Alamy Stock Photo; 24 Rafael Ben-Ari / Alamy Stock Photo; pp 26, 28, 29, 30, 32, 291 Destination NSW; pp 40 (top), 88, 144, 161, 219, 299 Shutterstock; pp 50, 67 Parks Victoria; p 72 (bottom) Philip Game / Alamy Stock Photo; p 124 Robert Wyatt / Alamy Stock Photo; p 140 Walk into Luxury; pp 142, 145, 146, 147, 165, 166, 167, 168 The Life of Py; p 174 Suzanne Long / Alamy Stock Photo; pp 210, 244 Tourism and Events Queensland; p 216 Tourism and Events Queensland / Jason Charles Hill Photography; p 255 Andrew Bain / Alamy Stock Photo; p 279 (top) Cradle Mountain Huts; p 280 iStock

Published in 2022 by Hardie Grant Explore, an imprint of Hardie Grant Publishing

Hardie Grant Explore (Melbourne)
Wurundjeri Country
Building 1, 658 Church Street
Richmond, Victoria 3121

Hardie Grant Explore (Sydney)
Gadigal Country
Level 7, 45 Jones Street
Ultimo, NSW 2007

www.hardiegrant.com/au/explore

In palawa kani, the language of Tasmanian Aboriginal People, with thanks to the Tasmanian Aboriginal Centre.

With thanks to Tasmania Regional Aboriginal Communities Alliance.

The maps in this publication incorporate data © Commonwealth of Australia (Geoscience Australia), 2006. Geoscience Australia has not evaluated the data as altered and incorporated within this publication, and therefore gives no warranty regarding accuracy, completeness, currency or suitability for any particular purpose.

Incorporates or developed using [Roads Nov 2020] © Geoscape Australia for Copyright and Disclaimer Notice see geoscape.com.au/legal/data-copyright-and-disclaimer

A catalogue record for this book is available from the National Library of Australia

Hardie Grant acknowledges the Traditional Owners of the Country on which we work, the Wurundjeri People of the Kulin Nation and the Gadigal People of the Eora Nation, and recognises their continuing connection to the land, waters and culture. We pay our respects to their Elders past and present.

Ultimate Walks & Hikes: Australia
ISBN 9781741177749

10 9 8 7 6 5 4 3 2 1

Publisher
Melissa Kayser

Project editor
Megan Cuthbert

Editor
Alice Barker

Trainee editor
Gemma Taylor

Proofreader
Cassie Holland

Cartographer
Claire Johnston

Production coordinator
Jessica Harvie

Design
Andy Warren

Typesetting
Megan Ellis and Post Pre-press Group

Index
Max McMaster

Content consultants
Kirsten Hausia and Patsy Cameron

Colour reproduction by Megan Ellis and Splitting Image Colour Studio

Printed and bound in China by LEO Paper Products LTD.

The paper this book is printed on is certified against the Forest Stewardship Council® Standards and other sources. FSC® promotes environmentally responsible, socially beneficial and economically viable management of the world's forests.

Disclaimer: While every care is taken to ensure the accuracy of the data within this product, the owners of the data (including the state, territory and Commonwealth governments of Australia) do not make any representations or warranties about its accuracy, reliability, completeness or suitability for any particular purpose and, to the extent permitted by law, the owners of the data disclaim all responsibility and all liability (including without limitation, liability in negligence) for all expenses, losses, damages (including indirect or consequential damages) and costs which might be incurred as a result of the data being inaccurate or incomplete in any way and for any reason.

Publisher's Disclaimers: The publisher cannot accept responsibility for any errors or omissions. The representation on the maps of any road or track is not necessarily evidence of public right of way. The publisher cannot be held responsible for any injury, loss or damage incurred during travel. It is vital to research any proposed trip thoroughly and seek the advice of relevant state and travel organisations before you leave.

Publisher's Note: Every effort has been made to ensure that the information in this book is accurate at the time of going to press. The publisher welcomes information and suggestions for correction or improvement.